THE UCHUCK YEARS

THE UCHUCK YEARS

A WEST COAST SHIPPING SAGA

David Esson Young

HARBOUR PUBLISHING

Harbour Publishing Co. Ltd.
P.O. Box 219, Madeira Park, BC, V0N 2H0
www.harbourpublishing.com

Front and back cover illustrations of *Uchuck III* by Bill Maximick
Author photo by Bob Cossar
Edited by Betty Keller
Cover design by Teresa Karbashewski
Text design by Mary White
Printed and bound in Canada

 Canada Council Conseil des Arts
for the Arts du Canada

 BRITISH COLUMBIA
ARTS COUNCIL
An agency of the Province of British Columbia

Harbour Publishing acknowledges financial support from the Government of Canada through the Canada Book Fund and the Canada Council for the Arts, and from the Province of British Columbia through the BC Arts Council and the Book Publishing Tax Credit.

Library and Archives Canada Cataloguing in Publication

Young, David, 1938–
   The Uchuck years : a west coast shipping saga / David Young.

Includes index.
ISBN 978-1-55017-582-0

   1. Young, David, 1938–. 2. Ship captains—British Columbia—Nootka Sound—Biography. 3. Nootka Sound Service Limited—Employees—Biography. 4. Coastwise shipping—British Columbia—Nootka Sound—History—20th century. 5. Nootka Sound (B.C.)—Biography. I. Title.

FC3845.N63Z49 2012   971.1'204092   C2012-900640-8

To the memory of my dad, Henry Esson Young.
He was an inspiration to a lot of people over many years.

Contents

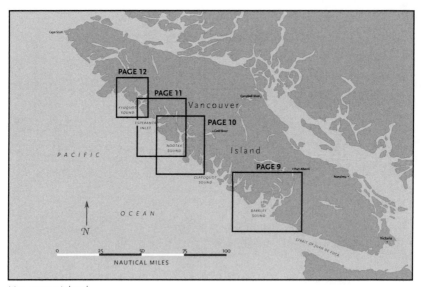

Vancouver Island

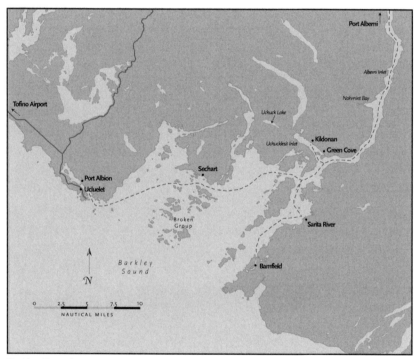

Barkley Sound

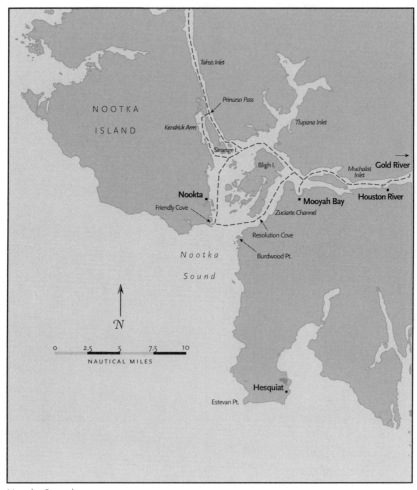

Nootka Sound

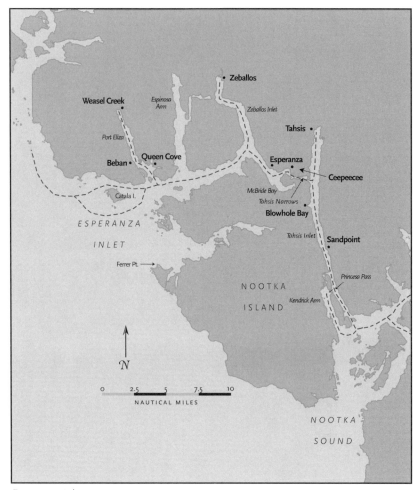

Esperanza Inlet

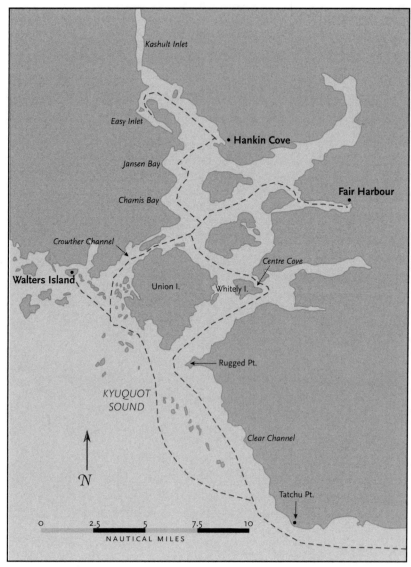

Kashult Inlet

Easy Inlet

• Hankin Cove

Jansen Bay

Fair Harbour

Chamis Bay

Crowther Channel

Centre Cove

Walters Island

Union I.

Whitely I.

Rugged Pt.

KYUQUOT
SOUND

Clear Channel

N

Tatchu Pt.

| 0 | 2.5 | 5 | 7.5 | 10 |

NAUTICAL MILES

Kyuquot Sound

Introduction

Coastal passenger/cargo vessels of all sizes travelled the whole coast of British Columbia for well over a century, but they have now virtually disappeared. Only two little ones are still in service. The *Uchuck III* is one of those two, and my family's history is inextricably bound up in her life.

I began writing about this vessel with the idea that perhaps my grandchildren might one day wonder what their grandfather and great-grandfather had done in their working lifetimes on the West Coast of Vancouver Island. Then it occurred to me that some of the tens of thousands of people who travelled with us as passengers might also be interested. Thus the idea expanded and became the story of the company that operated three of those passenger/cargo vessels and of the area and times in which that company operated. As it is largely written from my perspective, first as a youngster looking on, then as a young man working for the company and finally as senior master, president and half-owner of the company, it is also partly a memoir. The work ends in 1994 when my direct involvement with the company ended.

In writing the story of the early days of this company, up to 1960, I relied in part on a scrapbook containing letters, newspaper articles and photographs that was started by my mother, Peggy Young, in 1946. Other information has survived in the company files, although much was lost during office clear-outs. When we left Port Alberni, the files were thinned out by the simple expedient of bailing what we thought was useless into a dump truck parked below the second-storey office window. Undoubtedly, useful stuff disappeared along with the useless. I have also found some background information in the Alberni District Historical Society Archives.

To continue the chronology from 1960 to 1979, I relied on a series of five journals, two in my possession and three in the BC Provincial Archives. These were begun at the start of operations in Nootka Sound as a way for the two company principals and skippers, Esson Young (who was my father) and George McCandless, to communicate with each other on the affairs of the company. Esson's entries were sometimes musings on the state of the company with long passages on the direction that events were taking it and what he felt should be done next. George would add his comments on his watch the following week, although this type of entry was more common in the pioneering years of the Nootka Sound period. However, much of the information in the journals concerns ongoing business and notes about the work of maintaining the vessels. In scanning them for information, I often had to watch for little nuggets referring to matters previously discussed and not there in detail, but they served to prompt memories that had become buried. For example, I found one small note that says, "Found syrup is too cold for stars tonight." This reminded me that we had been practising taking star sights with a sextant but were having difficulty because we were at the wharf in Zeballos where we had no horizon to work with. To make an artificial horizon, we tried using a pan of water, but because the surface rippled in the slight breeze, we couldn't see the reflection of the star. Then we tried corn syrup, but it was too cold that night and the syrup wouldn't level itself properly.

As an owner and skipper I had full knowledge of company affairs from 1979 to 1991, but I still used the journals to pass word of the upcoming work to the skipper of the alternating crew, and these journals helped to remind me of events that were fading from my memory. The two ship's crews were reduced to one in 1991 so for that period I had to depend on my day-to-day working notes.

I have not tried to talk about all of the people involved in the company, only some of those who have influenced the direction that we took or for some other special reason. This doesn't diminish the contribution of the many people who worked hard at doing a good job under not very easy conditions. As my dad would say, "Given good men, you can take an awful licking before you have to throw in your hand."

CHART DISTANCES BETWEEN WEST COAST PORTS OF CALL

Distances given are in nautical miles:
  1 nautical mile = 1.85 kilometres
  1 nautical mile = 1.15 statute miles (1.15 x 5,280 = 6,072 feet)

The nautical mile is the distance on the earth's surface subtended by one minute of latitude at the earth's centre. The earth is not a perfect sphere so that length varies as we move away from the equator. The distance of 6,080 feet is accepted as a number to be used anywhere. For navigational purposes, the difference is not significant.

Port Alberni to Bamfield	30 nautical miles
Port Alberni to Ucluelet	46 nautical miles
Port Alberni to Tofino	68 nautical miles
Port Alberni to Nootka	109 nautical miles
Gold River to Nootka	24 nautical miles
Gold River to Tahsis	31 nautical miles
Gold River to Zeballos	39 nautical miles
Gold River to Kyuquot	66 nautical miles
Kyuquot to Fair Harbour	12 nautical miles

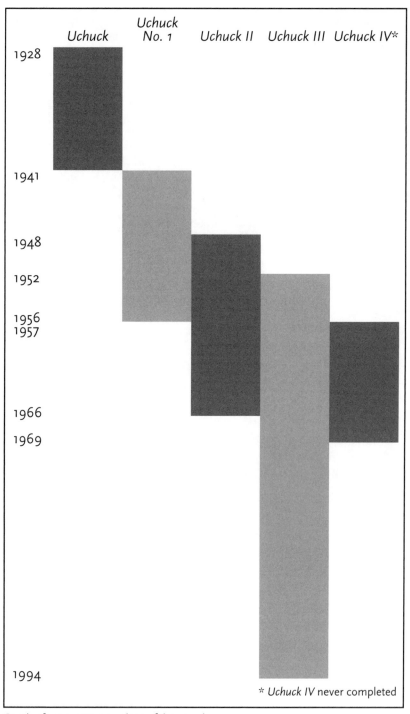

Graph of service time overlaps of the vessels.

CHAPTER ONE

A Brief History of Marine Companies in Barkley Sound

The story of the Barkley Sound Transportation Co. Ltd. and its three renowned motor vessels—*Uchuck I, II* and *III*—had its roots in events that occurred more than three decades earlier. In 1911 E.D. Stone arrived in the Alberni Valley of Vancouver Island, soon to be followed by his brother, Percy, and the two men went to work on the waterfront. Within ten years they were in the towing business and were also delivering mail around Barkley Sound, mainly to the people involved in the shore end of the fishing industry. In 1925 they built a passenger vessel named *Somass Queen* in their shipyard on the Somass River and began a regular service to the fish processing plants in the Sound. This ship was the first in a succession of vessels that they operated in that capacity. One of the men that they hired to run that service was named Richard Porritt, and sometime before 1936 he bought the part of the Stone's business that involved servicing the processing plants. (The Stone family carried on with their main towing business until 1974 when they sold it to Pacific Towing.) In 1936 Porritt bought a vessel from British Columbia Packers at Prince Rupert. This fifty-foot vessel, the MV *Uchuck*, had been built in 1928 and served him until he replaced her with the newly built vessel *Uchuck No. 1* in 1941. (In those times the second vessel with the same name was given the number one designation.) This was the first mail, passenger and freight vessel specifically built to run year-round in Barkley Sound.

It is not certain what the name "Uchuck" means but there are a lake and stream by that name at the head of Uchucklesit Inlet, and the name has some significance to the Native population. Some of the possible meanings of the word translate as good harbour, small spring, very wet and healing waters. The last of these seems to be the one most commonly accepted.

Perhaps before going further it would be useful to clarify the proper name for the territory served by the successive *Uchuck* vessels, which the people who ran them and used to them always referred to simply as "the West Coast." This could cause some confusion in other parts of Canada owing to different perspectives on what is meant by "west." In Central and Eastern Canada, the term "the West" applies to anything west of Ontario, and "the West Coast" applies to everything that lies beyond the Rocky Mountains. In BC, "the west coast" just refers to the point where the land meets the ocean. For the Hydrographic and Meteorological services it means the waters beyond the land, and they break it down into the North Coast, which includes the waters from Queen Charlotte Sound to the Alaskan border, and the South Coast, which includes the waters from Queen Charlotte Sound to Washington state. The part of the South Coast that is the concern of this book is that section that lies along the west

The MV *Uchuck No.1*, about 1945. ALBERNI VALLEY MUSEUM PHOTOGRAPH COLLECTION.

coast of Vancouver Island, extending from Pachena, which is just south of Bamfield, to Cape Scott at the northern tip of the island where it joins Queen Charlotte Sound. Among sailors, this stretch is simply known as the West Coast and we tend to follow that usage.

The West Coast was a busy place in the 1920s and1930s. There were fish canneries, salteries and reduction plants in the sounds employing hundreds of Chinese, Japanese and Native workers, who all lived out on the coast for the fishing season. Although a branch of the Esquimalt and Nanaimo Railway was completed to Port Alberni in 1911, most supplies and people were brought in by sea from Victoria and the Mainland and products shipped out the same way. In the years just before and during World War II the system began to change as larger fishing boats and packers were introduced that could take the catches to the processing plants on the Fraser River. After the war the huge production capability of US and Canadian factories was switched from war materiel production to the making of domestic goods. Better and cheaper engines and other equipment became available for the marine, fishing and logging industries, while at the same time activity on the West Coast ramped up as a flood of men came home from the war.

By 1946 fish processing had all but ended on the West Coast and the huge labour force had gone, leaving only remnants behind. The three places that were still operating were BC Packers' Kildonan cannery and the Green Cove saltery, both in Uchucklesit Inlet, and a reduction plant at Port Albion, across Ucluelet Inlet from the village of Ucluelet. The pilchard, a herring-like fish, was their mainstay species, but it mysteriously disappeared in 1947 in the same way that it had suddenly appeared in 1917.

However, from very early times the Alberni Valley had also been the centre for forestry on the west side of the island, and, as in both the southern and northern ends of Vancouver Island, logging by rail was the means of extraction here. The wood from the Ash Valley, northwest of Port Alberni, was brought to salt water at Polly Point, just south of the city. The logs from Franklin River, eight miles down the inlet from Port Alberni, and from small logging camps in Barkley Sound were towed up the Alberni Inlet to where sawmills, shingle mills, a plywood plant and finally a pulp and paper complex were built at the edge of the salt water

The *Uchuck No. 1* approaching a float at Ucluelet, September 1946.

at Port Alberni. The product was shipped out by rail or by cargo ships to anywhere in the world.

At the same time logging in Barkley Sound and Alberni Inlet remained small scale and in isolated patches in largely virgin territory. A-frame logging from the water was the method still in use here so the needs of all these operations were supplied by water transportation. Inland from these water-based operations, rail and, increasingly, truck logging was the way of the work.

The Pacific section of the world-girdling undersea communication cable that ran from Fanning Island, near Australia, terminated at the Bamfield cable station on the southeast side of the entrance to Barkley Sound. This station had been designed by Francis Rattenbury and built in 1902 on the site of a Nuu-chah-nulth (Nootka) village, and when the troll fishery developed, this sheltered place was the logical base for the fleet as it was close to the fishing ground. The last message to come through the cable arrived in June 1959, but the site reopened in 1972 as the Bamfield Marine Sciences Centre, a marine research centre for five universities.

On the west side of Barkley Sound the village of Ucluelet had grown up as a fishing centre. However, after the Japanese attack on Pearl Harbor in 1941, the federal government, concerned that the Japanese might try to land a force on the sparsely occupied BC coast, developed an air force base between the two settlements of Tofino and Ucluelet. Then, in order to move goods from salt water to the new base, they constructed a road between the two villages. By the end of the war there were small stable populations in all of these villages, and although the large fishing industry had faded somewhat, the logging industry had begun.

The Bamfield Cable Station in 1907, with the SS *Cascade* below. IMAGE C-07348 COURTESY OF ROYAL BC MUSEUM, BC ARCHIVES.

CHAPTER TWO

The Barkley Sound Transportation Company Ltd.

In February 1946 my father, Henry Esson Young, and his friend, George Bartlett McCandless, took over Richard Porritt's marine transportation business then operating in Barkley Sound from a base in Port Alberni. They named their new company Barkley Sound Transportation Co. Ltd.

Henry Esson Young (known to everyone as Esson) was born in 1910, the only son of Dr. Henry Esson Young, who had been elected to the provincial legislature in 1903 and served as minister of education and provincial secretary for a number of years. More importantly for BC, from 1915 to 1939 he was provincial medical officer and was largely responsible for the establishment of the University of British Columbia, a tuberculosis sanatorium near Kamloops and a mental health facility outside New Westminster. For all his good works, my grandfather was a tyrant in the family home in Oak Bay, and my father was afraid of him until he began asserting himself when he was in his mid-teens. My father attended UBC, but rather than go into medicine as his father had done, he chose the sea, and in 1933 he got a job as third mate on the cargo ship SS *Bright Star*. He then began studying for his second mate (foreign) certificate.

When the war came, my father joined the Royal Canadian Navy. His first posting was to the old fisheries patrol vessel *Malaspina*, a 162-foot vessel built in 1913 that had also been impressed into West Coast patrol duty for the navy in World War I. In March 1942 Esson graduated to the command of the brand-new, 110-foot Fairmile ML-069, another of the ships that patrolled the West Coast. But as all the action was on the East Coast, he soon began thumping people's desks until he was allowed to go east where he became executive officer of the corvette HMCS *Buctouche*. He assumed command of the *Buctouche* as skipper lieutenant in August 1943 and remained in that post until he was demobilized in August 1945.

Esson Young in 1933, just starting his maritime career as 3rd Officer of the SS *Bright Star*.

My mother (who was known to everyone as Peggy), my younger brother, Tony, and I very seldom saw him during these years. I remember that once he visited with us for just two days as it was a five-day train journey from the east coast. When I was six, the *Buctouche* went into Halifax for a refit, so my mother farmed Tony and me out while she went east to join him. I was sent to my grandparents in West Vancouver and had a magical time on their two and a half acres on Inglewood Avenue. Finally the day came just after VJ Day when father came home for good, carrying the decommissioned *Buctouche*'s bell in a sack.

With the war over, he was ready to restart his life, but he was now thirty-six and the best he could get was a manual labouring job at J. Fyfe Smith Lumber Co. Ltd. in Vancouver. It was a stop-gap job that provided an income, but it was typical of the come-down situation that many veterans found themselves in during those early post-war days. Then an old friend, Bob Rolston, head of Dale and Company in Vancouver, a major marine insurance company, told him about the small marine transportation business owned by Richard Porritt that was for sale in Port Alberni. Esson investigated and said to himself, "That's for me!" Then he looked around for someone to go into this venture with him.

George Bartlett McCandless was born in 1910 just two weeks after my father. His father, who had owned a clothing store in Victoria, died young, and his mother took George and his two brothers to California. He once told me of attending an institute there where he took three or four courses in rotation. Two of them were electricity and the third was art and when he finally got to the art class, the teacher told him that he should have come to her first because he was, in fact, a born artist and could draw and carve extremely well. However, when he returned to BC, he went to work for William York Higgs' tugboat company, towing log booms and barges in the Strait of Georgia. Later he was hired by Canadian Pacific Steamships for the north coast runs and by the time the war came he had become a junior officer. Like my father, during the war George skippered a Fairmile on the west coast, then became the navigating officer on a frigate that was taken to the east coast where he served for the remainder of the war. On his return in 1945, he went to work again for CP Steamships, but it was not what he wanted to do for the rest of his life, so he welcomed Esson's proposal to join him in buying Porritt's company.

George McCandless on the *Uchuck II*.
MCCANDLESS COLLECTION PHOTO.

Both men owned homes in Victoria and with the go-ahead from their wives, they sold their houses and then went to the banks to raise the rest of the $40,000 they needed. (Houses were only worth around $5,000 or less in those days.) In the end Esson raised 60 percent of the money and George 40 percent, but they always treated their arrangement as if it was a fifty-fifty deal.

The two men were very different in personality and the way in which they dealt with problems. George was rather volatile, but Esson was more thoughtful, a good talker who could form a reasoned argument on any subject that he was dealing with. Everyone listened when he spoke. As a result, there were a few bumps at the beginning of their relationship, but they soon sorted them out and found that they understood one another and complemented each other very well. They went at their new venture with pent-up energy and the work ethic they had developed in the 1930s. There was a lot to be learned quickly as they were taking over an existing operation with an established route and steady traffic in passengers and cargo travelling to the three main ports of Kildonan, Bamfield and Ucluelet.

When they started out, the partners brought a professional air to the work by wearing their navy uniforms, minus the rings of the RCNR on the jacket sleeves and with the merchant service cap badge in place of the navy one. But after a short while, Esson, who was of moderate height but in good physical shape as he had been a terror on the rugby field, abandoned the uniform jacket and hat, replacing them with a blue V-neck pullover and black leather jacket, but still keeping the white shirt and black tie, navy blue pants and polished black shoes. This became his uniform for the rest of his working life. George, who was taller than Esson but also muscular, abandoned the idea of a uniform fairly early on as well and adopted a more casual look that was patterned on the American naval khakis.

The *Uchuck I*

The winter of 1946 was warm, wet and windy—what today we would recognize as an El Niño winter—and it seemed that on each trip out the partners took a beating from violent weather. The route that Porritt had set up was somewhat sheltered on the first leg, starting at Port Alberni at the head of Alberni Inlet, going to Kildonan in Uchucklesit Inlet and thence along the east side of Barkley Sound to Bamfield. From Bamfield, the next twenty-mile leg included crossing the mouth of Barkley Sound to Ucluelet, a sometimes perilous beam-on-to-the-weather journey. The vessel travelled through open water and narrow passages between islands in wild weather in winter and sometimes thick fog in other seasons. The return passage from Ucluelet to Port Alberni was easier after the first half-hour as the vessel travelled along the west side of the Sound before getting back into the Alberni Inlet.

In the mid-latitudes on the Island's West Coast the weather systems consist of high and low pressure areas coming from the west, and before modern forecasting tools had been invented, vessels travelling along the West Coast didn't know what was happening out there on the ocean so storms came at them as a surprise. Of course, those who could read the clouds and knew what a barometer was telling them had some warning of what might happen, but they only got a few hours of advance notice at best. In any case, while there are natural rules of behaviour for weather systems and their wind regimes that were well understood even in those days, once those systems arrive on the coast, the shape of the landforms they encounter helps to dictate the local wind direction. The mountains, valleys and inlets redirect the airflow that is drawn from high to low pressure areas via a path of least resistance. Wind velocities, for instance, can suddenly change where venturi and corner effects at narrowings in the inlets and valleys come into play. As a result, the partners needed to build up a body of local knowledge to be able to predict what would happen in the various locations along their route when given a current weather forecast.

My first trip on the *Uchuck I* was nearly my last. It was shortly after my father and George acquired the vessel and I was not yet eight years old. I was lying down on the wide shelf above the bench seat in the wheelhouse, having been put there for my own safety while the vessel rolled her way across the mouth of Barkley Sound in a southeast gale. Then it came to be time for me to be seasick. I clambered down from my perch and started out the door, which my dad was holding open for me. In that vessel the deck of the wheelhouse was three feet above the main deck and level with the top of the guardrail around the deck. Just as I was stepping out, the vessel rolled down to starboard and I stepped off toward a black hole in the ocean. Fortunately for me, it happened that an Air Force serviceman was standing in the lee of the wheelhouse by the door, trying not to be sick, and as I was about to clear the rail on my way to the ocean, he grabbed a handful of the back of my jacket and brought me back inside the rail. The rest of the story has faded from my memory, but I do remember meeting that serviceman on another trip a few years later, and we recognized each other even though I had grown a lot by then.

The wheelhouse of the *Uchuck No. 1*, which was a twin screw vessel with wheelhouse control. The photo was taken from the shelf seen in the lower right hand corner, which was the same shelf that I lay on during my first trip, which was also nearly my last.

In spite of my near drowning, at the age of ten I entered the company fray on weekends and holidays and was earning twenty-five cents a day (out of Dad's pocket) by the time I was twelve. That began an involvement with the company that lasted for the next forty-six years.

In the beginning the *Uchuck I*'s run was designed to serve all the ports in the Sound three times per week: Mondays, Wednesdays and Fridays. The vessel's Port Alberni departure point was the fishermen's float in the inner harbour just across from Alberni Engineering on Bird Street, and passengers embarked from the foot of the gangway off the wharf-head. On the afternoon before a sailing, the vessel was moved forward from the float to a position beside the garage door of the freight shed at the wharf-head. The outgoing cargo was loaded through the sliding door onto the vessel, which when loaded was moved back to her berth. On the following morning, any late-arriving cargo—five- and ten-gallon milk cans, wire cages of rattling milk bottles (which tinkled all day with the slightest vibrations of the vessel), or cases of fresh bread and produce—was slid down the ramp and loaded by hand. The passengers boarded afterward through a lift-out gate in the rail.

That's me, seven years old, standing in front of our freight shed at the Bird Street wharf. ALBERNI VALLEY MUSEUM PHOTOGRAPH COLLECTION.

Landing a load of mail on a four-wheel dolly to be wheeled into the freight shed on the Argyle Street wharf. George McCandless is in the coveralls and I am on the winch.
FINNING TRACTOR PHOTO.

The *Uchuck I* was equipped with a simple system of cargo handling gear that consisted of a single swinging derrick, a friction winch and a bunch of snotters and slings. A snotter is a three-quarter-inch-diameter, ten- to fifteen-foot-long line with an eye spliced in each end; slings are made from the same diameter line, but the two ends are spliced together to form a big loop that is ten to fifteen feet long when stretched out. In addition to these, there were woven nets made from slightly smaller manila line with lifting ears in each of the four corners. These were used to handle small, irregularly shaped items like mail bags or small sacks of rice or anything too odd-shaped to sling.

The friction winch was simple but required some dexterity to use. It had a handle that the winch driver slowly employed until there was enough pressure on the friction blocks to cause the drum to turn and lift a load. When it was high enough, the handle was brought back enough to neither lift nor let the load fall but just to keep it in balance. A foot pedal was used to tighten a brake band on the end of the drum. One could lower the load with just the friction or just the brake or, if working with heavy lifts, by using the friction in combination with the brake. If you didn't use either, the load would free-fall. One day in Bamfield at low tide, John Monrufet was lowering a pinball machine from the wharf into the ship. He often got bored with repetitive actions, so this time he let the load fall for awhile before he tried to stop it with the brake, which was fine—except that the sling broke. There was a royal crash when it arrived in the hold in an explosion of springs, lights, nickels and a whole lot of broken wood and glass. Esson's comment was: "That was a little fast, John."

Monrufet worked for us for several years, first as engineer for periods of time in all of the company's vessels and then as mate after he qualified for that position. He designed the engine room and oversaw the installation of the machinery in the *Uchuck III*.

The loading procedure was to lay a stretched-out sling on the wharf, pile cartons of groceries, for example, in two side-by-side piles, one box on top of another, heavy items on the bottom, light on top. Then the two protruding ends of the sling were pulled up from each side of the pile and choked together over the top of the boxes. When the cargo hook swung back to the wharf for the next load, it was hooked onto the choked sling. The winchman took the strain, the man on the wharf set the lift by hitting the choked ends to make sure the sling had gripped the load securely, and then the winchman lifted it. The derrick swung over the ship and the load was lowered into the hold through the hatch. The man in the hold pushed the sling load to where he wanted it, signalled to the winchman to lower, and then released the hook, which went back for another load. The process went on, load after load, until there was a solid layer in the bottom of the hold, after which a second layer was started.

This method of handling cargo was the accepted way of doing things but certainly not the best use of the space, there being lots of air spaces between loads, and it didn't allow for special handling of more delicate items like eggs. An innovation came when the tray was introduced. This was a plywood platform about two and a half by four feet that was stiffened on the edges with oak runners and set with ringbolts at the corners. Lines were spliced to the rings to make a lifting bridle that would take the cargo hook. The tray was put on a four-wheeled dolly in the freight shed, loaded with boxes and then pushed out to the loading area beside the vessel. In the hold, the boxes were taken off the tray, sorted and hand stowed. The empty tray was set to one side on edge and the next one lowered in. The new load was unhooked, the empty tray hooked on and sent back. This was a better use of the space and improved the condition of the goods but was still a lot of work.

The load was built up toward the hatch opening and finally a net load of mail was set on top and spread out, leaving just enough room to put the hatch boards back in place. The canvas cover was pulled over and battened down. The top of the hatch and the deck space on either side was then filled with more trays, the boxes now left loaded on the trays, along with all other cargo that did not need to be sheltered or was too awkward to go below. This method was pretty much how the *Uchuck I* was loaded for her whole time in Barkley Sound.

There was no proper way to handle goods that needed to be kept cooled or frozen, so those goods had to be brought down on the morning of the sailing. In high summer there was a risk that we might lose some; in winter, the opposite was the problem, but could be addressed more easily, as the hold maintained the cargo heat for the duration of the trip. Ice cream and frozen food was shipped in large, green, heavily insulated hampers using dry ice (solid carbon dioxide) as the cooling agent. Packaged frozen food was still a new idea so there wasn't much traffic in that yet.

Refrigeration for the vessel's own supplies consisted of a top-loading icebox near the little coffee counter at the after end of the main cabin. The ice came from the ice house at Kildonan. Twice a week when we were delivering to Kildonan, I would take our little ice tongs and walk up to the ice house on the main wharf. This place was large and cold so I, in my rolled-up sleeves in summer, would enter through the meat-safe-type door to be hit with a blast of frigid air. Inside, two or three workmen, dressed in parkas, gloves and toques, would be moving slowly in the dim light, rather like a scene out of Dante's *Inferno*, only in reverse. They would push five-foot-high blocks of ice from where they had been formed onto a conveyor belt, which took them through an opening to the outside of the building and up a ramp over the wharf to a little shack. There, with a great roar that shook the whole structure, a machine reduced the block to shaved flakes that rattled down a chute into the hold of a fishing vessel moored below.

This load would keep the salmon cold during the troller's next ten days of fishing. Sometimes a block would break before it left the building and the pieces were put in a small room to one side. That was where I went to find a piece about the right shape and size to fit in our icebox and still small enough that I could carry.

The vessel left Port Alberni at 08:00 and the crew tried to have her back by 18:00 because the runs were tied into the bus schedule that connected the town to points south on Vancouver Island. Within a year the vessel was running six days per week to divide the traffic up. Monday, Wednesday and Friday were Ucluelet days and Tuesday, Thursday and Saturday were Kildonan, Sarita River and Bamfield days.

From the start, it was a very personalized business as Esson and George were in direct contact with the customers at all the ports. They were often asked to do or get things for people when they were back in Port Alberni. Someone wanted a pig, someone else a truck and another wanted a clock taken to the jewellers for repair. When the jeweller didn't want to deal with the clock, rather than take it back still broken, George figured out what was wrong and fixed it. Once Esson was asked to visit someone in hospital and then report on what he had discovered on his next trip out. Shepherding loose children or pets home from away was a normal part of their business.

Judging by newspaper reports of the time, nothing was too much trouble for the partners and the company was developing a good reputation as they brought new energy to the enterprise. However, from the outset they were aware that there was a movement to connect the existing road between Ucluelet and Tofino to the east side of Vancouver Island, and since Ucluelet was the single biggest port that the company served, they understood that when the link-up was made, traffic would fall off. As a result, they worked hard to provide additional services. One of the first additions to the summer schedule was a Sunday excursion to Bamfield, which allowed a four-hour stopover for people to enjoy a day at Brady's Beach. They had to take the trail across Mills Peninsula from the west side of Bamfield Inlet to this distinctly West Coast beach that faces the ocean, but it was about the only one available to people from the Albernis. (Alberni and Port Alberni were separate towns until 1967.) There were charter trips as well where groups such as service organizations, high school graduation classes and individual grade-school classes went for a day at the beach. The travelling time of three hours each way was short enough that there was adequate play time when they got there.

The two speedboat companies in Barkley Sound were in brutal competition with each other. Reece Riley had operated two fast vessels there since the mid-1930s—the *Maureen R.* and the *Black Hawk*—and he had cornered all the business of carrying marine pilots out to and in from foreign-going vessels coming and going from Port Alberni. He later bought a vessel based on a troller design, the *R.E. Riley*, especially for that job then built another bigger and faster one, the *R.E. Riley II*. As there were many ships in and out of the port, his boats were busy. The other speedboat company had two boats—*Commodore* and *Whirlaway*. Dorothy Clayton (Blackmore), the daughter of one of the original waterfront families, was the person in charge of this outfit when we arrived.

The competitive nature of these two companies was extended to Barkley Sound Transportation when Esson and George arrived, but they were not interested in fighting, so eventually everyone became friends. When one of Dorothy's boats broke down in Ucluelet, the *Uchuck I* brought in the parts that were needed to repair it rather than get the better of the competition by leaving her stranded.

The boats carried passengers to all points in Barkley Sound on a scheduled and charter basis. However, the waters were difficult for small boats

A full load for a Sunday excursion to Bamfield, about 1950.

to operate in as they had to travel in all weathers, night or day, in the long inlets that were littered with floating debris. Neither of these companies was around for long after Barclay Sound Transportation started up, but we saw them often while they were operating.

In 1946 when my family moved to Port Alberni and I first became aware of the Native people of the West Coast, they lived in many places in the sounds, some still travelling from place to place in dugout canoes. We would see canoes loaded with people towing a second canoe with their belongings, which were often contained in galvanized wash tubs with blankets tied over the top. By that time the canoes were powered with Briggs and Stratton inboard engines of four to five horsepower. Barkley Sound is not far north of tidal, saltwater Nitnat Lake where the Natives were renowned builders of seagoing canoes, living among huge trees as they do. I saw some of these fitted out with trolling poles and used in the commercial salmon troll fishery off Bamfield out to Cape Beale.

In Port Alberni on one summer afternoon with the customary strong inflow wind blowing, I had watched a twenty-foot plywood cabin cruiser powered by an outboard leave the fisherman's floats to head out across the inlet and then up the Somass River toward the village of Alberni. The white man aboard it had been planning to make the trip with his wife, child and dog, but the rough water generated by the afternoon westerly wind convinced the woman and child to take the bus. The man left, his boat leaping and bounding over the waves before disappearing safely up the river. Shortly after, a powered sixteen-foot dugout canoe with three large Natives in it followed the same route with no fuss at all. The canoe rose and fell on the waves so that, when the canoe subsided into the troughs, all that I could see were the heads and shoulders of the three men sitting stolidly in a row.

In those days business in general seemed to be conducted in a simpler way than it is today and this was true of the company's bookkeeping. Barkley

---

MV *UCHUCK I*

Built: Vancouver, BC in 1941
Length: 70 feet
Beam: 15.5 feet
Tonnage: GRT 68.67
Official number: 173412
Power: 2 D8800 Caterpillar diesels
Passenger capacity: 64
Cargo capacity: 9 tons
Cargo gear: single swinging derrick; Washington friction winch-
    powered from a P.T.O. off port main engine
Lifeboats: two sixteen-foot clinker-built on radial davits
Service speed: 10 knots
Crew: master, mate, cook. No engineer was necessary as the engines
    were operated from the wheelhouse.

Sound Transportation Co. Ltd. was just one of the clients of Gwynne
Wheatley, a public bookkeeper located in an office in the Ormand Block
on Fourth Avenue in Port Alberni. He had one assistant, Mrs. Audrey
Peterson, who worked on all of the accounts, but as Barkley Sound
Transportation's business increased, more and more of their time was taken
up with the company's affairs. When Wheatley died in 1960, nothing really changed where the bookkeeping was concerned: Esson hired Audrey
Peterson to be the company's full-time bookkeeper and at the same time
took over the rent for the office space. As our family home was in Port
Alberni, Esson was able to work in the office on any day that he wasn't
fulfilling his skipper's duties.

Within a few years the company's business seemed to be on the verge
of breaking out into something much bigger. One reason for this improvement was that Bloedel Stewart & Welch (that merged in 1951 with H.R.
MacMillan Ltd. to become MacMillan and Bloedel Ltd.) was establishing
a logging camp at Sarita River, five miles east of Bamfield. This camp,
when it reached peak production, employed about 350 men, many with
their families living in camp, and because there was no road between Port

Alberni and Sarita River there was a huge increase in cargo and many more passengers for the *Uchuck I* to carry.

The *Uchuck II*

It was soon evident that another vessel was needed, and in late 1947 the partners learned that the Corporation of West Vancouver, having ended its West Vancouver to Vancouver ferry service, was selling off its fleet. This service, which carried foot passengers only, had been running since 1909 and had even continued for another nine years after the Lions Gate Bridge was opened for traffic in November 1938.

At 03:00 on February 1, 1948, the *West Vancouver No. 6* departed from Vancouver with all her big forward cabin windows boarded up in order to make the trip to her new home port of Port Alberni. The weather was good, considering that it was February, and the passage was completed by late in the evening of the same day. The vessel was moved to the inner floats, just below the shipyard marine railway, across the float from the *Uchuck I*. Work began immediately. First, the twenty-foot-long forward cabin and the wheelhouse on top of it were broken up and removed. The removal was done by a Port Alberni man named Dick McMinn, whom

The *West Vancouver No. 6*, prior to becoming the *Uchuck II*. ALBERNI VALLEY MUSEUM PHOTOGRAPH COLLECTION.

George McCandless had known from his days with Canadian Pacific Steamships before the war. Dick paddled the waste material across the inner harbour on a two-log raft to a pebble beach just below the CPR railway tracks where it was landed and burned. He was to remain with the company as mate and then master until sometime after the company moved to Nootka Sound.

After the stripping was done, the forward part of the vessel rose significantly in the water. A cargo hatch was built in the middle of the newly created deck space and the area below deck was cleared out to become a cargo hold. The old mast was replaced with a new one in the same position and a single swinging cargo derrick was added in front of it. A new wheelhouse was built, this time behind the mast. Inside, the passenger accommodations took on a more modern and comfortable look with a coffee shop added in the main cabin and a crew's galley and messroom built below between the cargo hold and engine room. The machinery stayed very much the same. The four main contractors for this work were all local businesses—the Alberni Shipyard, Alberni Engineering, Bailey Electric and Ormond's Plumbing. By the end of May the work was nearly done. In just four months the vessel had been converted from a ferry to a small coaster, now named *Uchuck II*.

Cargo Handling

The cargo handling procedure in the *Uchuck II* was the same as that for the No. 1, only the scale was a little bigger. Where the No. 1 could carry about nine tons of general cargo, the No. 2 could carry about twenty-one tons. The trays were bigger and in the hold there were two shelves, one on either side, under the hatch opening where the trays could be pushed as they descended, two on either side. This arrangement allowed trays containing thirty cases of beer or milk to be left on the tray and not be hand-stowed, thus saving time and work.

The winch lifting capacity was about one ton per lift but could be increased by "doubling up the gear." This procedure meant lowering the derrick and slipping the cargo hook into an eye at the derrick head then putting a snatch block into the bight of the cargo runner. With the derrick back up, the new configuration created a tackle with a mechanical advantage of two, which nearly doubled the lift capacity. However, with a heavier lift in the air, it was more difficult to swing the derrick across the vessel because she would list over when the winch took the weight. The operator would have to pull the load uphill to bring it over the hatch opening. He also had to be careful not to let the load get out of control and swing over the other way; this happened to a vessel at Fair Harbour when a boom guy line parted with the result that she capsized and sank alongside the wharf.

Lifesaving Gear

The *Uchuck I* and *II* were equipped with very simple lifesaving equipment: each had two double-ended lifeboats lying in chocks on deck. They were handled with small cranes called radial davits, one at each end of the boat, and tackles made up of two triple blocks each—a system called "boat falls." The davits were mounted outboard, opposite each end of the boat, and stood on pivoting bearings that were mounted on the outboard hull guard, which allowed them to be rotated. One block of the falls was attached to an eye in the davit, the davit being bent in a curve to ninety degrees so that the end was directly over the centre line of the lifeboat. The second block was attached to a hook inside one end of the lifeboat. There was enough line in the falls to allow the lifeboat to reach the water from the vessel in light condition and listed twenty degrees either way. The coil of line was stowed in the lifeboat along with all of its other gear and the whole lifeboat covered with a fitted canvas cover.

The procedure to launch a lifeboat was to lift it out of the chocks with the tackles, secure the line, push the lifeboat straight back while pushing the bow outward, thus rotating the forward davit. Next, the lifeboat was pushed

Alongside the net float at Kildonan. Note the radial davits and lifeboats.

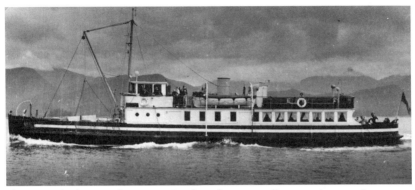

The MV *Uchuck No. 2* after conversion from ferry to small coaster, June 1948.

ahead until the stern cleared the after davit, which allowed the stern to be pushed outboard, too. Now the lifeboat was hanging over the water on the outside of the davits. The davits were lashed in this position, the lines were slacked off at the same time, and the lifeboat was lowered to the water where a man positioned at each end of the boat freed the blocks from the hooks, releasing the boat. If the vessel was rolling around or moving ahead, they had to be careful to hold the boat from swinging before easing off and lowering it. Once in the water, both blocks had to be released at the same moment in case the ship rolled back the other way while the boat was still attached by one end. In large ships, the crew and passengers would be in the boat during this procedure, but with vessels as small as the *Uchuck I* and *II,* it was safer and easier to have people embark later. This was accomplished by pulling the lifeboat up to the gate in the rail amidships on the main deck on the No. 1 or to the big side doors of the No. 2.

Each vessel was also equipped with five "buoyant apparatus," wooden frame platforms, four by four feet by eighteen inches, with slatted tops and bottoms and a line attached around the outside perimeter arranged in loops with a wooden handhold in each loop. To use these, the people were supposed to be in the water holding onto the handholds. Flotation was supplied by four copper air tanks that were fitted into the sections of the float. Each apparatus had a lanyard attached to it so all five could all be kept together in the water.

The *Uchuck I* and *II* were both equipped with six life rings made of cork and covered with canvas. Three had long lines so they could be thrown to a person in the water if the vessel was not moving. Three had canisters attached to them and to the vessel's rail so that, when the ring was thrown overboard, it pulled a plug out of the canister, allowing salt water to get in and start a re-action with the carbide crystals inside. This produced a smoky flame, which could be easily seen both night and day. Later these were changed to battery-operated lights with mercury switches that turned the lights on once the apparatus was righted in the water by the ballast weight in the light's barrel.

Both vessels were equipped with enough life jackets for all passengers and crew, plus 10 percent more as spares. In the No. 1 they were made of cotton canvas and filled with kapok, a light cotton fibre, and then sewn into plastic bags. They were in two joined sections, a front and a back, slipped over the head and lashed to the body with tapes around the pads and tied around the waist. The No. 2, having been built earlier, had canvas and cork jackets with four packets of thin cork sheets pegged together then sewn into panels for a front and a back.

To mark the occasion of the completed conversion of the *Uchuck II*, the partners organized a special celebratory day cruise for all those who had been involved in the work. The first commercial run was an excursion to Bamfield on the following day, a Sunday.

The fishermen's float and wharf that the *Uchuck I* had been using in Port Alberni was not big enough to handle both vessels, so they were moved to the town's new Argyle Street wharf. The long approach to this wharf, which was sandwiched between the old CPR wharf and the Port Boat House, extended from the end of Argyle Street over the mud flat. Today the Harbour Quay sits on the site of the Port Boat House, a collec-tion of buildings on floats where sports fishermen could rent sixteen- and eighteen-foot Briggs and Stratton-powered boats for seventy-five cents an hour. (The beautiful little fourteen-foot clinker-built rowboats rented for twenty-five cents an hour.) The targets for these fishermen were the spring salmon, some over sixty pounds, returning to the Somass River.

As the company was now operating two vessels, the six-day sched-ule was divided so that the *Uchuck I* looked after the Kildonan, Sarita and Bamfield ports, and the *Uchuck II* went to Ucluelet with intermediate stops as necessary. The two vessels sailed on alternate days, leaving Sunday open for tourist trips and charters in summer. These changes meant that there had to be two crews, so Esson and George each headed a crew that

The approach to the Argyle Street Wharf with all three vessels seen at the end, in 1954. The CPR wharf is on the left and the Port Boat House on the right.

sailed three days a week and used two of the off-days for maintenance and loading. This pattern, once established, was to stay in place for the remaining time that their company operated in Barkley Sound.

The only other ship providing freight services to Ucluelet was the Canadian Pacific Steamships' *Princess Maquinna*, which had been an institution on the West Coast since 1913. It operated on a ten-day round trip basis, starting out from Victoria on the first, eleventh and twenty-first of each month. It was the *Maquinna* that got most of the new government business in the Tofino/Ucluelet area during the Cold War construction of the Pine Tree Line's westernmost radar station at the Tofino Airport. And the ship got more business after the first radar equipment was deemed obsolete and even newer equipment had to be brought in. (Shortly thereafter it was found that Tofino's range overlapped with two others and the station itself was redundant.) However, the *Uchuck II* was making runs to Ucluelet three days every week, making it possible for the people and businesses there to import perishables and rush items reliably and often, so the company's business continued to grow as more and more shippers used their services in preference to the *Maquinna's* three-times-a-month service.

Then, in the midst of this improvement in business, very early on the

MV *UCHUCK II*

Built: Wallace Shipyard in North Vancouver in 1925 for the
Corporation of West Vancouver and named *West Vancouver No. 6*
Purchased: Barkley Sound Transportation Co. Ltd. in January 1948.
Length: 109 feet
Beam: 18 feet
Power: one Atlas Imperial Diesel 200-hp direct reversing air-start
engine. This was changed to a 300-hp Union Diesel in 1955 after
the crankshaft broke in the Atlas engine.
Cargo gear: a single swinging derrick and friction winch driven with a
V-4 Wisconsin gasoline engine.
Passenger capacity: 100
Cargo Capacity: 21 tons
Service speed: with Atlas engine 10 knots; with Union engine 12
knots
Lifeboats: two eighteen-foot clinker-built wooden boats on radial
davits
Crew: master, mate, engineer, cook

morning of February 11, 1950, just as the last minute cargo deliveries
were arriving for the *Uchuck II*, the McGavin's truck driver noticed a curl
of smoke rising from one of the midship cowl vents. He hurried off to call
the fire department, which immediately responded and, when ready with
their equipment and with Esson on hand to open up the ship, they burst
in to deal with the situation. The cause of the fire was a small coal-burning
stove in the engine room that was used to keep the chill off the vessel
in cold weather; it had failed through age, allowing the bottom to drop
out and hot coals to escape. The firemen's quick action saved the vessel,
but the mid-section was gutted. Fortunately, the machinery was not badly
damaged.

The restoration began with the wheelhouse being lifted off and set on
the wharf so that the wooden construction around the engine room could
be torn out and replaced. All the wiring and switchboards in the middle
part of the vessel had to be replaced as well. This work took until May to

complete, and in the meantime the *Uchuck I* took over both runs. This meant loading the vessel at night after she came back from the day's run. The volume of cargo taxed the smaller vessel, but she did the job successfully. Life returned to normal when the No. 2 resumed her runs.

The *Uchuck III*

As business continued to grow, it soon was once again apparent that Barkley Sound Transportation needed more equipment, and again the hunt was on for another vessel. The next new vessel was found in Vancouver—the stripped-out hulk of a US Navy YMS minesweeper. The US Navy had built 561 of these Yard class minesweepers in small shipyards across the country. They were a very successful design, intended for inshore mine sweeping, and they were present at all the landings of soldiers on Pacific beaches, going in ahead to clear the way for the landing craft. They were so sturdy that I have heard of one still active in 2006 for the Norwegian navy.

YMS 123 had been completed in 1943 by Kruse and Banks Shipyard of North Bend, Oregon, and then moved to a base at Mare Island, which is not far from San Francisco, to do patrol duty off the west coast of the US and Canada. After the war the vessel had been struck from the naval list, sold into private hands, then imported into Canada. When Esson came across her in his search, she had been lying uncared for in Vancouver Harbour for four years after having been stripped of all useful equipment. There wasn't so much as a light switch left. Esson took Bill Osborne, shipwright and

The reconstruction of the *YMS 123* into the *Uchuck III* is just about to begin. Note the gun mounts still in place.

The *YMS 123* being towed by the *Uchuck I* from Vancouver to Port Alberni, where it would be transformed into the *Uchuck III*.

owner of Alberni Shipyard, to see it, and Bill reported that it was sound and would have probably cost a half million in 1952 dollars to build to that level of quality.

The vessel was purchased for $5,000, and the *Uchuck I*, with George McCandless in charge, went to Vancouver to tow the derelict to Port Alberni. After passing Victoria and starting up the West Coast, George found that he needed to tow it stern-first in order to have it follow, more or less, in the wake of the *Uchuck I*. He arrived in Port Alberni with the sorry-looking wreck in tow and berthed it alongside the outer fishermen's floats while a space was prepared on the inner floats for the conversion to begin. Meanwhile, a huge garbage cleanup had to take place as someone had been living on board while it lay in Vancouver harbour.

Fortunately, when the hulk was at last hauled out on the marine railway of the yard, she was found to be in good condition underwater. Her conversion was to become a lengthy process, done as money was available, but at the same time, the simplicity of the new design would help make the vessel reliable and strong. The work had to be done as cheaply and simply as possible so the crews of the other two vessels were put to work on the job whenever they were available. They stripped off the gun mountings and tore out broken and useless parts. There was a royal splash when the castings that the three-inch gun had rested on were heaved over the side from the fo'c'sle. Then there was a general cleanup to see just what the company had acquired. I was part of the crew that stripped out all of the heavily armoured electrical wire from the engine room (and indeed the whole ship), cut off the bad parts and stretched it out to be used again. In later years people would remark on the strange positioning of some light switch, but

I knew this was because the length of some piece of the recycled wire had dictated that position.

In her original configuration, the housework of *YMS 123* was right up against the raised fo'c'sle head and reached to about midway along her length, and the rest of the deck space was open in order to accommodate the mine sweeping gear. For our purposes, the whole deckhouse with the wheelhouse on top of it had to be lifted, rolled back thirty feet and set down onto newly made sills. To make the move, the crew had to cut the hold-down bolts that ran from under the top of the covering boards on the outside edges of the cabin tops, down through the sides of the cabins, through the deck to the point where they were fastened to strong-points in the under-deck space. This had been the common method of stiffening the whole structure in wooden vessels, and some masters maintained a logbook recording when these bolts were tightened over the years of operation. As it would be too complicated to fasten the deckhouse down again in the original way, we had to invent a different way to stiffen the structure. With the housework pushed back, an expanse of bare deck was exposed, and we cut an eight-by-sixteen-foot hatch into this deck, then constructed proper hatch coamings, complete with sixteen hatch boards and notches put in on the inside of the coamings for king and sister beams. These eight-by-eight-inch beams were to be rigged whenever the vessel was loaded with cargo in order to put the strength back into the weakened structure. However, this practice didn't last very long as we found it to be unnecessary.

Once the deckhouse was secured in its new location, we built another section of deckhouse on behind to extend it almost to the stern of the vessel. It was built extra strongly to take the weight of the lifeboats and their lifting equipment. The original cabin had been divided up into separate spaces, but now we cleared it to become a large open passenger lounge with a coffee shop. The shipwrights put in many windows, built-in booths with tables, and then sheeted the bulkheads in light-coloured birch plywood.

Below the main deck and forward of the engine room was a second engine room that had housed the generating equipment that made power for the sweep gear. There were also compartments to house the asdic, the anti-submarine detection gear, and more fuel and water tanks plus living quarters. All of this had to be gutted out to make a thirty-four-foot cargo hold.

When reconstruction started in the engine room, the heart of the vessel, George McCandless stopped his regular sailing shifts in the two other vessels and went to work on the new one full-time. He often worked alone, but it was quickly evident that he was bringing forward motion to the project, and soon a welder from Alberni Engineering was assigned to the job on a nearly constant basis. Then John Monrufet, the overseeing engineer, began planning and laying out the engine room for the equipment that was to come.

By the summer of 1953 the reconstruction to create the *Uchuck III* was well underway and the vessel was taking form. Esson and George scrounged equipment from wherever it could be found. At that time Capital Iron Works of Victoria was breaking up surplus ships, including those of the Canadian Pacific fleet, and salvaging the parts for resale. There were mounds of propellers and steering wheels and deck equipment. There were masts and lifeboats and everything else needed to construct a ship. Boxes of light switches sold for a dollar. The partners paid scrap prices for the bridge telegraphs that had been on the *Princess Victoria,* a pittance for the *Princess Mary*'s wheelhouse steering gear standard and next to nothing for two of the *Mary*'s lifeboats. Some of the gear was rather bigger than the vessel really needed, but it was made to fit.

Dick McMinn was given the job of rigging the mast and derricks, which had been taken out of the *Princess Mary* and had arrived in a tangle of rigging wire and turnbuckles to be adapted to the *Uchuck III*. He worked on this project as well as his regular work as mate and then master in the *Uchuck II*, and when the job was done, received the princely sum of $100 as a bonus.

The mast was wooden and two and a half feet in diameter, the booms were octagonal and also wooden, one of them forty-four feet long, the other forty feet. The two DC electric cargo winches, salvaged from the afterdeck of the *Princess of Alberni,* were set in place at the foot of the mast.

One of my jobs on the new vessel was "slushing down," an old term for a procedure used to preserve the wire rope of standing rigging on ships. It involved hanging in a bosun's chair shackled to a stay or shroud in order to put a mixture of tallow (pig fat) and white lead on the wire by hand. The white lead by itself would have dried out, hardened, and then cracked, but with the tallow it stayed pliable. When applied to six-strand wire rope, it lies in the crevices between the strands and keeps the water out for years. White lead is made from sheet lead in a Dutch process that uses acetic acid, which eventually changes the lead to a white powder. It was traditionally used as the base of oil paint and also as a preservative and "never-seize" material. For that application, it came in tins mixed with oil and, when applied, allowed big bolts to be undone many years later.

As I was only fifteen, I had no problem with the prospect of getting covered with this gooey stuff for the slushing down job on the *Uchuck III*. First, I put a few pounds of white lead and a quantity of tallow in a ratio of five to seven into a bucket, then heated the mixture with a blowtorch till it became a steaming, smelly, melted mass. I then mixed it until it became a sloppy paste. Although the job is more safely done by two people, one attending from the deck below, I worked alone, first rigging a double purchase and hauling it up the mast on a gantline about seventy feet to the top of the topmast. Then I hung a bosun's chair at deck level below the lower of the two blocks and climbed in. With this tackle I was able to haul myself up, then once at the top I tied a hitch that would allow a stage-by-stage descent. (On the way up I did learn that the shackle holding the chair to the stay should not have the screw pin rubbing on the stay or else the pin would unwind either going up or coming down.) Once in place, I hauled up my pot of paste on another gantline, tied it off and I was ready to begin.

My procedure was simple. With rag in hand, I would scoop out a good gob of goop and apply it to the wire from as high as I could reach down to about opposite my nose. I would then clean off my hands somewhat in order to slip the hitches on the bucket and chair enough to descend to a position where I could repeat the procedure. And so it went for the length of that wire. On that mast, there were ten 7/8-inch-diameter wires to be done. The mess was considerable, both on me and the deck below. I was covered solidly up to the elbows and elsewhere in white stuff that, in light of what is now known about the effects of lead on the human body, was not a really good idea. (God only knows what was going on inside my lungs as I was heating the slurry.) It took a whole day to do this, leaving me hot, tired and sticky. As the wire rigging that I was treating was from

That's one new engine safely in the hold of the *Uchuck III*. It now needed to be rolled back through the bulkhead and into the engine room. John Monrufet is down there receiving it.

the CP's *Princess Mary*, it was already forty years old, but that rigging was still there in the year 2000 after another forty-seven years, although by that time it was holding up a different mast, so I guess the "slushing down" system worked.

By this time John Monrufet was almost ready to install the engines in the vessel. *YMS 123* had been equipped with two 600-hp Cooper-Bessemer engines, but now they were to be 500-hp Cleveland GM machines, so there was a lot of preparatory work needed to be ready the vessel to receive them. The Clevelands we had bought were still in a running submarine chaser named *Del Norte* and would have to be taken out. To simplify the process, that vessel was brought to Port Alberni from Astoria, Oregon, but as a result of customs problems, it had to be run back down to Lake Union in Washington state to have the engines removed there and then shipped back to Port Alberni by rail. One day the new *Uchuck* was towed to the Government Assembly Wharf and the engines lifted out of the railcar and lowered through the cargo hatch into the hold. They were left in that position, waiting to be skidded back to the engine room when the beds were ready to receive them. To supply some power and light, a two-cylinder Lister diesel generator was installed in the engine room on the starboard side. It was also fitted with a line shaft that had sheaves and clutches on it to run a belt-driven compressor and a bilge pump. While this generator was strong enough to run some lights and tools, it powered out on heavier loads; as a result, we could use our ten-hp DC electric cargo winches to bring construction materials on board, but we had to stop frequently to let the generator catch up.

In the 1950s marine electrical equipment was still quite simple. Generators produced DC current only, which was used for light, heat and running electric motors that drove winches, pumps, compressors and blowers, and they had switchboards with a dozen or fifteen big simple knife switches. No ordinary household appliances could be used with this power as they would burn out in an instant, and while DC appliances were available, they were very expensive. As a result, the only galley equipment we could afford in the beginning was a two-burner range with an oven that had big ugly DC switches on it and a simple two-element heating coil hot plate. No thermostat was possible so toasters and kettles and suchlike could not be used. We also installed a small hot water tank in the galley, using the DC generator to run it, but it had a manual switch. The trick was to remember that you had turned it on. If you forgot and then didn't use any water, the tank would start to boil and pressure up the system with steam, and then you had to open a valve and let the pressure off. I made that mistake more than once and filled the whole cabin area with wet fog almost down to the deck amid the roar of escaping steam. But the system must have been tough because it withstood that treatment many times and the tank itself lasted much longer that any I have encountered since. Fortunately, the *Uchuck III*, like the other two, was to be a dayboat only, so that the systems and equipment that would make it a live-aboard were not necessary.

The round-fronted steel wheelhouse was narrow, but we didn't have much equipment to put in there. We had the two engine room telegraphs, originally from the CP's *Princess Victoria*, but only one of them had to be installed inside as Esson and George were still thinking of their navy days and ways and felt that, when manoeuvring the vessel, the master should be outside where he could see all around. Thus, the second telegraph was mounted on the half deck above and behind the wheelhouse. There was a voice pipe from that position into the wheelhouse so helm orders could be given to the quartermaster at the wheel. (In 1983 when these bridge telegraphs reached the age of eighty years, we dismantled the whole system to look for wear and damage. There wasn't any.)

On the evening of July 23, 1955, as had been done at the end of the *Uchuck II*'s conversion, Esson and George organized a run to take out the crowd of people who had done the work of rebuilding the vessel—everyone from the bank manager to the youngest labourer. I was at the wheel as quartermaster at the end of this first run as we went alongside the dock, but it was probably the only time that a landing was done that way because the skippers soon figured out that it could be docked quite nicely from within the wheelhouse. On the following day the vessel went to work. The first crew started out as seven men and a cook, but having a quartermaster was a luxury left over from the days when labour was cheap, and that position was soon scrapped. Then over time, as labour-saving equipment found its way on board that reduced the amount of hand-stowing of cargo, the crew was pared down to just four men and the cook.

MV *UCHUCK III*

Built: at Kruse and Banks yard in North Bend, Oregon, in 1943 for US Navy and named *YMS 123*.

Purchased: Barkley Sound Transportation Co. Ltd. in 1952. Conversion to *Uchuck III* completed in July 1955.

Length: 136 feet

Beam: 24 feet

Draught: 10 feet

Tonnage: GRT 279

Official number: 179475

Power: two 8-268A 500-hp Cleveland GM diesels taken from US Navy submarine chaser *Del Norte*; these engines were replaced in 1984 with a pair of the same type.

Cargo gear: two forty-four-foot derricks in union purchase—SWL 3.2 tons. Later the mast and derricks, which were originally from the CPR *Princess Mary*, were changed to the mast from the *Princess Alberni* and the derricks from a 10,000-ton cargo ship.

Winches: DC electric 10 hp

Cargo capacity: 200 short tons (approx.)

Passenger capacity: 100 day passengers

Life boats: two twenty-foot clinker-built wooden boats; in 1985 these were replaced with two sixty-five-man rescue platforms and two twelve-man covered life rafts. There was also a twelve-foot Davidson lifeboat with a 25-hp outboard to serve as a rescue boat and a means of collecting rafts together when deployed.

Crew: master, mate, engineer, oiler/deckhand, cook. However, the size of the crew varied from four to twelve depending on what was happening.

Handling Cargo on the *Uchuck III*

The cargo handling gear on the *Uchuck III* was very different from that on her two predecessors: she was fitted with two winches and two derricks rigged in union purchase. Here, the cargo runner from each winch went to the gin block at its own derrick's head and then down to the cargo hook. The winches were DC electric with automatic brakes, a system allowing for close control. The derricks were fixed in position outboard on either side, so when one winch was operated down and the other up, the hook moved from one side of the vessel to the other. A load could be lifted off the wharf and swung across the vessel and set down on deck or even right over the other side onto a barge. This system allowed more control over the movement of cargo, thus making a safer working environment.

The new vessel could handle one hundred tons of general cargo with a five-ton, single lift capability. To get this much lift, the cargo gear was permanently doubled up, in the same way that we did it on the *Uchuck II* when we were preparing for a heavy lift. This setup, of course, slowed the hook's travelling time by one half and, although this was sometimes annoying, it added to the safety of the operation.

The winches had been designed to run with half-inch-diameter wire rope on the drums, but since we were going to use the lifting gear permanently doubled up, there had to be longer and larger diameter wire used instead. The larger wire caused a problem because there wasn't enough room on the winch drums for the wire to spool properly. As well, the small diameter of the drum caused the larger wire to be bent unnaturally, which introduced kinks and overrides and eventually caused the individual wires to break. A runner would last about a year before it needed to be changed, but since the winch runners were 180 feet long and only damaged in sections, the remainder was useful for lifting straps, sets of double hooks and

The *YMS 123* as we received her in 1952.

mooring line pendants. It seemed that I was always splicing up old winch runners for something.

The *Uchuck III*'s cargo was moved on pallets, each measuring four feet by six and made of five pieces of two-by-six lumber, each piece six feet long, laid over three spaced four-by-fours, each four feet long, and five more two-by-sixes for the bottom. The whole structure was bolted and nailed together. The lifting arrangement was an assembly of wire rope and one-inch-thick horizontal steel bars that hung from the cargo hook. The bars were slipped under the ends of the pallets for the lift and then released to go for the next one.

In addition, over the years we developed a number of special pieces of gear to handle different types of cargo. There were lifters for the large reels of wire used in the logging camps and tongs for smaller reels, two types of car-lifting gear, travel trailer gear, cages for oxygen and propane cylinders, hooks of several descriptions and big nylon straps for lifts of lumber. There was a tool for lifting just about everything.

From the beginning the *Uchuck III* was able to handle cars and pickup trucks. George built the first car-handling gear based on what Canadian Pacific used on the *Princess Maquinna*. It was a system of bars that locked around the front and back wheels of the vehicle and a cage affair hanging from the cargo hook with wires in all four corners that fastened onto hooks on the outside ends of the bars. For tiny cars like Austin 850s and

The MV *Uchuck III* at the end of conversion in June 1955. Since then, nearly all the equipment, seen here on deck, has been changed.

Here I am using my own car to practice loading and unloading vehicles using the union purchace gear.

Volkswagen Beetles, there were simply two small I-beams that were slid across and under the vehicle near the wheels. The regular pallet lifting bars were then hooked under the notches in the ends of the I-beams. As balance was so important, there was always a little jiggling and balancing before the lift was made. One day when we were lifting a Volkswagen out of the hold in this fashion, it was a little off-balance as it was difficult setting it up in the hold. It rose a few feet then slipped and fell out of the rig, landing on its bumper, and flopped back onto its wheels. There was no damage but those watching were not impressed.

Three large vehicles would fit fore-and-aft on deck, and up to five small ones in the hold, depending on how big they were. There could be three in the after hold, one on the square of the hatch and sometimes one on a special rig hanging in the hatchway over the car below. Once in awhile there could even be one hanging in the rigging over the centre car on deck, held in place by chains from each corner, but this was only done in good weather.

All cargo handling procedures are very labour-intensive and time-consuming, and this became an issue as cargo volume increased. We began designing gear and procedures to make it all happen as fast as possible.

In 1955 when the *Uchuck III* came into service in Port Alberni, delivery trucks off-loaded onto the floor of the freight shed, and at loading time the goods were piled by hand onto pallets, which were resting on four-wheeled dollies that were pushed by hand out to the loading area. But if the timing was right, we could load cargo directly from a truck onto pallets at the ship's side, saving one set of moves. This meant trucks had to wait in line if they arrived at nearly the same time. In places like Ucluelet the trucks were all there when the ship arrived, parked in a semicircle, so that we and the drivers loaded them from the pallets as they were landed on the wharf from the ship.

We next acquired a forklift truck that changed the procedure on the dock at the Alberni end. A freight truck could now come at any time and just park. We then used the forklift to set a pallet into the back of the truck, loaded it and then stored that pallet load in the freight shed until ship-loading time when it was moved again out to the ship's side; this resulted in one less handling of the individual pieces.

An overhead rail system in the after hold of the vessel carried a pallet-lifting rig similar to the one that brought the pallets on board. We used this to lift the pallets that had been run aft in the hold on a dolly and set

Loading the *Uchuck No. 1* directly from the truck, saving us a step by bypassing the warehouse. Pictured is George McCandless on the dock, Dick McMinn running the winch and Frank Bledsoe with his back to the camera. Mickey's Transfer was also a local Port Alberni outfit.

them down on shelves built on each side and on horses beside the shelves. This left an alleyway for the dolly in the centre, allowing three rows of four pallets each to be set down and one on another dolly in the middle of each of the three rows. This arrangement could represent as much as fifteen tons of cargo that didn't have to be double handled. It was still heavy work but definitely an improvement.

One day the engineer, Dave Wisk, having repaired the overhead track for the umpteenth time, came up the ladder from the hold and announced, "We need a forklift down here." A few days later, he, Esson and I climbed into Dave's old Mercedes 240D and went off to forklift land— Vancouver—to find a small electric forklift truck that could be kept in the hold to stow pallets and move other stuff around. Manarch Holdings was our first stop. We watched them move steam cleaners around their warehouse with a small electric forklift. This was interesting, but we wanted to see what else there was available in the city. As we were leaving, the manager told us that we could go to Wajax and all the other places, and at the end of the day we would come back and buy this machine. And that is what we did.

Now with a forklift on the dock and one in the hold, we could use smaller pallets that we moved aboard by using one of the larger lifting ones as the transporter, which meant that two forklift drivers and a winch driver could load the whole vessel. The small pallets could be fitted more easily into the irregular spaces in the hold and piled on top of each other. This loading method also helped with the perennial problem of sorting for different ports by keeping groups of things together, and they could be made more stable by wrapping them in plastic shrink wrap.

Passengers

A wide variety of travellers came with us for all sorts of reasons, but often because it was the only way they could get to their destinations. Salesmen from the big stores and the industrial houses came on a semi-regular basis. In the late 1950s there were air force personnel going back and forth to the new radar station at Tofino. The families attached to the COTC cable station at Bamfield as well as all the fishing families living there travelled with us. People running for political office, union organizers, circuit preachers and piano tuners came from time to time, and each year the Royal

Canadian Legion at Port Alberni gathered up the First World War vets, a shipload at a time, and took them out for a riotous time, re-fighting the old battles and generally carrying on.

At the end of a school term and at holidays, the Native kids from the Christy Residential School at Kakawis on Meares Island near Tofino went home to their reserves in Clayoquot and Barkley sounds. We also delivered some to Uchucklesit Inlet. Once, when we were not scheduled to go into the inlet on that day, Percy Williams came out to meet us in his long Briggs and Stratton-powered dugout canoe to pick up the inlet contingent. I remember watching six or eight little kids scamper down the ladder over the side of the vessel and into the canoe to end up sitting in a row of little black heads, happy to be going home. Another time it was Kelly Cootes who was the ferryman, and when asked if he had them all, he replied, "I don't know, are there any more that look like me up there?" A week later we brought out the teaching sisters dressed in their habits and under the strict control of a mother superior. They all piled into one car in Port Alberni and went off in a cloud of exhaust.

YMS 123 was a strongly built vessel that was designed to withstand the shock from the exploding mines that had been cut loose by its sweep gear and then detonated. As a result, more had gone into its construction than would go into a vessel of similar size built for other purposes, and that is one major reason that, as the *Uchuck III*, she survived for so many years. The other big reason for her longevity is that she worked steadily after the original conversion was completed in 1955, although there were a few six-month layups in the mid-1960s that caused moisture to get into electrical and mechanical equipment. The lack of forced air ventilation also allowed some wood rot to take hold in some enclosed spaces, which meant more repair work in subsequent years than might otherwise have been necessary.

CHAPTER THREE

Weather and Navigation

Weather

Travel in winter was wearing on us as darkness faded later in the morning and arrived sooner in the afternoon, leaving only a few working hours of daylight for us. Everything we did became more difficult and we seemed to be always wet. One effect of all the rain was, of course, swollen rivers and streams.

Like any large-scale land clearing, logging denudes the land and makes it unable to hold water. Then the accumulated rainwater that comes with storms and sometimes with added snow-melt water runs off rather than being released slowly into the river systems. Without the tree root systems in place, the land can turn to a slurry of mud, and when it gets wet enough, it starts to move. Because coastal logging is conducted in mountainous country, these effects are widespread and we saw them everywhere that we operated.

One night in a time of heavy sustained rain in the Alberni Inlet in 1954, the *Uchuck II* was on her way back from Ucluelet to Port Alberni. She came upon a mass of logs and debris floating all over the inlet near China Creek, seven miles from Alberni. There was a small logging camp on the beach at that position and our vessel's crew, while carefully moving through the debris, saw flashing lights ashore, which the master took to be a warning to the vessel regarding the logs. In fact, the camp buildings had been washed out to sea leaving the people on the beach and some in the water. The small stream running down on one side of the camp had been blocked by logging debris up the hill so that a dam had formed. When the pressure was great enough, the dam broke and the pent-up water roared down, taking out the camp and all in it. One man was lost and others nearly so.

More than once the Gold River rose quickly because of heavy rain, flooding the highway at the Big Bend, five miles up from the waterfront. The water swept around the bend, gouged out the bank and the fifty-foot-wide parking turnout and then piled large logs in a jumble on the road. The upper watersheds had long been logged out so this kind of activity will likely continue until the second growth is well enough established to be able to hold the water back again.

Along with the washouts upriver, at the river's mouth the current was running at ten to fifteen muddy knots and bringing with it a continuous stream of logs, roots, stumps and other debris, pushing it all out into the inlet. It boiled by close to the floats connected to the government wharf. If the small boats and especially the aircraft, which necessarily had to be tied on the outside of the float, were not moved, they would be damaged by hits from the parade of stuff coming down the river. In one event two aircraft were swept away. The smaller Cessna was recovered but the Beaver sank, and since it was largely intact, flew off underwater to who knows where. It didn't help that the water is twelve hundred feet deep just a short way off the floats.

At Mooyah Bay, Jim Taylor realized when he started up his camp there in the mid-1950s that the hillside above the camp was unstable. He resolved not to log that portion until just before finishing up in the area and leaving. But Jim died accidentally in a flight to Blowhole Bay, and the operators following him in that tree farm licence didn't understand why he had devised that plan and logged the hillside before the end. In due course the land slipped and pushed part of their camp right out into the bay. Fortunately no one was injured in that event.

Another glaring example of poor logging practices is visible on the seaward- and weather-facing very steep bluff just above the Bunsby Islands in Checkleset Bay, which is just west of Walter's Cove in Kyuquot Sound. This bluff was logged in the past so the earth was washed away to leave a bare rock scar that can be seen from well out to sea, a scar that continues to grow in the wind and rains of winter with an accompanying rumble of boulders tumbling down. The Bunsbys are a favourite destination for kayakers, some of the most environmentally conscious people around, so it seems poor advertising for the industry. Of course, these events have been repeated everywhere on the West Coast, not only in logging areas but wherever land has been cleared for development.

Another kind of weather situation develops when there is an Arctic outflow. It arises when a huge mass of very cold air moves down from the Arctic on the east side of the Rocky Mountains, heading toward the Gulf of Mexico. Some tongues of this air spill out through the Rocky Mountain passes to the Coast Mountains and then down through the mainland inlets onto the coast. These downslope winds can be ferocious. Temperatures drop to well below freezing and velocities in the mainland inlets can rise to sixty knots or more. Vessels travelling can ice up from the freezing spray and can be lost if they capsize from the added topside weight.

On the west coast of Vancouver Island, we are spared from the worst of this wind, as the backbone of the island stands in the way of the blast, but we get our own reduced version as a cold outflow from the Vancouver Island mountains. The worst that I can remember was a time we were

The road between the town and the waterfront washed out by the Gold River, about 1975. This happened more than once.

approaching Gold River and the temperature was minus twelve centigrade, while the wind coming out of the Gold River valley had hit forty knots. The *Uchuck III* was not set up to deal with weather like that, so we had to take extra precautions. We couldn't run around with the eight-foot by sixteen-foot cargo hatch open or the cold air would flow down into the hold and freeze groceries stacked there as well as the water pipes leading forward in the vessel, nor could we have any cargo stowed on deck that might freeze. But there was little we could do to keep our passengers warm because heat to the cabin spaces was mostly just what escaped from the engine room, which was always semi-tropical. The wheelhouse and cabin/office attached to it were heated by electric wall heaters, which didn't compete very well with the extreme temperatures outside because there was no insulation anywhere.

One January day, this outflow condition was happening while we were transiting from Kyuquot Sound to Esperanza Inlet. At lunchtime we happened to be between the two entrances where there was no wind at all, only bright warm sunshine, so some of the boys took their lunches out onto the main hatch. Just as they finished, we ran back into the bitter outflow wind from Esperanza Inlet, and they scurried back inside.

A washout at Mooyah Bay in 1975, when the rainsoaked, logged-off hillside above the camp let loose and pushed part of the camp into the bay.

Another winter problem arose because the fresh water coming from the streams and rivers flowing into the heads of all the inlets lies on top of the salt water. When the temperature drops much below freezing, ice forms and then thickens when there is little wind to disturb the surface. The noise while the ship is moving in ice is terrific as the ice is smashed up and sent sliding and skittering across the unbroken ice sheet. But there were times when we didn't attempt an approach to an iced-in camp because, once stopped, we would not have been able to manoeuvre to turn around. The men from camp would then bash their way out to us in a steel boom boat towing a small float to collect their groceries and parts.

We found that we could travel through as much as four inches of ice, but at six inches the vessel tended to ride up and crash through. With that action, the hull planking above and below the gum wood sheathing at the waterline would come into contact with the ice, which stripped off the anti-fouling paint, our protection against teredos, the marine borers. We came into contact with these bugs whenever we travelled to logging camps and their nearby booming grounds because teredos are attracted to floating logs. They could easily transfer to the ship when we were stopped there, and left alone, they could honeycomb the hull planks.

We don't think about a fresh water supply until it's hard to find. Wherever our vessels had a home base, there was a water supply piped down to the wharf head, but once in a while the above-ground waterline would freeze. Suddenly we would have a real problem. We had to scout out another supply, even making a special run to somewhere that had running water. On one occasion we had to go alongside a chemical barge at Gold River and drag one of our firehoses over the barge and up into the pulp mill grounds to find running water. In hot summer weather the local water sources would sometimes run short, not quite drying up but getting to the point of being unsafe to drink without boiling. When that happened we tried to find a safe source somewhere along our route. This work all took time out of our schedule but the alternative was strict rationing.

In sustained hot weather, the coast would be closed to all activity in the bush. Logging crews would leave so the freight business would get very quiet, leaving only tourist work for us to do and in the later days fish farm work. These periods were usually a week or two long but once in a while fire season could extend to a month. This hot weather was fine for the tourist business but we had to remember to warn them that the sun is double in strength out on the water because of the reflection off the calm water.

Fog occurred mostly in late summer and fall, especially in the area west of Estevan Point. Today the majority of vessels have radar, so finding their way is not as difficult as in the days when Esson and George began their company, but even with radar, care must be taken to avoid opposing traffic, and passengers have to be warned that the ship's whistle will be sounded every two minutes.

There are anomalies in the weather at any time. In winter we could run into a stretch of clear and warm conditions. One Saturday in a January, when we had finished at Port Eliza and were about to start back to Gold River, we took an hour off and went over into the Neuchatlitz village through its narrow and winding approach. We shut everything off and just lay there in the sunshine for a half hour so that everyone could come out on deck and sit in the sun for a bit. But in August 1988, two proper southeast gales struck, just two weeks apart. One was a major gale loaded with rain—I heard twelve inches in twenty-four hours—that caused washouts worse than winter washouts all over the region. In Tahsis Inlet across from the exit from Tahsis Narrows, a normal little babbling brook turned into a torrent, coming down the logged-off hillside and taking out the automatic navigation light on its little point of land at the side of the inlet. At the end of that day, there was a wide, boulder-strewn riverbed where the little stream had been, although the stream itself had returned to a trickle once more.

In each of those summer gales, I had to make trips to Friendly Cove with almost full loads of tourists; a passenger from one of those trips returned to take the trip again later that month because he said that on the previous one he couldn't even see the colour of the trees through the rain. During the other gale that summer I was to go over to Burdwood Point, nearly three miles across the mouth of the Sound from Friendly Cove, to pick up a group of Strathcona Park Lodge leaders who were out on a camping sabbatical. When the gale came up, I tried to contact them on VHF to arrange for their pickup the next day when there might be less wind and sea action in that exposed location. I also didn't want to cross the mouth of the Sound in a beam sea that would have us rolling badly while I had nearly eighty people on board, most of them past middle age. However, I couldn't reach the group on VHF, and though they were probably all right, I couldn't know that for sure. Finally, to avoid crossing the mouth of the sound, I decided that I would go back the way we had come on the north side of Bligh Island, around the east side of the island and out Zuciarte Channel on the south side to a point close to Burdwood, a total distance of sixteen extra miles. This trip took an hour and twenty minutes, but we found them having a ball, bodysurfing onto the beach and quite happy to stay another day. It could have been called a wasted trip, but I did have to find out if they were all right.

We were always conscious of weather because it could determine how we did business. It could be fun, or serious, or even scary, but it was always interesting.

Navigation

The coasting vessel is constantly in and out of rock piles, passages and inlets, day and night, as she goes about her work of taking cargoes to settlements and camps. Great and constant care has to be taken to keep the vessel safe. On a black night among the islands and inlets, the skipper must know exactly where he is within one minute of travel—as those travelling on the *Queen of the North* found out in 2006.

Navigation is the term used to describe the process for taking a ship from one place to another, though this term was normally applied to those crossing oceans, and in the old days it was accomplished by observing the positions of sun, moon and stars using a sextant to measure the angle of the celestial bodies to the horizon. Then a mathematical position was found using plane and spherical trigonometry. But not many sailors are mathematicians, so systems of inspection tables were developed, simplifying the practice of navigation so that the master didn't have to work from first principles each time. Coastal navigation or pilotage, on the other hand, is the method of position-finding that primarily requires taking bearings on landforms and man-made objects using a compass and then plotting those lines on a large-scale chart against the identified objects and landforms. Today, electronic navigation is used in both coastal and oceanic travel and has spot-on accuracy, always providing that the on-board equipment works properly and the signals generated ashore and from earth satellites continue to be supplied.

There isn't much room in the wheelhouse, considering all that needs to be done in it. Sean Mather, one of the new owners after me, is at the wheel. ANDREW SCOTT PHOTO.

When Esson and George began Barkley Sound Transportation with the *Uchuck I* in 1946, they had only the most basic of tools to work with in that vessel, but this was true for most other small vessels of the time. The *Uchuck I* was fitted with an air whistle with air supplied by a compressor, a few charts, a good-quality magnetic compass, a large-faced clock, a pair of binoculars, an aneroid barometer and a seven-pound hand leadline.

The Whistle

The whistle gave a high-pitched note and was made so that it sounded quickly and cut off quickly, allowing a short sharp blast. When they were travelling in fog, that is, in restricted visibility, the collision rules required that the whistle must be sounded every two minutes in a four- to six-second blast. This announced the ship's presence to other nearby vessels, but the sharp blast also produced echoes off any nearby landforms. Sound travels at not quite 1,200 feet per second in air. If the whistle is sounded and an echo returns in one second, the skipper knows that an object is about 600 feet or one tenth of a nautical mile away. But a problem cropped up when they were travelling in falling snow: the whistle would plug up with snow so that only a squeak and the sound of heavy breathing came out of the forward-facing horn. The nearest or youngest crew member would then have to be sent up on top of the wheelhouse to scoop out the opening. Afterward, he kept his coat on as he knew that he would be going there again soon.

Charts and Chart Work

When deck officer candidates go to school to get certificates of competency, a large block of their training concerns charts and the information on them that applies to everything from the largest of vessels, which have all possible equipment available, down to the smallest with its minimal equipment. The *Uchucks* fell into the latter category.

In small vessels, charts are often stowed as rolled-up scrolls between the deck beams overhead and, because of the stiff paper, they tend to be very springy and roll up like a blind if you relax for a moment while trying to work with them. Ideally, charts should be stowed flat in a cabinet of drawers and there should be a three-by-four-foot work table available. The *Uchuck I* and *II* had a half-measure shelf to work on. The No. 3 had a piece of plywood, not quite the size of a chart, that was hinged to swing down from the overhead in the wheelhouse; it was stopped by chains at an angle of about forty-five degrees. When working there at night, it was difficult to hold a pencil and run the parallel rulers over the chart on this surface while holding a red-lensed flashlight in one's teeth and balancing against the movement of the vessel. This situation didn't encourage complicated chartwork so a lot of rule-of-thumb was employed.

Canadian hydrographic charts are very good with huge amounts of information on them, although in recent years some of the extensive portrayal of land features and on-shore constructions have been simplified or discontinued. The water areas are now printed in shades of blue to indicate depth rather than marked by just a thick carpet of numbers; this is definitely a plus because in the past anyone older than forty needed to have a good magnifying glass to work his way through the numbers.

In 1986 in the midst of the reconstruction of the *Uchuck III*, a folding chart table was built into the wheelhouse so, for the first time in any of the three vessels, we had a proper working surface. That we mostly went over a familiar route meant that after the first few trips, we had a good set of courses and times recorded and pretty well committed to memory. As a result, it was not always necessary to do the chartwork, but we wanted to have an open chart of the area that was instantly available for reference.

Charts must also allow the skipper to deal with the relationship between the true north and the magnetic north poles. The latter is not at the true pole and is moving in a direction and at a rate that varies but is predictable in the short term. Depending upon where you are on the globe, the two poles will be in line with one another or be separated by many degrees. The compass rose, which is printed on each chart, shows the relationship diagrammatically as simply a circle within a circle. The outer true one has north or zero degrees at the top, and the inner magnetic one has its north point rotated to one side or the other by the amount in degrees of the difference in angle of one pole to the other for that point on the surface of the earth. Each circle is graduated in degrees to 360. There are also figures printed on the rose that indicate the annual angular change between the two poles so that with an older chart, one can work in the correction needed. In recent years there has also been a website available that shows the current magnetic variation for any given spot on earth at any time. This resource allows navigators to use even very old charts and still have the magnetic information up to date.

Compasses and Procedures

When we travelled on our regular routes, the compass courses were carefully observed and written in a logbook with the name of the feature just passed and the time of passing. As the vessel travelled at a constant speed, the elapsed times on the courses from point to point were the same each time, except when errors were introduced by the effects of weather and current. These effects had to be estimated and allowances made. This procedure was followed on every trip so when travelling in fog, one opened the log for the last trip on that route and did as was done the last time. The result would be nearly the same each time. The navigators in the Canadian Pacific coastal passenger steamers took one extra precaution. When travelling in fog, they had open in front of them the logbook they were currently working with plus the logbook for the last voyage as well as the one for the voyage of the year before as a further check.

At night or in fog when moving along in close quarters and arriving at a position at the end of a timed run, the skipper of a coastal vessel must verify that he has actually come to his next position before he moves on. The whistle's echo in fog or a stab of light through the dark might be enough. If not, then he may have to stop and, in the case of fog, carefully move in toward the beach until he can identify the feature. Normally in fog, a beach can be seen from one-eighth to one-quarter of a mile off, so usually it comes into view in time. Only when the position is assured can the ship head off on the next leg to do it again. Today, a skipper can usually rely on radar information alone, but we didn't have that equipment until 1960, although we still travelled the inlets night and day in all weathers and kept to our schedule.

Large vessels have gyro compasses while smaller vessels generally have magnetic compasses, and they work on totally different principles. The former references the true north pole using a gyroscope and a system of mercury ballistics and is not subject to error in the same way as magnetic compasses are. The magnetic compass references the magnetic north pole by means of a rotating card that has a magnetized needle or needles attached to it. This card is enclosed in a bowl of fluid and rests on a jewelled bearing, which makes it practically frictionless as it turns. (Really, the card stays still and the vessel turns under it.) A helmsman has to understand this relationship or he can chase the compass and head off in some other direction in the dark.

Besides the difference between the true and magnetic poles, there are other errors that can be introduced to a compass reading that must be recognized and allowances made for them. A second set of errors can be caused by the singular magnetic field that exists in every vessel: it is the sum of all the magnetic influences created by the physical ferrous metal and the electrical fields—for example, those produced by wiring and electric motors. The navigator certainly doesn't want someone standing near the compass with a wrench in his hand or even a sheath knife on his belt. The compass must be compensated with carefully placed magnets fixed in position around it, this being done periodically by a compass adjuster. Any leftover error after compensation, called deviation, is discovered by the compass adjuster or ship's officer in a process called "swinging ship."

Compass adjusting is something of an art. When we were studying charts and magnetism in school, we were cautioned that at the end of it we would *not* be compass adjusters. We would be able to swing a ship for deviation, that is, we would be able to determine the error present and make the proper allowances, but that was about all.

When the compass adjuster comes, he first determines what the errors are. He does this by having the ship go around in a circle as he takes many bearings of a distant object or landform that he has identified on a chart. He compares the compass bearings to the magnetic bearing as shown by the chart and notes the differences. He then adjusts the correcting magnets and iron elements that are part of the binnacle until on a further swinging, the differences are less or gone. When this process is complete and adjustments made, he swings the ship around again, taking another set of bearings to find any remaining difference. Those differences are written onto a card to become a table of deviations. When the navigator lays off a magnetic course on the chart, he allows for variation if the chart is not brand new, then refers to the deviation card and applies that correction to the heading that he has just laid off. That becomes the course to steer.

Larger vessels have a proper free-standing ship's binnacle, a five-foot-high wooden structure housing the compass with its many magnets and pieces of soft iron in specific positions, all of which can be moved about in order to adjust for the magnetic situation in that particular ship. We had an incident in which the unlocked magnet door on the port side of the binnacle swung open when the ship rolled sharply. The rectangular wooden plug that blocked those magnets in place fell out and the magnets followed, rolling away to the side of the wheelhouse. The question then was: which way around did the poles face and from which holes did they come? We had no idea, so we tried to guess. When there was no hope of figuring that one out, we put out a call for the compass adjuster.

Before electronic navigation equipment became available, the compass was the vital piece of equipment for finding one's way around on the coast and on the ocean. I can't conceive of going anywhere, even now, without a compensated compass and the charts of the areas that I will be going to. I will use any other means that are available—indeed, one is required to do that by the Collision Regulations—but I am hugely uncomfortable without the old standbys. Even with redundancies, the electronics can fail.

Night Running

Running at night is another aspect of the work that presents problems for the coastal vessel. It is not as bad as running in fog but has its own challenges. Distance at night is difficult to judge as, for example, when looking out at a single white light. It is hard to determine if it is a faint light close up or a bright light far away, especially if the weather is less than perfectly clear and if there are no other reference points available. Inexperienced navigators can and often do get into close-quarters situations with other vessels before they are aware of it.

In overcast conditions at night, the inlets are darker than the ocean because the little bit of skylight is shut off by the surrounding hills, but with practice the navigator can discern a faint skyline shape, making this one more item in his tool box. By going over the same run again and again, he begins to recognize the outlines, adding weight to his presumed position. There are a few nights in every year when there is absolutely no light, and one can see nothing. Zero. I recall one night like this when suddenly a small rent in the cloud cover appeared and the planet Venus showed through. The hill outlines became visible and the outline of the forward part of the ship reappeared. I also remember a dark night when I was handed something to eat while we were running offshore. It was so dark that I could not see the object at all and although I liked it, I didn't recognize what it was until I got to the stone in the middle and discovered that it was a peach. That is *dark*. During the long nights of winter, we especially looked forward to those where the moon—or even a small slice of the moon—appeared. It made all the difference, even with heavily overcast skies. For that week-long shift we could see the beaches and landforms, which took some of the work out of what we were doing.

The wheelhouse was kept in absolute darkness to preserve the night vision of the watchkeepers. It takes two minutes to be able to see a little in the dark, twenty minutes to see well and four hours to see as well as possible. If someone strikes a match to light a cigarette, the watchkeepers must start all over again; a young crewman may make that mistake once, but the reaction from the others in the wheelhouse will impress upon him not to do it again. Next time he will give a warning so the others can close their eyes. A navigator also learns to use peripheral vision to see better, moving his head around to be sure not to miss anything. Binoculars are invaluable, too, as they are good at gathering light, exposing things that would otherwise be missed.

The *Uchuck III* presented an extra problem as the wheelhouse was placed amidships with all the cargo gear between it and what was ahead, so we had to look through round ports at the series of triangles and rectangles made by the rigging. One little trick we used in this vessel was to turn off the navigation lights for short periods as long as there was no opposing traffic; this routine gave us a little better chance to see past the backscatter that the navigation lights bounced off the rigging, even though the lower parts of the wires were painted black. That little advantage sometimes made the difference between seeing or not seeing a nearby object. The only little bit of light anywhere during these times was the tiny spot of red light aimed at the lubber line of the compass, which showed the helmsman the ship's heading. In the modern day there is much more equipment on the bridge, a lot of it having lighted screens that destroy the ability to keep a proper nighttime lookout from inside the wheelhouse, thereby increasing dependence on that equipment.

Running in Fog

In the days before radar the Canadian Pacific's *Princess Maquinna*, if caught in fog in Clayoquot Sound, would sometimes anchor until the fog lifted as it was too hazardous to travel among the sand banks and strong currents that abound in that area. But times changed as competition increased and coast-wise vessels were expected to keep to a schedule, fog or no fog.

Ideally, when running in fog in the daytime in the *Uchuck III*, we should have had three people on hand: a watchman, a helmsman and a radar observer. The older radars, one of which we had on that vessel after 1960, were only usable in daylight if the observer kept his head right inside the viewing hood, shutting out the daylight in order to see the display. At night we could take the hood off and see the display from across the wheelhouse. So that brought our need for crew in the wheelhouse down to two people at night. In fact, often only one of us was there unless we were in heavy traffic or some other situation where more hands were needed, but I finally decided that, whenever we travelled in daytime fog, it was necessary to have one man with his head in the radar while I steered. This way, I could run the logbook times, steer and be the lookout. I always knew where we should be by watching the elapsed time from the last reference point, and I could have that confirmed—or not—by the man at the radar.

Depth Finding

For centuries the only way to find water depth was to drop a weighted line into the water, throwing it out ahead of the moving vessel and measuring the line when it became vertical and slack as the weight landed on the bottom. The hand lead was a seven-pound tapered piece of lead with an eye on top to fasten the line to and an aperture in the bottom into which the seaman would put a bit of tallow. When the lead hit the bottom, a sample of sand or whatever was down there stuck to the tallow, helping the sailors know where they were through the nature of the bottom material. The line was marked at set intervals with various materials of different colour and texture, so the sailor could tell by day or night what the measurement was. And this is all that the *Uchucks* had to check for depth in the early years in Barkley Sound.

CHAPTER FOUR

The Barkley Sound Years

Reversals of Fortune

During the three-year conversion of the *Uchuck III* the wharf was busy with two working vessels and one under construction taking up all three sides of the wharf head, and at times there could be eighteen or even more people going home at the end of the day. The *Uchuck II* lay across the outside face of the wharf, the *Uchuck I* on the right side and the *Uchuck III* in behind the wharf shed on the left with her stern stuck well out into the fairway. When the No. 2 was in position to load cargo, her stern overhung the right side of the wharf so when it was necessary to get the No. 1 out or in, the No. 2 had to be moved up to a point where she was touching the No. 3, allowing just enough room for the No. 1 to move.

This placement, at least at one time, created a problem partly because the engine in the *Uchuck II* had a unique character, requiring the engineer to understand its personality. Some engineers could talk to it, others couldn't. However, on a positive note, the skipper and engineer could converse via the engine room telegraph, which was a great help—especially when problems arose. To indicate what he wanted the engineer to do, the skipper would move a handle on the dial of his bridge unit, which was connected by wires and pulleys that set a pointer on the same segment of the engineer's identical dial. To get the engineer's attention over the noise of the machinery, there was also a very loud bell geared to this movement. The urgency with which the handle was moved in the wheelhouse and the

Looking over the engine room of the *Uchuck III*. The man in coveralls is John Monrufet, one of our long-time engineers, and the man in the foreground is Robert Allan, naval architect. Also note the telegraph head to the right, which was how the wheelhouse directed the engine room. ALBERNI VALLEY MUSEUM PHOTOGRAPH COLLECTION.

urgency of the clanging of the bell would let the engineer know a little of what was going on up above.

The problem mentioned above arose because the *Uchuck II* was powered by an Atlas Imperial 200-hp direct-reversing air-start engine. When the engineer wanted to change from ahead to astern power, he had to stop the engine and restart it turning in the opposite direction. Compressed air would be injected into a cylinder, according to the firing order, to start turning the engine over. Once this began to happen, fuel was injected and started the engine running. Although the restart usually worked, occasionally it didn't. Once in a while when the shot of air went into the first cylinder in the line, its piston would be right at the top of its travel, that is, at top dead centre (TDC). (Said differently, the connecting rod would meet the journal on the crankshaft exactly up and down.) Nothing would move. In fact, there could be no movement until that piston was off TDC. To accomplish this, the engineer would go to a rack, extract a heavy four-foot bar stored there for this purpose, insert it in one of the holes in the one-ton flywheel at the front of the engine and bar it over a little bit. He would then replace the bar in the rack and return to his control station to try again. In the meantime, the vessel, if she had been in motion at the time, would still be moving according to Newton's first law of motion, although with the engine stopped, she would be moving in utter, eerie silence. If the order from the wheelhouse had been to make the engine go astern, there were probably going to be consequences if the vessel continued to go forward. This did happen in our crowded wharf situation at least once when No. 2 rammed No. 3, which was directly ahead, causing some damage to the No. 2's stem but fortunately not to the new vessel, although there was a lot of noise and fury. On one other occasion, this time at Ucluelet, the vessel was going alongside the wharf but couldn't stop and crunched into two small commercial aircraft tied up to the attached float. One was a bi-wing Waco and the other was a fabric-covered Fairchild (that's how long ago this incident occurred), and they suffered considerable damage.

Sometimes this problem could also crop up if there was no air in the air receiver. If the vessel had been travelling in fog, for instance, with the air whistle sounding as prescribed, and if the engineer had not been told of this, it was possible that he did not have the integral air compressor running. In this case, the air receiver may not have enough pressure to restart the engine on the next manoeuvre, and it would become necessary to start up the auxiliary air compressor and build air pressure back into the air receiver before he could change the ship's direction. In the *Uchuck II* the equipment for this was a seven-hp, 1925 model, single-cylinder, dark green Atlas Imperial gasoline engine weighing about two tons. It was started by rolling the 400-pound flywheel by hand until it chuffed into life, emitting the smell of old rotten gasoline, since it wasn't run very often. The engineer then had to wait for about fifteen minutes until there was sufficient pressure to get going again. I leave it to your imagination what may have been happening above during that interval.

Reversing also became a serious problem when the vessel was near a booming ground and the bag booms were blowing around. Then the ship could easily be boxed in, and it would become necessary to turn short-around, and to do that we had to back and fill a number of times to get headed in the right direction. For times like this the skipper had an arrangement with the engineer whereby he would ring up half ahead and then half astern without stopping the indicator at "Stop" on the way, and from this the engineer understood that there were going to be a number of quick manoeuvres coming up. The problem was that he only had a limited amount of compressed air—enough to make only as few as eight changes of direction—so he went into a procedure that would allow him to start the engine up again in the opposite direction without using a full shot of air, thereby increasing the number of manoeuvres that he could do. This was possible because the engine, as it slowed to a stop, would roll back a little on the last compression stroke. On that roll-back, the engineer would inject fuel, and if his timing was just right, the engine would start up in the opposite direction. The record, as far as I know, was twenty-three changes of direction without using air.

One Sunday night in 1954 the man at the wheel of the *Uchuck I* fell asleep on the trip back to Port Alberni after completing the usual run to return loggers to their camp at Sarita River. It was midnight and the vessel was crossing Nahmint Bay when it wandered off course enough to drive her at her full ten knots right into a bluff near Whitecliff Point on the east side of the bay. George McCandless was sitting at a table in the galley adding up the day's fares when the hit came, and he was flung forward, taking out the table but not breaking any of his bones. The single passenger was sitting in the main cabin and she suffered minor injuries; the cook was uninjured. The man steering was already leaning against the wheel, so he was all right.

George took over at the wheel, backing the vessel away from the rock wall, but it was quickly obvious that she was making water through her shattered stem. He was able to back across the inlet to the Franklin River flats and lean her up against a dolphin where she settled into the mud on the falling tide. A tug brought pumps down the next day and the crew was able to effect temporary repairs so that the vessel could be moved the ten miles to Port Alberni. It was a sad sight for Esson and George to see her up on the ways with a right-angle step of shredded timber in her curved stem.

In those years the yard had several shipwrights employed full-time because they were frequently called on to make repairs to the extensive troller fleet. To stay busy in winter they built new fishing vessels, some on speculation. Two of these men came over to see the damage to the *Uchuck I* and took many measurements before going away to build a new stem. In the meantime all the broken wood was removed and the site cleaned up, ready for the new piece. A few days later the two shipwrights came back with the new stem piece made from two pieces of twelve-by-twelve fir. It was slipped into place, fitting the first time. The planking was refastened to the stem rabbet, the whole structure caulked and she was done.

In December 1954 it was the *Uchuck II*'s turn for a major problem. While on a regular run and going at full speed, an ominous rumbling and major vibration began to come out of the engine. Then it stopped of its own accord. It didn't take long to discover that the crankshaft had broken at one of the main bearings. It was not repairable. Fortunately, the *Uchuck I* was out that day as well and happened to be not too far away, so she was diverted to take the No. 2 in tow back to Port Alberni.

A new engine was needed, and as I remember the story, Esson discovered that the Burrard Iron Works had a salvaged 300-hp Union Diesel in their Vancouver shop at that time. This engine had come from a sunken vessel on the East Coast and had been shipped to Burrard for the company's apprentices to work on as they learned their trades. This is the same

The replacement engine being lowered into the *Uchuck II*. The boat deck needed to be removed to let it down. The new engine was a 300-hp Union Diesel weighing 18 tons. Speed was boosted from 10 to 12 knots.

type of engine as can be seen in the RCMP's *St. Roch* at the Maritime Museum in Vancouver; it weighs about eighteen tons and is fourteen feet long, seven feet high and four feet wide.

A deal was struck with Burrard and we began removing the old engine and replacing it with the new. I was just sixteen but I remember working with the engineer on Christmas Eve of 1954 as we began dismantling the Atlas. That ship had an overhead rail with a chain block on a car that could be placed over any part of the engine in order to lift off and replace cylinder heads when needed. This time we used it to pull the heads, then the pistons and then the individual cylinders, each of which had been fastened down to the base with four large bolts. When released, each bolt gave off a puff of really stinky dead air, and it took us a while to figure out that it was air that had been trapped there since the engine was installed in 1925. As we worked, we piled all the discarded parts on the deck outside the engine room casing, giving the vessel a decided list to starboard.

At the end of the day, since it was Christmas Eve, I thought that I had better get a haircut before I walked home. I arrived at the barbershop without thinking of what I might look like after working in the engine room all day, which is probably why the barber asked if I had been firing coal in a boiler somewhere. I suppose that was a reasonable thing to ask in those days.

As the conversion of the *Uchuck III* was still underway, for the extended time that the *Uchuck II* was out of commission the *Uchuck I* had to take over both runs. However, the business had grown much larger since the last time that No. 1 had been required to do double duty—after the fire on the *Uchuck II* in February 1950—so that it was a real challenge to find space for all the cargo. The hold was filled first, then the foredeck, then the forward passenger cabin, then both side decks, the boat deck and even the top of the wheelhouse. I remember that for one trip we piled a bedspring on top of the wheelhouse, and this caused a problem on the next day's run when the magnetic compass inside the wheelhouse malfunctioned.

The Crew

In both vessels—and the No. 3 after she came on line—there was a minimum crew size below which they could not be operated efficiently. In the *Uchuck I* the number was three: master, mate/deckhand and cook. (The master operated the engines from the wheelhouse.) The *Uchuck II* had four: master, mate/deckhand, engineer and cook. The *Uchuck III* needed five: master, mate/deckhand, engineer, oiler/deckhand and cook. It was cost that limited the manpower to these minimums, but we were not alone in that; Northland Navigation also operated with as few crew members as they could manage to do the work.

The crews of the Barkley Sound Transportation Company could not be paid as highly as those in large companies, but the type of work offered attracted the sort of people who were not looking for the most dollars as their reason for being there. Some came to get more varied experience than could be found in large or single purpose vessels, and when they were with us, if they wanted to learn other aspects of the work, they were encouraged to do so. Men who could do more than one job provided useful back-up for others when needed in a short crew. And because of our long hours, young men starting out to train and study for their marine certificates found that the required time to serve before being able to write the exams built up faster. In my time in the company 150 or more people passed through, coming and going for all different reasons, some there for a few days, others for twenty years or more. Many who came to us had no marine experience, so we trained them to do what we needed done.

At times, crew strength was increased depending on what was

The crews in 1949. Note the fedora hats. From left: David McCandless, Jack Howitt, John Monrufet, Esson Young, George McCandless, Dick Hardy, Arvid Petri and Dick McMinn. In front: Dave Young and Peanut.

happening, such as a strike of longshoremen in Vancouver or of Northland Navigation personnel. At those times the *Uchuck III* took up the slack for Canadian Pacific or Northland Navigation vessels' runs and had much more to do than usual so the crew was increased. On one of the occasions that the CP vessel could not do her run, all the cargo was sent to us at Port Alberni, but because the run was still the CP's responsibility, the master from their vessel came on board as pilot, and the purser came to oversee the cargo paperwork. The resulting collection of old salts on board added a holiday atmosphere to the voyage, though one problem did occur. While travelling from Ucluelet to Tofino at night, the man on the wheel looked out to port and wondered out loud if there should be a group of rocks out there on that side. It turned out that we had wandered to the inside of Gowland Rocks and would soon be coming to grief. A smart about-face was ordered to get us back to where we belonged. (The vessel did not have radar in those days.)

Around 1951 the sawmills in Port Alberni began bringing in workers from Denmark and neighbouring countries. Arvid Petri, our wharfinger, although Norwegian-born, had been raised in Denmark and was still fluent in Danish. As soon as this fact became known, new immigrants began coming down to the wharf for assistance with English and help with paperwork. Out of this contact, we acquired some very good employees, the first being Gunnar Sorensen, who stayed with the company for the next ten years. Then there were three Norwegians and another Dane who became the crew that settled into the *Uchuck III* after she went into service in July 1955.

Masters, mates and engineers are required to be certificated to certain levels as determined by the types of voyages sailed and the tonnage of the vessels. Some came to us with the necessary certificates. Others were moved up through the ranks to be a master, mate or engineer, usually before they had served the requisite time needed to sit the examinations for a certificate. In those cases, the company would apply to the minister to have an exemption issued that would allow the man to serve in the position until he had enough sea time accumulated to write the exams. This was only allowed if no qualified man was available to fill the job.

Our mates came mainly from within the company. When a deckhand showed that he had learned enough to become an acting mate, he was promoted as soon as a space opened. This was so because our work depended on knowledge of the day-to-day business of the company almost as much as the business of working and navigating the vessel. The only reason that this upgrading was possible was because the vessel was tied up at night, so technically the master was always on watch. Usually, once the acting mate had served enough time to write for and get the proper certificate, it was time for him to move on to get different experience and rise in the industry. The company would then move the next man up and go through the procedure again.

For us, a good engineer was a heavy-duty mechanic who liked boats because this was very much a hands-on job where the man worked alone, although sometimes with an assistant, operating and maintaining many types of equipment. As long as he liked working with engines, he could learn the marine way of thinking along the way. And the first thing he had to understand was the value of preventative maintenance because on the water, when a breakdown occurs, the results can be disastrous.

Finding cooks for that challenging post on board our vessels was difficult because the facilities could have been better. In the *Uchuck I* the coffee shop was in a tiny nook in the after part of the main cabin, right by the booby hatch over the stairs to the after deck. In the No. 2 the coffee shop was at the forward end of the main cabin in a nice airy spot right in the centre of the vessel. Each of these shops had a two-burner gas stove, a surface on which to make sandwiches and a glass-fronted case that held baked goods, cigarettes and chocolate bars. There were two percolator-type coffee pots, a bunch of heavy enamel cups, a sink with a hand pump—and that was about it. In each of those vessels the crew's galley was directly below the wheelhouse and in front of the engine room. Since on the *Uchuck I* the galley was low in the vessel, the sink drained into a five-gallon bucket, which had to be carried up through the cabin and dumped over the side. And because the galley and coffee shop were separated, the mate/deckhand was given the job of cooking the mid-day meal for the crew.

Right from the beginning the *Uchuck III* was a little more modern, having a two-element DC electric range with an oven and a two-ring hot plate. There was water under pressure and even a hot water tank. But the first refrigerator was an Astral of about two cubic feet without a compressor because the DC current would not allow electronic controls. Sometimes

The tiny coffee shop at the after end of the main cabin. Note how people generally dressed when they travelled.

it would quit and the remedy was to empty it, turn it upside down un-plugged for an hour and then set it up again and plug it back in.

In the five years that the company remained in Port Alberni after the No. 3 came into service, the crew still came on board having already had breakfast and they went off to have supper at home, but the cook looked after their noontime feeding because the coffee shop and crew's galley were in the same space. This layout was much more efficient than in the other two vessels: the cook worked facing the cabin, and the crew's mess room was entered through a door behind her. At the very beginning of the No. 3's operation, there was a ventilator pipe, two and a half feet in diameter, that passed from the ventilator head on the deck above to the hold below to force air into that space. Unfortunately, it passed directly through the centre of the space where the cook worked. In a very short time cook Grace MacQueen decreed that it was to be taken out. And so it came to pass.

Our long-term cooks were nearly always older women, partly because we carried many female passengers who sometimes wanted to talk to a woman about female concerns and partly because it seemed there were fewer crew problems created with an older woman in that job. Young men behave differently when there are young women around, and having an older woman on board meant that, instead of flirting, the young ones had someone to talk to about their problems. Having women in the crew also helped to clean up the language and generally keep a higher degree of civilization on board.

There were always two women working on the separated runs in Barkley Sound, each making three trips a week. One stayed on the Bamfield run and the other on the Ucluelet run. Dina Kronstrom came with the *Uchuck I* and stayed with us for another fourteen years. Her opposite number, Betty Whitlock, another long-timer, stayed until 1955, which was when the *Uchuck I* was retired; it was the only one of our vessels that she wanted to work on. Grace MacQueen served in all of the vessels while they oper-ated out of Port Alberni. There were a few other cooks serving for shorter times in between and around those three, but the job at that time was such that a woman could have a home in the normal way and work more or less normal hours, so once settled in and liking the work, they were content to stay for a long time.

There was a camaraderie built up when a crew worked together for awhile, sharing hardships and the not-so-wonderful living conditions, but having lots of fun along with the work. It had to be that way for anyone to want to do this. When the dynamics of a crew worked properly, they were a tight little group who knew each other well, allowing for personal oddities with good humour. Sometimes there were rough patches but they generally adjusted until it was running evenly again. Very occasionally there were misfits in the crowd, but they soon found the work not to their liking and moved on. The company was not very good at firing people, so a few stayed too long, causing an entire crew to be infected and unhappy for a time. But in the whole time I was with the company there were only three or four actual firings, mainly for incompetence in a position that required expert knowledge.

Passengers often remarked about how smoothly the loading and un-loading operations went as each man seemed to be at the right place at the right time with few or no words being exchanged. Men moved back and forth in what my mother described as a ballet, the vessel gradually absorb-ing the cargo lying all over the wharf. Occasionally work stopped while they got together to plan the next several moves, then away it went again. All the while, the galley was in operation producing smells that wafted about the deck, drawing in passengers and giving the crew something to look forward to.

No one could be too proud to do even the most menial of jobs. Masters and engineers cleaned their own spaces and were involved in all aspects of ship maintenance, operation and cargo work. It was not unusual to see the skipper or engineer loading a portable freezer, operating a forklift or scrambling into the back of an incoming freight truck to unload cargo.

The Junior Deckhands

The group known as the "junior deckhands" was a subgroup within the company structure and was composed of David and Henry McCandless, Gordon Petri and me. There was about a five-year spread in our ages and I was the youngest. Gordon's father, Arvid Petri, was the man in charge of the dock office whose duty it was to receive cargo, take reservations and distribute outgoing cargo as well as a myriad of other jobs. He was also the unofficial supervisor of our little group. He even established a "strike fund" for us that was kept in the dock office in a small, white-painted plywood box with a coin slot in the top. This fund was powered by the sale of empty beer and pop bottles that had been left on board the vessels plus any change that had fallen out of the pockets of people sitting on the slatted deck seats. Once a year it would be raided and distributed to the four of us just in time for Christmas.

We worked on various shifts, which became more serious as we got older. We were ship or dock crew as needed, although our work schedules always allowed time for schooling and Sea Cadets and sports activities. But we were not a pressed crew, and from the age of fourteen on I couldn't get enough

Three of the "junior deckhands," though perhaps a few years before we started working. From left: David McCandless, Henry McCandless and Dave Young, 1947.

of it, being there after school, on weekends and during summer holidays. We even got paid a little.

On Saturdays one of the junior deckhands would sail in the *Uchuck I* as mate; this was quite a responsibility as on that vessel the crew was comprised of just master, mate/deckhand and cook. By the time I was fifteen, I was the only one of the four junior deckhands left and therefore became that mate/deckhand—temporary, acting—every Saturday. I really enjoyed this work and thought about it as I sat in school during the week. By that time I was able to do most of the tasks that needed to be done, and I had been instructed in the handling and manoeuvring of the vessel since I was ten. In fact, after our regular stop in Nahmint Bay, while the skipper was busy collecting fares, I was usually the one at the wheel when the vessel stopped so that Gus Beurling's boat from his Nahmint Lodge sport fishing camp could come alongside to get his bag of mail. No one could have been prouder than I.

I had a girl in all the ports, although they didn't know it, but it was fun hoping to see these gals each Saturday. In that couple of years I was a happy guy, whistling and singing in the wheelhouse all by myself as we went along. And I must have been able to do the work well enough as I wasn't kicked off.

Changing Times

In July 1956 the *Uchuck I* was sold to Harbour Navigation Ltd. of Vancouver, and it became the task of George and me plus Ron MacQueen, who was a chum of mine, to deliver the vessel to Vancouver with an engineer from Harbour Navigation. By this time the *Uchuck III* was working steadily on the Ucluelet run, so the *Uchuck II* had taken over from the No. 1 on the Bamfield run. As an ex-ferry, the No. 2 had done very well on the tougher Ucluelet run, always fully loaded with cargo and passengers, but she worked better on this shorter run where she was not so weather stressed in winter as she was now on the more protected side of the Sound.

The Ucluelet run had always been the heavier of the two, and discharging cargo there now took two to three hours three times a week. In summer it was hot, dusty work as the cargo was hand-stowed around standing loaded pallets in the hold and on deck. But the cargo usually included pallets of beer for the hotel, so the shout would go up to the winch man from the hold for him to ask the skipper if we might break into a case. As a result, the hotel was always short one case in summer, though it was always replaced on the next trip.

There would always be people standing all over the wharf, either there to receive goods or just to watch the progress of the cargo being landed and then hand-loaded onto waiting trucks. The skipper dealt with the paperwork of the arriving cargo and signed for the outgoing cargo while at the same time distributing the beer and liquor that he had bought the day before in the liquor store in Port Alberni. As there was no liquor store in Ucluelet, this was a perfectly legal transaction as long as there was a written order with enough cash in it to cover the cost of the goods with some extra for the freight charge.

With everything going along so well in spite of incidents and accidents, there seemed to be general euphoria in the company, and at one point, George announced, "They can't touch us now." Esson immediately reached for the nearest wood, wishing that he hadn't heard that comment.

A fun time by all at a log rolling contest in the Ucluelet harbour, in 1947. IMAGE I-26212
COURTESY OF ROYAL BC MUSEUM, BC ARCHIVES.

Not only did he have a healthy amount of sailor's superstition but he also had a Scottish Presbyterian heritage with all of the dour foreboding that can come with that.

It was at this point that Esson and George decided to buy another vessel in order to repeat the *Uchuck III* experience, and they purchased another YMS, one that looked even worse than the last, and used the *Uchuck II* to tow it to Port Alberni. *YMS 407* had enjoyed a more illustrious career in the South Pacific than *YMS 123* had on this coast. One bit of evidence of that career only showed up when we were cutting up the old mast for firewood and found a stitching of Japanese machine gun rounds in its centre. One idea for the conversion of *YMS 407* was to go with a hard times venture and complete it as simply and quickly as possible, using the engine from the *Uchuck II* along with some of its other gear as well. However, just the act of changing the vessel to single screw would have been too big of a job, and as a result, that idea never went very far.

There had been only one logical reason for the partners to buy another vessel: they felt that the *Uchuck II* was coming to the end of her useful life because of age and small size and would need to be replaced. Other than that, it is unclear to me, except for this need for replacement and the euphoria caused by the growing volume of business, why the partners acquired this vessel at that time as both of them knew that roads were coming to the Barkley Sound area soon. Right from the beginning of their business there, they had been told they would only have ten years of operation ahead of them until the roads would be built around the Sound and there would be no further need for a shipping service. (It turned out that they had fourteen.) But it seems that they hoped to put their ships out to charter in other trades with other companies. There were even preliminary plans to charter the *Uchuck III* to carry explosives to Central America where governments would rather have explosives arrive in small amounts so they could keep track of who had the product and where it went. Those plans never got beyond the initial planning stage.

By late 1957, the road from Port Alberni to Sarita River was open and being used to haul freight to the MacMillan Bloedel logging camp there. On the other side of the Sound, the road to Ucluelet and Tofino from Port Alberni was nearly complete as well. But Esson and George still did not believe that the current setback in revenues was permanent and decided to go ahead with plans for the full conversion of *YMS 407*. By early 1958 preliminary work had begun on producing another vessel similar to the *Uchuck III*. John Monrufet was again the designer of the mechanical work and he set about finding used equipment for the project. Engines and gears were found at Nelson Brothers Fisheries Ltd., mufflers and auxiliaries elsewhere, and by the end of the year, the plans were basically done and some of the equipment acquired. Unfortunately, that is when they discovered that a lot of the hull planking had rotted and needed to be replaced, a cost that was not welcome at this time. Esson then began researching the possibility of fitting the vessel with a crane instead of the conventional mast and derricks, and he corresponded with Jacques Cousteau since his vessel, *Calypso*, also an ex-YMS, had been fitted with a crane. Approval for Esson's choice of name, *Conchilla*, arrived from the federal ship registry, but he was outvoted as everyone else continued to call the new vessel *Uchuck IV*.

Work went on whenever funds were available, but by March 1959 progress was slowing as the company had become overextended and revenues had dropped by 40 percent. They needed another year to finish the

---

UCHUCK IV

Built: Henry Grebe and Co. Inc. in Chicago as *YMS 407* and
completed on December 8, 1943.
Purchase: sold out of the US Navy on February 19, 1947 to Union
Steamship Co. of Vancouver. Barkley Sound Transportation Co.
Ltd. agreed to buy on December 12, 1957.
Reconstruction and renovation project never completed.

---

project but, realizing that they couldn't continue, they offered the vessel to
BC Packers in its partly finished state to be used as a fast packer, similar to
the YMS conversion they already had in their vessel *Western Express*. This
offer came to nothing.

Esson was now coming to believe that there was no way to continue
operating in Barkley Sound and, after some research, decided to take
the company to Nootka Sound, which was on the verge of opening up
to industry. In March 1960 he and George moved the *Uchuck II* north
to the Sound, leaving the *Uchuck III* to finish up the light work left in
Barkley Sound. In the middle of June the *Uchuck III* travelled to Ucluelet
with fifty-seven members of the Port Alberni Chamber of Commerce and
friends to attend a luncheon given by the Ucluelet Chamber of Commerce.
Esson was to be the guest of honour in a farewell tribute to the fourteen
years of service that the company had given. He was quite moved by this
gesture, which provided a fitting end to the era. He was presented with a
two-foot-tall totem pole carved by a local man; on its stand was a plaque
commemorating the company's service, and in the years that followed this
pole had a place of prominence in each vessel serving in Nootka Sound.
It is still there today. He was also presented with a cake made to look like
the ship; this was to be put on board the vessel for the crew, and a few days
later when the No. 3 was on the ways in the shipyard in Port Alberni, it
fell to me to get this cake on board. As it was in a box of the right size for
transporting, I started up the long ladder to the deck with this thing under
my arm. However, the end of the box was not properly secured and came
open as I approached deck level. And out it came. All that was left for me

The Port Alberni harbour taken from the mast head while the *Uchuck III* was under construction, about 1953. In the foreground is the Port Boat House and its rental fishing boats, with the *E.D. Stone* tied to the fuel float, the *Maid of Nahmint* in the harbour, all overseen by the mills. GORDON PETRI PHOTO.

to do then was to climb back down the ladder and kick the mess under the rail carriage.

Operations in Barkley Sound ended for the *Uchuck III* with a charter run on June 11 to Ahousaht in Clayoquot Sound and back, and on June 16 at 12:53 the vessel sailed for Alert Bay, via Victoria, to go out on charter to Murray Marine Services. She would replace the *Lady Rose* on the run from Kelsey Bay to Alert Bay, Sointula, Port McNeil, Beaver Cove, Minstrel Island and a few smaller places. Meanwhile, Esson and George planned to expedite the conversion of the *Uchuck IV* to replace the *Uchuck II* in Nootka Sound or to put her out on charter. But by April 1963 it was evident that the company's financial reversal was such that work would have to be totally stopped on the conversion. (The new vessel lay in Port Alberni until it was sold to John Monrufet, effective April 1, 1969, with the idea that it would be used as a floating restaurant and fish market.)

The service in Barkley Sound was uninterrupted after the June 1960 departure of the *Uchuck III* to Alert Bay. John Monrufet and Dick McMinn felt that there was still enough work to be done in the area, although on a smaller scale, and they formed their own company, Alberni Marine Transportation Ltd. At first they chartered the *Uchuck I*, bringing her back to Barkley Sound from Vancouver, but they soon let that vessel go and chartered the *Lady Rose*, later buying her. In addition, they added a trucking operation from Port Alberni to Ucluelet and Tofino and for a time worked one service in conjunction with the other. The *Lady Rose* served them well until they sold out and retired twenty years later. Although the *Lady Rose* has since been retired, in 2011 there is still a service in Barkley Sound, nearly a century after one first began. The current vessel in service is the MV *Frances Barkley*.

CHAPTER FIVE

The Early Nootka Sound Years

During the final years of the Barkley Sound Transportation Company's service in Alberni Inlet and Barkley Sound, I was attending the University of British Columbia so I was not in regular contact with my father, though I did come back to work on the ships during the summer holidays. As a result, I didn't follow all of Esson's planning for the move to Nootka Sound and I have not found any documents relating to the move. I do know he and George were aware that the Gibson Brothers had built a sawmill at Tahsis, because back in 1947 they had served for a short time as alternating pilots for the Gibsons' MV *Machigonne*. The brothers were using that vessel, a converted 112-foot RCN Fairmile, to transport mill crews from Port Alberni to Tahsis, but in order to get there, the ship had to round Estevan Point, a feature that during a typical West Coast winter can be considered a scaled-down version of Cape Horn. Unfortunately, Fairmiles are very active vessels so this was a very rough trip, and I've heard many horror stories from people who vowed never to make that trip in the *Machigonne* again. Sadly for them, the only other way to get to Tahsis back in those days was the CP's *Princess Maquinna,* which only docked there three times a month, so many of the mill workers suffered through that journey on the *Machigonne* a number of times.

Though Nootka Sound was new for us and seemed like the end of the world for the mill workers, Native villages had existed there for thousands of years by the time European explorers arrived in 1778. Traders were not far behind and it was not long before they began a trade in sea otter fur to the Far East. This remained the main economic activity through the early 1800s. Missionaries arrived during that period, but there was little white settlement because the area was so remote.

Logging and sawmilling began in the early 1900s, but the product was mainly for the local market as there was no way to export lumber. The fishing industry began here around the same time but did not really expand until pilchards arrived mysteriously on this coast in 1917. When the pilchards disappeared in 1947, many of the processing plants closed down.

Prospectors found gold at Zeballos in the early 1930s, and when ore samples were sent to a Tacoma refinery, they were seen to be the richest anywhere in this part of the world. A hectic but brief gold rush followed, but with the start of World War II, the cost of mining and lack of labour made mining there uneconomic. One day it stopped and everyone left. The population dropped from around fifteen hundred to less than fifty persons. From 1962 to 1969 an iron mine operated there.

In 1937 the Nootka Mission Association, an offshoot of the Shantyman's Christian Association, established a hospital and mission at Esperanza to serve the whole area. Dr. Herman Alexander McLean was the driving force and the only doctor for most of the fifty years that it existed

Actually fairly normal for a leatherback sea turtle, this giant weighed in at 1,200 pounds. It was caught off of Nootka Island in 1937, and was brought to the Nootka Cannery in Friendly Cove for weighing. IMAGE C-04901 COURTESY OF ROYAL BC MUSEUM, BC ARCHIVES.

there, serving fishermen, miners, loggers and their families, as well as the Native population. The hospital closed in 1973 with the opening of the Tahsis Health Centre, but the Esperanza facility remained open for a time as an occasional dental clinic.

Tahsis, which had been the winter home to the Mowachaht people for centuries, became the site of the Nootka Wood Products sawmill in 1937, followed in 1945 by a sawmill owned by the Gibson Brothers with backing from the Danish East Asiatic Company (EAC). This mill burned in 1948 and was immediately rebuilt; Gibson Brothers sold their interest to EAC in 1952, and the enterprise became the Tahsis Company Ltd. in 1960.

At this time, there were serious rumours that EAC planned to build a pulp mill somewhere in that area, which would have helped to cement the transition from mining and fish processing to industrial scale forestry. I'm sure this information must have greatly influenced Esson's thinking. On the other hand, he must also have known that access to Nootka Sound via road across Vancouver Island from Campbell River had just been made possible by the connection of the road systems created by the Elk River Timber Co., an American company operating west of Campbell River, and EAC's Tahsis Company with timber holdings in the Sound and around Gold River. The two road systems had been private and closed to the public as there was active logging throughout the area, but once their networks were connected, they began to allow access to the public although they limited it to runs by Vancouver Island Coach Lines Ltd. (VICL) (and later their freight trucks) with times and conditions of travel strictly spelled out. When Barkley Sound Transportation moved north in 1960, VICL had already begun a service from Campbell River to bring passengers and package freight as far as the Tahsis Company's Gold River beach camp where the Gold River meets Muchalat Inlet, as well as to two camps belonging to Elk River Timber along that road.

Esson met with the coach lines people, and they worked out a way for the two companies to interline in order to move people and goods beyond the Gold River camp. He also secured permission to use the Tahsis Company wharves and floats from which to operate, and then he had to start generating traffic. He began by finding out who was working in the area, apart from the two main companies, and arranged meetings with them to promote the new service. There was not much boat traffic in

Nootka Sound in those days, although many individuals and small logging outfits had power boats in which they came and went from the villages of Tahsis and Zeballos. The hospital and mission at Esperanza in Nootka Sound also had some boats they used for their medical and missionary work. The *Chamis Queen* and the *Lou B.* were the two water taxis running in the Sound when we arrived, but they were later replaced by the *Le Gar* and the *Zeballos Lady*, clinker-built fast boats. The two operators, Slim Beale and Red Wilton, saw us as competition to their service, but a major factor in the reliability of the service they offered was that the runs they were asked to make were very long, and they were operating in remote waters that were full of floating and fixed dangers for small fast boats. In fog they would sometimes follow the *Uchuck*, and on more than a few occasions the *Uchuck* towed in or rescued one of them, always with cheerfulness and courtesy as had been the way in Barkley Sound with the speed boat competition there. This helpful attitude did no harm in assisting the new service to become welcome in the area. Slim Beale carried on for a long time doing a liquor run from the government liquor store in Zeballos to the people of Tahsis, which at the time had no store. We occasionally covered for him when for some reason he was not able to run.

Queen Charlotte Airlines had pioneered air service into Nootka Sound, beginning in the early 1930s when gold was discovered in Zeballos and lasting into the early 1950s. They were followed by local companies such as Island Air, which set up a service between Campbell River and Gold River, stationing their small Cessna at a floating office/cabin in Gold River. Conditions were difficult for small aircraft because of the strong winds in summer and even more challenging conditions in winter, but plane service was essential throughout the region because planes could do many things that ships could not, such as carrying out medivacs and bringing in rush goods. Eventually there was enough traffic for a proper base to be set up and a succession of companies operated in the region, each with several aircraft. As their service complemented ours, there was a good-natured rivalry, but the crew of the *Uchuck II* would sometimes help a pilot struggle to get awkward freight goods, such as a logging truck transmission, up a plank and into a Beaver, simply because it was so important for the local economy that machinery get on its way for repairs.

The only real competition for the company in Nootka Sound came from Northland Navigation, which operated out of Vancouver on a weekly basis, having taken over Canadian Pacific's West Coast route in 1958. This company operated several vessels in turn, the longest to serve being the MV *Tahsis Prince*. The freight rate this company charged was lower than the combination of that charged by the *Uchuck* plus the rates charged by the Coach Lines and the other carriers with which the company interlined, so this was an impediment to the growth of business for Nootka Sound Service. Even so, our traffic began to increase because of the difference in the service level.

Realistically, it had probably been too soon to try to set up a service there as neither Esson nor George had any idea what industries would be successfully developed, but if they had delayed, someone else might have seen an opportunity and moved in. In addition, it would have been less difficult if the company had some fat to live on in this start-up period, but it was pretty well broke. This difficult time lasted for nearly ten years as the business slowly became viable. In the meantime it was all very wearing on the partners, who were both fifty years old at the beginning of this phase of their company's existence.

Two days prior to the *Uchuck II*'s first scheduled run in Nootka Sound, the partners took her on a preliminary run, going over the route to find out how long it would take and to get a good set of compass courses and elapsed times written down. Without radar, it is necessary to have the courses and times between points figured out and recorded to keep to a schedule in times of limited visibility. As he had always done at the approach to any port, on that first entry into Gold River, Esson blew the *Uchuck II*'s air whistle, a distinctive sound that was very much like a steam whistle. It so happened that Mike Weymer and his wife were living in the Tahsis Company beach camp three-quarters of a mile up the road from the company wharf, but Mike had previously worked and lived at Sarita River so he and his wife knew the vessel well. Now when its whistle sounded at Gold River, she raised her head and said, "There's the *Uchuck*!" And they went outside and there she was! They had not known that the vessel was due to begin service there.

❀ ❀ ❀

At that time Gold River was only a large logging camp on the river flats. It had been established by the Tahsis Company in 1955, and besides providing homes for the loggers, it had a dock, a post office and a co-op store. But when the company began making plans to build a mill on that site, the camp had to go, and a new Gold River was established at a point fourteen kilometres east where the Gold and Heber rivers meet. It began with forty houses for the future mill workers as well as all the amenities for family life in the wilderness. A bonus for those living there was that the rank smell from the kraft mill had dissipated by the time it reached the new settlement. The District of Gold River was incorporated on August 26, 1965, and it was reincorporated as the Village of Gold River on January 1, 1972.

The initial schedule for the *Uchuck II* was designed so that the runs began at Zeballos at midday, stopping wherever necessary to pick up cargo and passengers and arriving at the Gold River Camp by 17:00 hours to meet the bus from Campbell River. Incoming freight and passengers would leave the bus and the outgoing passengers would get on. That done, the

The *Uchuck II* prior to 1952. Note the Canadian Red Ensign, Canada's unofficial flag until the adoption of the Maple Leaf in 1965. MCCANDLESS COLLECTION PHOTO.

vessel would start back up the line. This was to happen five days a week: Tuesday, Wednesday, Friday, Saturday and Sunday.

Voyage number one on March 18, 1960, began at 11:30 hours at Zeballos. The vessel picked up ten passengers, one at Tahsis and nine at Mooyah Bay, before proceeding to Gold River to connect with the bus. There were no passengers for the return trip. Voyage number two began the next day at the same hour, but this time there were only two passengers from Tahsis and none on the return trip. There was some cargo: three bundles of newspapers, a ring gear for the Tahsis Sawmill and a bundle of plywood for Mooyah Bay.

Within a month the passenger loads had increased to as many as forty or fifty people, and the cargo volume began to build as people got used to a service that promised to be ongoing. When the Coach Lines added a second bus that left Gold River at noon to make connections for down-island points beyond Campbell River, the *Uchuck's* schedule was changed so that the vessel left Zeballos at 07:00 on four days, except on Fridays when it left at 11:00. Soon that too changed to the earlier time, and then departure time was pushed back to 06:30 for all runs and stayed at that hour for all future sailings from Zeballos. The five-hour layover in Gold River before the afternoon sailing allowed time to load cargo brought in by the first Coach Lines bus of the day and later by freight truck, which was the only way to get cargo in, or to do small onboard jobs. In winter the wait between buses could be as much as eight hours if the road conditions were bad, so the *Uchuck's* printed schedules were considered only a guide. In summer this interval was used to make a tourist run to Friendly Cove (Yuquot) at the southern tip of Nootka Island and sometimes short-distance extra freight runs. At about 17:00 when the second bus of the day arrived with the incoming passengers, mail and package freight, there was a great scurry to get the vessel loaded, and the *Uchuck* began the return journey to Zeballos.

One rainy afternoon as we headed for Gold River after a late night trip to Zeballos, we were looking forward to the four-hour wait for the afternoon bus to come and made plans to use some of that time for a little sleep. But as we came around Gold River Point, we saw two school buses on the wharf. Oh no! We had forgotten that today we had eighty grade sevens going out to Friendly Cove on a charter run. We didn't even have a coffee girl on board for this trip. But the kids came on board in the rain and away we went. The driver, the deckhand and I went hard at making sandwiches and selling pop and chocolate bars steadily all the way out to the Cove. Such energy those kids had!

Adjusting to Nootka Sound

At the beginning of service in Nootka Sound, most of the *Uchuck*'s crew members still lived in Port Alberni and they elected to commute, so Esson and George established a week-on/week-off work schedule. Once a week the incoming crew arrived on the bus from Campbell River, having left a car at the bus depot there for the out-going crew to take back to Port Alberni. The car was usually George McCandless's 1956 Oldsmobile Delta 88, a big, comfortable car that could carry everyone. At Gold River there was a hurried exchange of news, the retiring crew piled onto the bus and then the new crew had lunch and picked up where the other crew had left off.

We could usually count on half an hour in Gold River for the process of passing news of the week's events to the incoming crew—and so did the Coach Lines driver. If the time extended to more than he was happy with, he would begin moving the bus ahead by inches, with a few words shouted out the open door to make us hurry up. Eventually, we five retiring crew members would get on the bus with a few more words, often profane and directed at the driver, and then we would settle back and go to sleep for the ride to Campbell River. No one had much oomph left at the end of the week-long shift.

One day there was a difference. The driver was new and didn't know about this ritual so, when his passengers were aboard and his freight loaded, he drove off. We watched, figuring that he was just going off to the beach camp to pick up some freight and would come back for us. But he was gone a long time, and then it dawned on us—he was not coming back. So now what? At that time Vancouver Island Coach Lines was the only non-forest company traffic allowed on the private logging roads between Campbell River and Gold River. We were stuck. It was time to phone for a plane.

Island Air of Campbell River agreed to come out on a charter trip to pick us up. An hour later Bobby Langdon, president and owner, landed the Beaver on the water near the ship and taxied up to the airplane float. Dennis Bye, our engineer, was not a fan of flying in small aircraft, and unfortunately his friend Ray Mitchell, who was along for the week as oiler, knew this and began describing all the things that could and probably would go wrong on our flight. Then just as we were about to climb into the plane, Bobby Langdon, who was standing on the pontoon, looked all around, hands on hips, and asked, "How do you get out of here, anyway?" Dennis was nearly destroyed with that. We flew out of Gold River with Dennis hunched down in his seat and very quiet for the duration of the flight. No amount of pointing out the sights below cheered him up, not even the herd of Roosevelt elk that we saw crossing the Elk River to the lower pastures for the winter.

In terms of where to live, however, my father and mother decided to move to Campbell River in order to be closer to Nootka Sound. As far as Esson was concerned, the move was permanent, but as the company office remained in Port Alberni, he now had to commute to both the office and the vessel from a home midway between the two. The decision to leave the office in Port Alberni had been made, first, because that was where Audrey Peterson lived, and second, because it would be upsetting to uproot an office and try to get that word around when there was so much else to do when setting up the new operation. So while in the beginning Audrey Peterson had been mainly the company's bookkeeper, she now took on the job of office manager as well. She had to make business decisions on her own, checking them with Esson later because there was no phone service to Gold River. While George McCandless had elected to remain in Port Alberni after the company move and was available to her when needed, he was not by nature inclined to paperwork. This had never been a problem in the past as it had been an understanding between the two partners from the beginning that Esson would look after the business end of things. Fortunately, Audrey Peterson had a thorough knowledge of how the company worked, so Esson soon developed a routine of travelling to Port Alberni one day every other week, usually on the day after he came home from Gold River, to deal with any of the previous week's finances and other events that she couldn't resolve. (In 1967 "Mrs. Pete" retired and her assistant, Florence Kapchinsky, took over the job, but the office remained in Port Alberni for another seventeen years. The road from

Punching tickets. Note the gas mask bag as a ticket bag. I was still using one just like it in 1994.

Campbell River to Gold River was opened to limited public access in 1967 and three years later parts of it were rerouted and then the whole distance paved and opened as Highway 28.)

Esson instituted a formal but simple freight and passenger paperwork system. He and George collected revenue, sometimes in cash, but mostly on a charge account basis for both the Coach Lines and the shipping line by adding the Coach Lines freight charges to their own on goods coming in that had not been prepaid. The Coach Lines did the same on goods going out. Esson set up charge accounts for local businesses and for some regular travellers, and he sent out pads of travel vouchers to the hiring halls in Vancouver to be made out for travelling mill, logging and mining employees. They turned these over to the skipper on board and then our office billed the employers. A system of passenger tickets was evolved that looked like the old Vancouver streetcar tickets with all the destinations printed on them. The double ticket was punched with the date, amount and place, and one half was given to the passenger as a receipt. Occasionally a passenger would be confused about where to get off, and a glance at his ticket would quickly settle the question.

Many of the single loggers arrived on the dock at Gold River straight from the hiring halls of Vancouver, heading out to yet another camp in the wilderness or to the sawmill at Tahsis. They had been travelling all day, starting at 07:00, by bus and ferry and here they were at the end of the world with one more journey in front of them. They each had a travel warrant from the hiring hall, which had the camp name on it. The skipper, while collecting fares en route, had to be aware of who wanted to go where, as that would determine what stops the ship would make on that trip. At each place we would have to be careful that everyone got off that belonged there. Some would be asleep when we arrived and many would not know when the next camp was theirs, so we had to check through the vessel at each place. Occasionally we over-carried someone and had to go back to the last stop.

One man went to Santiago Creek in Tahsis Inlet and was let off in the dark at the camp float. Next morning he went out with the crew and looked up, way up, to where he was to be working and said, "To hell with that noise." When we came by later in the morning, we picked him up to take him back to Gold River, but on the way he leaned over the rail at each camp we stopped at to ask if they needed a chokerman. Then at Mooyah Bay they did. He tossed his gear off and went there instead.

One day an unlikely looking pair of men got on at Gold River bound for Tahsis. They seemed to be a little different to the types that we usually carried. The smaller of the two was the speaker and paid the fare for both as I went about collecting. It turned out they were repo-men, going in to seize some cars that had delinquent payments against them. The big, quiet but very pleasant fellow was probably the enforcer.

But one older woman, an old hand on the coast, knew exactly where she was going. We were travelling to Zeballos on a trip on which we were very late, and I told her that it would probably be about 03:00 before we got there. She wasn't bothered by this and said, "That's all right, son. I'll be tits-up over there on the bench. You can wake me."

Sometimes we would get apprentice marine pilots who were checking out the routes that deep-sea vessels take as they come in to the ports of Tahsis and Gold River. City girls appeared occasionally, coming to be with loggers they had met in town. They looked bewildered as they set off in their high heels up the steep ramp off the logging camp float into the black night. They had not imagined anything close to this.

If for some reason the vessel arrived back in Zeballos before midnight, we might send our young deckhand up to the beer parlour before "last call" to fill a table with glasses of beer while we finished up the work. As this didn't happen more than a few times a year, about halfway through the run on such a day we would begin to think that we might just make it, so everyone got into high gear and worked as efficiently as possible to get the trip done quickly. Mostly we hoped that the old hand-cranked, air-cooled, Wisconsin engine on the winch would start easily each time we needed it because, if it didn't, that might be enough to foil our plans.

But normally it was after midnight when we arrived in Zeballos, so the object was to get to our bunks as soon as possible because we would have to do it all over again the next day. We usually managed to have a snack on the way to our bunks, since by that time supper had been six or more hours earlier. Then it was into the bunk and, as with a child's doll, the eyes closed as you lay down. Sometimes I woke up in the morning with my hair still combed from the day before. Crawling out of the bunk in the morning was always hard, but things soon improved with the first jolt of high-test coffee. The body responded, the stiffness wore off and the hands quit being sore as the day got going. This all happened five times a week.

Life Aboard

Sleeping arrangements in the company's vessels, since they were day boats, were not good in those early days. The *Uchuck II* had just one bunk in the galley that was used by the skipper; the rest of us had mattresses that were stowed during the day and brought out for the night. We simply put them down someplace on the deck that we thought might stay dry. If the vessel had a slight port list, it was usually safe to sleep on the starboard side. This situation improved a little in the No. 2 when we robbed some of the fold-down bench space in the waist to build a couple of bunks for the engineer and mate. The last thing the engineer did at night was shut down the old single-cylinder Gardner generator, which because of its heavy flywheel took some time to wind down, allowing him time to come up and climb into his bunk before the lights went totally out. I would hear it slowing down, but usually by the last compression thump I was asleep. In the morning the first thump of the old thing starting up again, as the flywheel was rolled over by hand-crank, was enough to tell all of us that the next day had begun.

As the skipper's bunk in the *Uchuck II* was in the galley where the stove was, it was his job to make the coffee in the morning. This was not ordinary coffee. This was seagoing coffee, made in the old aluminum perk, the guts of which had long since been lost. The recipe was simple: first, you put a whole bunch of coffee in the bottom of the pot, then you topped it up with cold water, brought it to a roiling boil for a couple of minutes and then set it aside for another minute. Next, you lifted the pot and gave it a good thump on the table to settle the grounds. It was ready. It was strong. In fact, stirring in the sugar could be a two-handed affair. But this was necessary stuff, being the starting fluid for the sailors.

The white enamelled mugs being plunked down onto the galley table is what the sailors awoke to after their short night in their bunks. The mugs hung on hooks over the galley sink. They all faced one way so, as the ship rolled, they didn't run into each other, but most importantly, they faced away from the nearest salt water. Observing this superstition was just about as important as not opening the can of Pacific evaporated milk upside down. If one did that, it went over the side. (In these more enlightened days, such anti-environmental behaviour would probably get you a major frown.)

The design of the mugs was important. They had ring handles that you could get a thick finger through, a good flat bottom, straight sides so the coffee wouldn't slop out and were made of thick material so that the heat was held in for a trip outside to another part of the ship. A good sailor could deliver one, two or even three mugs to any part of the ship under any conditions. To get across a heaving deck, he had to plant his weight over each foot with each step to keep his balance. (This accounts for the rolling gait that sailors have at anytime anywhere.) He needed one hand free to be able to climb ladders, open doors or grab handrails when the ship dropped off a sea. He had to be bold, stepping out smartly to get the rhythm of the ship, and the carrying arm had to be clear, so the wrist could work like a gyroscope, turned by instinct to keep the tops of the mugs level with the horizon. If he stopped suddenly, he thrust the mug bottoms forward enough that Newton's first law of motion did not come into effect and slop coffee onto his fingers. If the wind was above thirty-five knots, he would only fill the mugs three quarters full, so when the whitecaps rolled across the surface of the coffee, they wouldn't climb over the rims. This coffee parade happened many times a day, although sometimes the fluid was tea, made in much the same way, in the old enamelled teapot. At the end of the day it felt like you had fur on your teeth, and I won't even discuss the added effect of cheap tobacco.

Spreading the Word

To let people know about the service they were offering in Nootka Sound, the partners met with all possible potential customers, including the president of the Tahsis Company, Mr. Frederiksen, and the local mill manager, Doug Abernathy. Several times they invited these people and others to travel on the *Uchuck II* to see for themselves how the system worked. However, Abernathy was not easily convinced, and he told some of his department heads that he only gave these new guys six weeks before they folded and left the area. When that prediction proved wrong, he gradually became a supporter, but still he did not want to lose his freight connection with Vancouver, fearing that this small company might not be able to perform well enough to cover all his company's needs, leaving Tahsis vulnerable. As a result, he continued to patronize Northland Navigation Ltd. as well.

However, other companies in the area became early supporters of the new service. Taylorway Logging at Mooyah Bay was one of these, along with A.C. McEachern Ltd., a road building contractor working at Marvinas Bay on Nootka Island. Ray Grumbach, the towing contractor for Tahsis Company and a man Esson and George knew well from their Barkley Sound days, also used their services. Others soon saw the advantage of using the *Uchuck* as it made possible earlier and more frequent deliveries of needed goods. Very early on, the Comox Creamery at Courtenay began sending in a regular supply of milk products, and this was the sort of steady business that the company needed to build a base.

By 1960 logging had become the major part of the economy of the Nootka Sound area, supplanting the forty-year dominance of the fishing industry, though at first the trees were cut mainly to supply the sawmill at Tahsis. That company also had its own truck logging division at Gold River. After the *Uchuck* was sent on several occasions to Fair Harbour in Kyuquot Sound with bridge building lumber from the mill at Tahsis, it began to be generally recognized that our service had many capabilities.

The vessel was always available, versatile and the crew willing to do anything or go anywhere at any time. It remained for people and companies to remember that she was there and ready.

But while logging was important to our company's growth, it was also important to us that an iron mine was in the planning stages at Zeballos where a magnetite ore body was to be exploited and the ore sent to Japan. This was going to be a large operation, and Esson and George began to think that the unfinished *Uchuck IV* could run directly from Vancouver with passengers and freight for this mine. However, even in this early stage of their operation in Nootka Sound, they both thought that it might be possible to sell their whole company to one of the big players in the area. This idea had come up during a conversation between George and Mr. Frederiksen, head of the Tahsis Company, who had mused—as did the iron mine people did later—that it might be a good idea for each of those companies to have its own vessel. Nothing came of these musings.

Tourism

While operating in Barkley Sound, the company had built a good tourist business. People from everywhere had come to see what a working coastal vessel did. They were not catered to, they just took what came, and every trip was different. But in Port Alberni it had been easy for them to just drive into town and get on the vessel in the morning for the day trip. For

The *Uchuck III* pictured on a postcard. ALBERNI VALLEY MUSEUM PHOTOGRAPH COLLECTION.

the company's early tourist efforts in Nootka Sound, this type of travel had to be set up with Vancouver Island Coach Lines in order to get people as far as the Gold River logging camp. The first run of this kind was on July 6, 1960, when a few people came along for the ride, having arrived on the noon bus with plans to leave on the afternoon one. Taylorway Logging provided a logger lunch in their camp cookhouse at Mooyah Bay and gave them all a chance to see what a real logging operation looked like. After an hour's stop there, the vessel sailed westward via Zuciarte Channel on the south side of Bligh Island to give the passengers a look at the ocean and to make a quick visit to Friendly Cove before returning to Gold River. It was immediately obvious that this idea had potential and it would grow in the years to come because in those days there were not many places of this kind that were as easily accessible to the public.

Radar

During their first September in Nootka Sound Esson and George installed a Raytheon radar on the *Uchuck II*, but the two partners had to learn how to tune and use the new equipment and then to trust what it was telling them. Lots of old sailors had trouble with radar at first, preferring to trust their gut feelings rather than this new box of tricks. However, having radar further enhanced the reliability of the service and helped to ease the strain on the partners, a strain that had been well illustrated on one of George's trips back to Nootka Sound from a refit in Port Alberni. He encountered fog most of the way, and though the clock told him he should be getting near Estevan Point, he couldn't see it and he couldn't hear the horn. He stopped the vessel, which stopped the engine, to listen. Even then he didn't hear the horn so, assuming that he must be about abeam of the point by then, he altered ninety degrees to starboard and moved in one mile and then stopped again to listen. This time he heard the horn so then he knew for sure where he was. He had given up smoking some time earlier but this trip started him smoking again.

Unlike the present-day solid state radar sets with transistors, microprocessors and integrated circuits, the early sets were power-hungry machines with vacuum tubes in the circuitry, which made them more susceptible to failure. The common feeling among the old sailors then was that a radar set had only a certain number of turn-ons in it and they didn't want to waste them. It was also a fact that there were very few repair technicians around—especially on the remote West Coast—and those who did exist certainly weren't right handy. So for a time the old navigation practices were kept up, with radar only used as a second opinion, but eventually the old ways faded with the coming of new generations of sailors and more reliable equipment. Double and triple redundancies have helped to assure steady operation. And other more modern equipment has been developed since 1960, so that today an old-time sailor would hardly recognize anything in an up-to-date wheelhouse where there may not even be a wheel.

Repairs and Refits

As in Barkley Sound, the *Uchuck II* met with floating and half-sunk logs on a number of occasions. At least four times she was beached alongside the inner side of the wharf head in Zeballos, twice to straighten the propeller and twice to change it for the spare. These were long and difficult jobs, and there are full pages in the journal describing how and exactly where the vessel was secured to the wharf and what tools had been made to straighten the blades. These notes were all made in an effort to have a detailed plan ready for the next time it happened—as there would surely be a next time. The master's other option when this kind of thing happened was to run the vessel to Port Alberni, but it was twelve hours away and it would take another twelve back plus work time and then it was only possible if the tides were big enough in the cycle for a haul-out. And all those times could increase in winter.

The vessel's wiring was an ongoing problem, too. When the conversion to coaster from ferry had been made, a new type of surface wiring had been used, which consisted of paired wires encased in a lead cover. This made a very neat installation that could be bent smoothly around corners. No one knew then that after some years of heat, but more especially vibration, the lead covering would harden, crack and let in water, which in turn produced grounds and shorts, so that you never knew what you might get a shock from. It also had the potential for fires. Gradually it had to be replaced as the problems were located.

The first nine months of pretty continuously running meant repairs to gear and vessel were all done by the crew in the few hours between runs and on the couple of harbour days per week that they were in Zeballos. But only small jobs and temporary repairs of the larger things could be done at these times. And although the mill and logging camp shops were always willing to help out in emergencies, there were no machine shops or ship-yard facilities anywhere nearby to perform mechanical maintenance. This meant that the crew had to be very resourceful, and in the journals kept by Esson and George there are many references to how they had resolved problems, at least temporarily. The new radar gave them a lot of trouble, too, taking up more time than they wanted to spend on it. Most major machinery repairs had to wait for the annual inspection and refit when the vessel was taken out of service for a week or two.

When we went to Port Alberni for refit, we took cargo both ways to help defray the running costs. On our way out of the Sound we would deliver last-minute parts and gear to the camps, sometimes generating traf-fic that we would not ordinarily get. Once when we were heading back to Nootka Sound from Port Alberni we carried a brightly finished, classy looking, twenty-foot motor vessel on deck. At the same time we loaded a prefabricated house to deliver to the Ahousaht reserve on Matilda Inlet. When we arrived at the government wharf in Matilda Inlet, it was neces-sary to put the boat in the water while we lifted the prefab house out of the hold. By the time we finished, it was dark and the weather had turned miserable—blowing and raining. That's when the skipper asked where the boat was. My brother, who was working as deckhand at the time, indicated a line leading over the side and said, as he put his hand on the line, "If this line is tight, we're laughing." It wasn't. Our searchlight revealed the boat on the other side of Matilda Inlet, soon to go ashore if we didn't get there right away. We commandeered a local boat and went off to retrieve it. Then we carried on.

Wharves and Roads

The floats and wharves that the *Uchuck* used in Nootka Sound were still very rough in those days. At Gold River one arm of the river came out very near the Tahsis Company wharf, and when the river was in spate, there was the very real danger of logs, roots and stumps charging down and taking out the wharf. At those times it was dangerous to tie the vessel up as the added weight might be the little bit needed to tear everything loose, espe-cially at low tide when the flow against the wharf was greatest.

Once the kraft mill was built at the mouth of the river, we moved to the newly built public wharf at the other side of the complex. But there was now a new problem for us. The wood room part of the mill complex was just behind our berth. Here, the logs were taken from the water, debarked and then chipped, a very noisy, steam-powered operation that worked twenty-four hours a day. The exhaust from this operation was aimed in our direction, making it hard to talk to anyone on deck. One day George McCandless went to the mill office, found an engineer there, brought him over to the *Uchuck*, poured him a gin and told him that he would have to do something about all that noise. The engineer agreed that cutting it was quite doable and promised to make it happen. He did tell George not to expect results right away, but in due course it did happen.

Meanwhile, the land route leading into Gold River was also still very rough and ready, and both the road and the many bridges across it were subject to washouts every time the rivers rose with heavy rain and/or melting snow. If a bus was trapped west of a washout, as happened on several occasions, another bus had to be sent out from Campbell River to the site. After a squared-off log was put in place across the washout, the freight was carried and the passengers walked across it from bus to bus, every passenger carrying something—his own baggage or some of the freight. When the bus was late like this, the *Uchuck* waited at the wharf as long as was necessary so that sometimes the run would be completed in Zeballos just in time to start the next one. The crew would have a cup of coffee and pretend that this was a new day after a night's sleep.

Snow was also a problem because the road across the island went through the mountains. When snow became too deep for the logging companies to operate, they simply shut down and didn't try to keep the road passable, at least in the short term. One year the snow came during the Christmas holiday shutdown when no men were in the camps, so there was no snow removal and eventually the road was totally impassable. To get it open again, D8 cats were brought in to push the snow off the worst parts. One year they even brought in a snow blower from the Fraser Valley, and that machine created a wall of snow twenty feet high out at Camp Ten, halfway along the road. That year the snow was still deep on the ground in late March. There were even a couple of years when the *Uchuck* had to be sent to Port Alberni to pick up cargo because the Campbell River–Gold River road had been closed for too long. Since this was winter, it was not a good time for the vessel to get to Port Alberni and back at a specific time.

On one occasion when the road was a sheet of very slippery packed snow, the bus going out met the VICL freight truck on its way in. The road bed was very narrow because of the banked snow on each side, so when the vehicles were easing past each other and the drivers stopped for a moment to talk to one another through their windows, the bus slid gently sideways, allowing the outside mirrors on the two vehicles to lock together. As everyone pondered what to do, Esson suggested that the passengers could try pushing. Half a dozen of us got out and pushed the front of the bus backwards and up the slight slope, then got back in and continued the journey.

The public travelling on the Campbell River–Gold River VICL run were required to sign a waiver stating in essence that the logging companies would not be responsible for any mishap befalling them. The windows of the coach were to be kept closed and there was to be no smoking on board. The driver was required to announce these rules when the bus got to the first Elk River Timber gate, which was located at the trestle bridge over the lower end of Upper Campbell Lake, but he always gave a warning about five miles before the gate that there was still time to light up that last cigarette. At the gate the list of people was handed down to the gate man who then raised the bar for the bus to go on. A driver named Ray Fontana, having become bored with the ritual spiel, came up with, "Okay folks, none of this, none of that and keep the windows closed."

During the trip west, the bus would encounter up to a dozen off-highway logging trucks, loaded and heading toward the Campbell River log dump. At sixteen feet wide, these trucks were twice the width of anything on a regular highway, and since they couldn't stop quickly and the road was narrow and winding, the bus had to be prepared to get onto the shoulder immediately or stop at a widening whenever one of these monsters suddenly appeared. Often, on meeting a bus, the truck driver would hand signal to indicate that there was another truck following him. In summer the dust clouds would help to give warning of an approaching truck, but as it rumbled past, the dust was so thick that it was necessary for the bus to stop until the air cleared. When there was snow on the road, the trucks tended to drive in the middle of it, so that a bus, coming around a curve, would find a wall of truck and logs bearing down on it. Bus drivers often steered wide into an outside turn in order to see farther down the next stretch, and they would sometimes pass on the wrong side of the truck in the middle of a big turn because log haulers liked to keep to the cliff side. These bus drivers reacted quickly, expecting to have to do any of these things, but it also helped if the bus driver had been a truck driver in his past.

No one talked much on the winding stretches of road, and nervous passengers sat on the edge of their seats. (Our engineer once counted 525 curves in the road.) On one surprisingly cold morning, we passed nine loaded logging trucks that were either in the ditch or stopped in the middle of the road to avoid sliding off on the slick surface. They should not have been sent out that day but no one had known how bad it was. Our bus had to ease around each one in turn. In one place all the passengers were told to get off while the driver took the bus to the extreme outside edge of the road above Campbell Lake. From his seat he could not see the edge of the road beside him. He made it, so we all piled back in and carried on.

The incoming traffic on the bus was usually light on the morning run, often consisting of just the *Uchuck*'s crew. We knew all the drivers well, so there was always banter back and forth. It happened that VICL had bought four coaches especially for that run, and they all had a type of clutch system that made it hard for the driver to shift gears without grinding them. Some drivers could shift better than others, and my brother, Tony, enjoyed chiding those that ground the gears until one day, while the bus was in motion, the driver, Glen Hilchey, stepped out of his seat while we were still underway. "All right," he said, "see if you can do any better." Tony couldn't and he said no more.

By the end of the 1960s, the village of Gold River had been created, the pulp mill built, and the logging road made into a public road by twinning parts and adding new pieces. One joint use section remained in the Gold River canyon because there was nowhere else to put a second road along that stretch, and the public road was now on the south side of Campbell Lake and crossed the Buttle Narrows. This lengthened the travel distance by eight miles, but since the road was no longer shared with logging trucks, no one complained. The public road that was created is a one hundred-kilometre winding highway that still mostly follows the routes of the original logging roads.

Another problem for the *Uchuck*'s crew was the lack of telephone service on the coast. On one occasion the air start valves on the No. 2 would not operate properly so that the engine could not be started at sailing time in Zeballos. It took five hours for that problem to be sorted out and dealt with, but it had not been possible to contact VICL in Campbell River to tell them to hold the bus. So it had duly arrived, and the passengers had sat on their suitcases in Gold River for the full five hours, waiting for the *Uchuck* and not knowing what was going on. But such things were a part of life on the West Coast in those days and not really unexpected.

CHAPTER SIX

The Lean Years

Running for Work

In May 1961 I graduated from the University of British Columbia with a bachelor's degree in economics and geography and looked forward to a summer on the *Uchucks* before entering law school in the fall. I headed for Alert Bay where the *Uchuck III* was to end her service for Murray Marine Services and became a member of the crew as we took her back to the West Coast of the Island. Esson and George planned to use the No. 3 on a regular freight run from Port Alberni to Kyuquot Sound as it appeared that the logging companies were going to restrict access to the Gold River road for some time yet, which would make it a real bottleneck for freight movement at a time when economic activity was finally increasing in that area. They believed that with the *Uchuck III* doing the main freight work from Port Alberni north and the *Uchuck II* looking after the light freight and passengers from Gold River, they could cover all the Coast's requirements. Looking further ahead, they saw the possibility of replacing the No. 2 with the No. 4 when that vessel was completed. That project had been on hold for some time, but with a major effort they felt that it could be completed in another nine months.

It was going to be difficult to attract cargoes for this new West Coast run as the pattern had been broken when Canadian Pacific ceased its run, and the freight rate would have to be higher by a meaningful amount than that of Northland Navigation unless the cargo actually originated on

The SS *Princess Maquinna* at Bamfield. She served the West Coast for almost forty years, from 1913 to 1952. ALBERNI VALLEY MUSEUM PHOTOGRAPH COLLECTION.

Vancouver Island. But when the CP ships had been running, Woodward's Stores had provided an outport service to the West Coast from its outlet in Port Alberni, and Esson thought he could get some of that traffic going again to make up part of a regular cargo.

The *Uchuck III* arrived in Port Alberni from the east side of the island on May 19, 1961, and immediately relieved the *Uchuck II* for a much-needed refit. When that was completed, the No. 2 returned to work in Nootka Sound and the No. 3 commenced the new West Coast run. It started at Port Alberni and ended at Chamis Bay in Kyuquot Sound with occasional stops in Barkley Sound, Clayoquot Sound, Nootka Sound and Kyuquot Sound, in a partial replication of the old *Princess Maquinna's* run. The round trip took three days of continuous running. Meanwhile, the No. 2 gathered up southbound outgoing cargo and transferred it to the No. 3 for the trip south. The company was now running two vessels and the debt was mounting, so the partners knew that traffic would have to build quickly on the new run in order for the company to survive as there was no cushion to tide it over until better days.

However, on June 23, 1961, Esson left a note to George in the journal that the time of reckoning had come and that the No. 3 had just three weeks left to show that she could really bring in the money. After that three weeks the insurance would run out and, if she wasn't earning sufficiently, she would have to be tied up. Coincidentally, A.C. McEachern was finishing up its road building contract in Marvinas Bay, which meant a good customer from the company's first days in Nootka Sound was not going to be there for the *Uchuck II* anymore. Although a mail contract was all but awarded and there were very positive signs that a small subsidy was going to be approved by the Water Transport Board in Ottawa, neither would come soon enough. In early July the *Uchuck III* had to be pulled out of service and tied up in Port Alberni.

Northland Navigation was also having difficulty on its West Coast run at this time as roads were being pushed through from the east side of the Island to some of its other ports of call as well as Nootka Sound. The company's traffic was going down steadily and this showed in the condition of the *Tahsis Prince*. She had been built in 1920, and because the company didn't have the funds for refits, her condition was steadily worsening. We got along quite well with her crew, sometimes delivering their small orders to save them long trips to the ends of inlets for very little revenue. In return, when we had been delayed by late arriving trucks and buses, they would sometimes lie off the wharf at Gold River and delay their deliveries while we scurried about trying to get loaded and get out. Sometimes, if the *Tahsis Prince* was already at the wharf, we would lie alongside and their crew would swing a few lifts across from the wharf, rather than have us wait for them to finish discharging before we could go alongside to pick up our cargo.(In March 1968 the *Tahsis Prince* was run ashore after hitting a rock near Estevan Point; she was salvaged by Bobby Wingen of Tofino and cut down to become a pontoon for logging operations.)

On one occasion George was talking to the Northland Navigation public relations man who had come out to see what was wrong with morale, why there were so many freight claims and why there were so many other problems. He intimated that maybe they should just give up the whole West Coast run. And that is what eventually happened, but not until 1976 because by then all the old patterns of transportation by water were gone, replaced by land routes to a coast that was also much less densely populated than it had been.

The summer of 1961 was Nootka Sound Service Ltd.'s lowest point.

The debt was mounting with no way to stop it. All the logging camps were shut down for fire season. Traffic for the *Uchuck II* was low and there just was not enough revenue to keep going. However, Esson felt strongly that if they could hold on a little longer the situation would improve, so Esson decided to put my brother and me, who were both working there full-time, on his own pay cheque for a while, and he asked George if Robert, his son, could go on his, an action that would reduce the monthly payroll from $3,300 to $2,200. Hopefully this cutback would help to get the company through until better times. I was in my early twenties by this time and had accepted that this kind of thing was the normal way of life and normal business practice. I couldn't believe that there would ever be money for anything the vessels needed or things we wanted and that we would always have to make do with what was at hand. I remember knotting rotten manila tarpaulin lashing lines that had parted in order to get a little more service from them. Even now there are vestiges of this bent in my thinking.

The root cause of the company's financial problem was simply that Esson and George could not put the freight rate up to the level it needed to be. Traffic had increased to the point where they could not do much more without employing more people, and they couldn't employ more people without increasing costs. Customers would come looking for special freight rates but we just could not give them what they wanted. Esson told one of them that after seventeen years in the business he had just $38 in the bank. But until the rates could be raised, this situation could not change much. If they had been younger businessmen, they probably would have seen what the rate had to be and simply applied it. No one else would do the work they were doing for this little compensation, but Esson and George came from a time when even the prices they were charging seemed exorbitant.

Some of the politicians they talked to recognized the company's need for a subsidy if it was to continue providing regular service to even the smallest places, but there was the question of whether it was a federal or provincial responsibility. At this time the federal government was trying to get out of the direct subsidy business, but an agreement between governments was not yet in place, so Nootka Sound Service would just have to wait. In any event, where government is involved these matters move slowly.

That summer Esson and George made extra little runs to pick up revenue, taking the Evergreen Club of Tahsis out for a moonlight cruise after a regular run or taking children out to Esperanza's summer camp at Ferrer Point. At the same time they still tried to do little things for people beyond normal expectations, such as on one occasion taking a cocker spaniel named Sandy back to his home at the Nootka Light Station. He was set down on the float below the station and the whistle blown to alert the keeper that his dog was there.

One of the good things that happened during that summer of 1961 was a visit by a team from *Beautiful BC* magazine who wanted to film the area. Two people from the Department of Recreation and Conservation came along as part of the project as well, and this group plus a few people from Zeballos travelled with the vessel for two full days of scheduled runs with some extra side trips added to let them see the whole area. There was a holiday atmosphere over the whole two days of shooting, and as the group stayed at the Pioneer Hotel in Zeballos, there was a cheerful gathering in the pub there (actually a beer parlour in those days) in the evenings. The team's finished project helped to spread the word that there was something for tourists to see in Nootka Sound, but the best part of this adventure was the nine-page spread in the Fall 1961 edition of *Beautiful BC* magazine entitled *"Uchuck II."* It was very shortly after the *Uchuck III* was tied up that summer that I became ill with a nasty virus that put me in hospital for three weeks and then in recovery at my parents' home for another month. As my earnings would now not be enough to let me return to university that fall, I stayed on with the company throughout the winter of 1961–62, only taking time off in the spring to attend navigation school at the Vancouver Vocational Institute to get my mate's ticket. All the years of part-time work—a week here, a summer there—had added up to the thirty-six months I needed to qualify to write the exams. The studying was the easy part of getting my ticket as I had just finished four years of it.

By October 1961 there was still no subsidy contract, and Standard Oil began threatening to cut off the company's credit for fuel. And then George became ill with pneumonia and was ashore for more than six weeks. Esson stayed on board for all that time except for four days when he was relieved by Dick McMinn in order to attend my grandmother's funeral. To try to keep Esson abreast of company business during that six weeks, the book-keeper, Audrey Peterson, came to Gold River on the noon bus on two occasions to deal with urgent company business and to bring letters for signing as well as other correspondence that was accumulating. She went out again on the late afternoon bus.

Then finally toward the end of that year, things began to look up. Commonwealth Construction started work on the International Iron company's new mine at Zeballos. At the same time more logging compan-ies signalled their intention of moving in, and the tourist business began improving, helped along by the article in *Beautiful BC* magazine. Even so, it was still too soon to use the larger vessel in Nootka Sound, and it was decided that the *Uchuck III* should remain tied up in Port Alberni for the rest of the winter.

However, the *Uchuck II*'s cargo gear was taxed to the maximum and more whenever it was necessary to load heavy cat tracks and large reels of wire rope on board. On one occasion we struggled to load a 3,650-pound reel of wire that was destined for Green's Logging in Tahsis Inlet. It had been delivered to Gold River on a flatbed truck, and we had to put a wire sling around the body of the reel in order to be able to grab it with our cargo hook and swing it from the truck bed into our cargo hatch. The physics of the situation is that the weight would be instantly shifted to the derrick head as soon as the reel was lifted clear of the truck bed, so when we started to lift, the hook had to be off the dock by the height of the truck deck plus the height of the reel plus the distance to the choked sling eye—that is, more than ten feet. The only thing that made it possible was the fact that we were loading at high tide. Later at Green's camp and in the dark, we tied the *Uchuck* directly under the rigging of their log dump machine. A man from the camp came on board wearing white gloves and stood in the beam of a searchlight to direct the dump machine operator by using hand signals to have the rigging lowered out of the black night into the No. 2's hold. When the gear appeared, we hooked up the reel of wire, and a moment later it vanished up into the black.

The first ore ship came into Zeballos in April 1962. These are large vessels of seven hundred feet or more in length. The ore was brought to the beach in Arrow Transfer hopper trucks and trailers and dumped onto three cintrons, or shaking gratings, which dropped the ore onto a belt. The belt moved the ore to a large pile on the beach, and when a ship was in place, the ore was moved by another belt and dropped into the ship's holds, one by one, as the ship was moved along the berth. Each ship was gone again in about two days.

On March 7, 1962, our federal subsidy came through, Esson having worked for months with the sitting member of parliament for Comox–Alberni, Harry McQuillan, to achieve this end. In the lead-up to the subsidy, Esson had contacted all the customers who were affected to ask them to send letters of support to the government. (As it came up for renewal every five years, Esson asked them all to do this for subsequent applications, too. I remember after one of these blitzes, the government official that Esson dealt with calling to say, "All right, Esson, call off your dogs! It's coming!")

The next good news was the announcement that the company had received a contract to carry the mail, beginning on July 2, 1962, to all the villages and some of the camps in Nootka Sound, including Tahsis, Zeballos, Esperanza and the Mooyah Bay logging camp. Esson and George now felt that they could switch vessels, counting on traffic to be greater in summer, and then switch them back again in the fall. The *Uchuck III* with her five-ton lift and her greater car-carrying capacity would be an asset in the busier season. On the change-over day in May, we shifted from one vessel to the other in Zeballos, transferring cargo gear, all the paperwork pertaining to cargo and even some food. The totem pole that had been the parting gift from the Chamber of Commerce in Ucluelet when the company left there was unbolted from its stand in the smaller vessel and moved to its proper place in the No. 3.

The *Uchuck II* then went out on charter to Young Life of Canada to carry young people from Vancouver to a summer camp at Malibu at the mouth of Princess Louisa Inlet in Jervis Inlet. But this $900 per month charter came to an abrupt end in August when the one-ton flywheel came loose from the engine. The vessel was taken to Burrard Iron Works for repair, but by the time she was ready to return to work three weeks later, the season was over and the vessel was no longer needed. In October she went back to work in Nootka Sound for the winter, replacing the *Uchuck III*.

Continuing Problems

The journals from this time are filled with discussions of the company's ongoing problems and concerns, some small but persistent. At one time, a bag of laundry went missing. It had come from Taylorway Logging and was going to the laundry at Tahsis but had not come back. For several weeks hints of what might have happened to it came in, but all proved unfounded. This was all duly noted in the journal and the topic went back and forth between Esson and George week after week, until finally they just ran out of ideas and told Taylorway to order new stuff and bill the company. But even small bills like this were unwelcome, and the discouraging truth of the missing laundry case came out later when Esson discovered that it had been theft, but he never let on to anyone who had done it.

Meanwhile, the company's vessels really had no home. There was no wharf that they could use exclusively, so all supplies, tools and spares were carried on board. In the *Uchuck III*, the hold was much bigger than we needed for the current volume of cargo, so our extra stuff was stored in an untidy jumble on both wing shelves in the fore and after holds. Our gasoline-driven, three-wheeled Mobilift forklift truck was of no use to us at this time so it was also simply parked in one corner of the after hold. Some of our other equipment was stored on top of the small interior office in the government shed at Zeballos. One item parked there was the crow's nest from the foremast of the *Uchuck III*, which we couldn't use for lack of crew. On the Port Alberni runs it had been used by a lookout at night to watch for floating logs in the beam of the bow light, an act of desperation to try to keep from crippling the vessel with hits to floating logs. During her first winter of operation there, she had to be hauled out nine times to change propellers. But in Nootka Sound the crew had been reduced to four men so there was no one left to ride around in the crow's nest.

There are many references in the journals to where sunken logs and deadheads were located, often with sketches to illustrate. In places like Princesa Pass that leads from Kendrick Arm to Tahsis Inlet, it was not uncommon for the crew to find a deadhead, its lower end hung up in the shallow water. Many times we put a line on one of these to pull it out so at least it wasn't right in our line of passage as we really did not want to get jill-poked some dark night. The hope was that it would hang up somewhere out of the way. Some logs and deadheads just got more waterlogged

A crew change, about 1964, on the old Gold River company wharf. Note the bus next to us that served as our transport. From left: Tony Young, George Smith, Barney Ririe, Robert Verchere, Harold Bridgen, Crystal Schoppel, George McCandless, Esson Young and myself.

with time and eventually sank to the bottom and out of the way. Hitting one of them could result in a bent propeller or shaft, which would mean a slower speed and much vibration until time and tides were right to haul out or beach the vessel. The No. 3 was more at risk because her twin screws were outboard of the centreline, so were vulnerable to logs sliding down the sides of the vessel. She also had bilge keels that actually funnelled the wood right into the propellers. In a later refit we removed the bilge keels to prevent this; by doing so, the rolling of the vessel in a seaway increased, but this was considered the lesser of the two evils.

The situation regarding floating logs finally improved when the value of lost logs increased, causing operators to find better ways of transporting them. The introduction of dryland sorting and scaling of logs made it possible to set up a system of bundling before they went into the water. A boom of bundles being towed is less likely to lose whole bundles in transit in lumpy water than a flat boom is to lose single logs.

Last Gasp of a Run

At one point in the mid-1960s Esson was skipper on the crew I served on; my brother, Tony, was oiler/deckhand and I was mate. This was still in the leaner times, and as we came toward the end of these runs to Zeballos, it was usually 01:00 hours at least and we were all weary. We needed to come up with the one more burst of energy to finish off the day. We had passed Burrah Island, fifteen minutes out from Zeballos, and were on the home stretch. All three of us had gathered in the wheelhouse to wait for the right moment.

When that moment came, Esson would reach behind the radio phone and withdraw a bottle of VO whiskey, take off the cap, take a pull from the neck and then pass it around. That stuff bites, and everyone would go, "Ahhhh," after his turn. We would talk some more, the jug would go round one more time, then with the cap back on, it was returned to its home behind the radio.

By this time we were minutes away from the wharf in Zeballos. Tony and I would suit up into our heavy-weather gear, riding on a wave of new energy. Timing was now crucial. We would have this new impetus for only a short time, and in that time we would unload the remainder of the cargo and secure the vessel for the night. We just had time for a quick snack before collapsing into our bunks. Day done.

Two trips later, that jug would be empty and we sent it over the side to join its predecessors, always at about the same place. We began to think that at some time the next empty would land on top of the last one, but I guess not as it was about a thousand feet deep at that location.

After a week on board, it was crew change or "going home" day. Everyone hurried around, getting the vessel cleaned and ready to hand over to the incoming crew. There were lots of smiles and the euphoric feeling of reaching what in the old days was called "the channels," when ships that had been away from England for a year or more were finally in the English Channel and almost home. We had not been gone that long, though often it felt like it. Then there was the bus waiting on the wharf and a fresh-faced new crew wandering around, critically watching the vessel's approach to make sure that we did everything right.

The new crew came on board, was filled in on the week's happenings and given news of what to expect in the days ahead. They had lunch and picked up where we left off. We climbed on the bus and were all asleep a mile or two up the road.

CHAPTER SEVEN

The Beginning of the Turnaround

Joining the Family Firm

One evening in early October 1962 I found myself sitting in the UBC law library, looking out the window at English Bay. The sun, about to set in the Strait of Georgia, was bathing Point Atkinson in golden light. I was a brand new student in a subject that seemed eminently civilized, sensible and fair, but sitting there on such an evening I wondered if I belonged. I remembered what the downtown lawyer had told the group of us newbies on the first day. "Look at the man on your right," he had said. "Now look at the man on your left. Next year one of you won't be here." I realized that I had come to law school in part because I thought this was what others expected of me—I should become something more than just a simple sailor. I had thought that I might find my niche in some law firm that handled marine cases because at that time there were only two men in Vancouver who specialized in that field. It would be a good job, and I would need that because I would be getting married soon to Nancy, who had almost finished her nurse's training at St. Paul's Hospital. I was sure my future wife would prefer a lawyer husband to a sailor who wandered off to sea all the time.

By mid-November the courses had become a blur. I didn't seem to be able to sift through a whole bunch of cases and pick out the relevant bits quickly, and I didn't know who to go to for help. One day at the end of classes I picked up my briefcase and walked out the front door of the Law

Here I am off to HMCS *Quadra*, a sea cadet camp in Comox. It was July 1952, the year that the camp opened. Previously the *Quadra* was a Royal Navy establishment and then a Royal Canadain Navy training facility during WWII. For a short period, Esson Young was executive officer there in the early part of the war.

Building, and when I turned the corner between the buildings, I suddenly realized that I would not be going back. A great weight lifted. This was the right thing to do.

A few days later I walked the waterfront looking at fish packing companies and towing companies to see if there were any mate's berths open, but it was the end of November and not much was happening. Next I went to the shipping agents to see what might be possible there. At Kingsley Navigation, agents for a number of shipping lines, a nice man told me there was a bulk carrier heading for the Orient that might need a seaman—but no, they were a pretty rough bunch—however, he said, there was a Swedish ship docked in Powell River that needed an able seaman. He phoned the ship, spoke to the master, had me speak to him and soon I was back on the sidewalk with a bus ticket to Powell River in my hand. I left my old Vauxhall with all my stuff in it parked outside my wife-to-be's apartment and hoped that no one would notice that one of the back doors couldn't be locked.

In Powell River I walked down through the pulp mill and along the wharf to the MV *David Salman*, a brand new ship just out of a Finnish shipyard. She was 420 feet long with eight sets of union purchase cargo gear, exactly the same sort of gear I was used to—only there were many more of them and they were much bigger. I discovered that out of a crew of forty-two, only two of us were Canadians, but it turned out that the other Canadian was an old friend of mine.

I sailed in the *David Salman* for six months, making twelve trips to California, but I took two weeks off in March so that Nancy and I could be married. We found an apartment in Powell River, but this was not too satisfactory as the ship was only there for three or four days every two weeks, and during those days I sometimes had to work day shift. In May 1963 I was offered the third mate's berth but decided to come ashore instead. When no work was available in Powell River, my wife and I headed back to Port Alberni. Soon I was back aboard the *Uchuck*, and Nancy and I found a place to live in Courtenay. The distance to Gold River was not too great and the week on/week off rotation was not so onerous that family continuity was strained too badly, but Nancy had to become self-sufficient for the weeks that I was away. We settled in and made the system work for the next thirty years.

Still Struggling

Each year on or about March 18, Esson would write in the journal, "Here we are, another year later in Nootka Sound, and still we survive." He kept careful track of expenses and discovered that, when the *Uchuck III* was running, there was a general loss of $100 per trip at any time other than in the full summer season, and this was a significant sum in the 1960s. However, when the *Uchuck II* came back in the fall, there was a general break-even situation or a little better. As a result, the partners were becoming confident enough of a future for their company in Nootka Sound that on February 5, 1965, they officially changed the name to Nootka Sound Service Ltd.

However, the hard times had resulted in inefficiencies being perpetuated. We could not afford to buy new line when we needed it to make more cargo slings for the *Uchuck II*. At the same time the lifeboat lifting lines were in need of replacing, so we borrowed the lifting lines from the No. 3, which was tied up in Port Alberni at the time, rigged them on the No. 2, and then took the No. 2's old lines, cut out the bad parts and used the rest for the slings. Around the same time, two of the three self-righting lights on the life rings were in need of replacement. We bought one, but at $27 we could not afford the second one, so we used salvaged parts and made do for a while with that. All this took time and in the end only delayed buying the necessary equipment anyway.

The spread-out nature of the area's settlements and camps meant that we often went long distances with very little to deliver. Whenever possible, we tried to arrange to have everything destined for a particular port delivered to us for shipment on a set day of the week. But often we couldn't make this happen so we were forced to go several times to each place with small amounts of cargo. For example, Friendly Cove was at an outside part of our runs with not much business generated at any time other than in summer, but in one week alone we found that we had to go there eleven times. This is an extreme case, but such things did happen. By avoiding these situations, we could lower the cost and speed up the runs, which was better for the passengers as they could get to their destinations a little sooner. When we knew that goods were being moved just to build up a depleted inventory, we could schedule their delivery a bit more conveniently for ourselves, but there was never any question of not making the deliveries if the customer had a large enough volume of cargo moving or had an urgent need of a small item.

One of our inefficient practices that probably could have been fixed early on was the way we purchased our ship's supplies. From the beginning we had always bought them at straight retail prices, usually through Alberni Engineering. It is likely that we had no choice in the early years, but one day I was approached in Courtenay by Ted Ellison, a traveller for Western Marine Supply, and learned over a cup of coffee that at some point the rules had changed and we could have been buying wholesale and paying 40 percent less. The result of that cup of coffee was that we set up an account with Western Marine to purchase ship supplies at a 40 percent discount, something that would have been a great boon in the company's early days in Nootka Sound.

Business Improves

International Iron's mine at Zeballos had closed less than a year after they began shipping ore when it was found that the open pit method was not going to work, but in August 1963 Falconbridge bought them out and opened an underground mine. That ore body was exhausted six years later but in the meantime the mine had provided a good source of income for Nootka Sound Service. And the positive legacy from that period was that many new navigational aids had been established to help guide the big ships into Esperanza Inlet from the ocean, something our company appreciated when we started regular service to Kyuquot Sound in 1982.

About the same time that Falconbridge moved in, Fleetwood Logging set up Northern Hemlock as a larger-than-average-sized logging camp just around the corner from the mine on the Little Zeballos River. Fleetwood was one of a number of outside forest companies that came to the area around this time, putting an end to the lock that the Tahsis Company had on the region, although Tahsis remained the dominant company. Stoltze Logging moved from the head of Espinosa Arm, where it had been served by Northland Navigation, to Kendrick Arm on Nootka Island and began importing some of its supplies through Gold River. In time this company became one of our biggest accounts, and it remained so through two more owners and name changes right to the present day.

Eldred River Logging took over from Taylorway Logging at Mooyah

Bay, a place that we had served from the beginning of our Nootka Sound days. The timber there had always been held by BC Forest Products, which had been the only other timber holder in the Sound when we arrived. Art Mangles' Newcon Logging had begun operating in Plumper Harbour in January 1962, and it remained there for many years. This company had satellite camps elsewhere, including on the west side of Nootka Island at Beno Creek, where the logs had to be put into the ocean and towed around the corner past the Nootka Light and into the Sound. They also worked at the head of Tlupana Inlet on some of the road right-of-way for the Tahsis to Gold River road. Russel and Lilly Logging worked on Nootka Island from a base at Blowhole Bay and at another site at West Tahsis. Beban Logging of Nanaimo moved into two sites at Port Eliza, becoming the largest contractor of all that we dealt with in the Sound; they had an account with us for over thirty years. Hayes and King Logging from Duncan came to Houston River and other sites and became another very important contractor to use our services. These last five companies were all Tahsis Company contractors, but there were many other smaller companies contracting to Tahsis and other major forest companies scattered all through the sounds, some for a short time, some more or less permanently. Some camps stayed in one place for so many years that they developed a huge network of roads.

When we had first arrived in the Sound, almost all the logging camps except the Tahsis Company's Gold River operation had been A-frame operations on log floats. With the beginning of cat-and-arch logging and skidder operations, the camps stayed in one place for a little longer as the machines worked on simple roads radiating for a short distance from their starting point. The buildings were usually still on floats but some had been pulled ashore and set up there. That was possible because they had been built on skids so they could be dragged off the floats, with the object of being dragged away again when the work was finished.

When truck logging became the main method of extraction in this area, the road systems reached back for many miles into the tree farm licence (TFL), which allowed the camps to stay in one place for years. The living quarters, cookhouses, offices, machine shops and powerhouse were arranged together on a piece of flat ground so that in time the camp took on a permanent look. The camps at Port Eliza

A-frame logging in Kyuquot Sound. The A-frame is on floats so that it can follow the work around and pull the logs into the water.

and Kendrick Arm were there for thirty years and more, and even had schools that were part of School District 84. In this area, a camp could grow to have a hundred or more people employed, depending on the size of the TFL to be worked.

The contractors who came in during the 1960s set up semi-permanent camps that were, in fact, small villages with schools and amenities for all. Even the smaller camps had a house/dining hall, a timekeeper's office/camp office, bunkhouses, a mechanics shop/tire shop and a shack for the generator. The single men lived in bunkhouses while a number of families lived on-site in small houses on skids or later in manufactured trailers. In time there were companies that built trailers of all kinds especially for these camps—bunkhouses, cookhouses, offices, first aid stations, recreation halls. The families living there generated significant traffic for us in groceries and supplies and provided a fairly regular list of passengers, travelling for all the same reasons that people in town travel.

All of these camps had to be located in protected bays where the logs could be dumped and sorted into booms. There also had to be a float system for docking planes, small boats and freight carriers such as the *Uchuck*. As we were already in the area as a means of freight transport when most of the 1960s camps were established in Nootka Sound, they built their floats with ramps wide enough for a truck so that we could lift cargo directly onto them for delivery to the camp.

Although our traffic increased with the arrival of each of these logging companies, we were still trying to meet Northland Navigation's freight rates. Unfortunately, our rate was added on to the freight rates of one or even two trucking companies that we interlined with to move the cargo from the same Lower Mainland suppliers that provided Northland with cargo. We began to win the rates war when some of our cargoes originated on Vancouver Island and when some suppliers—the tire companies, steel and welding gas suppliers, the brewers agent and grocery wholesalers—started bringing goods out to Gold River in their own trucks for us to deliver to the logging camps. Then in 1964 the Federated Co-op decided to bring its supplies over the road as far as Gold River for us to take to its store in Tahsis rather than using Northland Navigation for the entire trip. This had become possible for them because the Co-op had other stores on Vancouver Island by this time, so it meant sending one full trailer from Vancouver to service them all. This created significant business and was very welcome as it represented a steady volume of cargo for us on a twice-weekly basis.

But occasionally we got too much business. This happened when there was a strike somewhere in the transportation sector, creating huge problems down the line for companies such as ours that supplied the outlying places. Prior to the road between Gold River and Tahsis opening, there was a strike that shut down Northland Navigation, which meant that all the tonnage that usually came by sea for Nootka Sound had to come by land to Gold River for us to distribute. Suddenly we had more than we could easily cope with. We arrived in Gold River from Zeballos at noon to find as many as three forty-foot-long Canadian Pacific trailers—minus their tractors and drivers—parked side by side on the wharf, each full to the doors with general cargo. Our crew of four, with sometimes a couple of extra kids from town, had to unload, sort and check these mixed loads against thick stacks of waybills. We might be loading for the rest of the day and well into the night before sailing, or we might take time off to sleep for a couple or three hours and then finish off loading before sailing the next morning. On more than one occasion we arrived in Zeballos in time, or even late, for the next day's 06:30 sailing. On one such day two people came down to the wharf at 06:30 to go with us, but when we were not there, they assumed we had sailed early. In fact, we had not yet arrived. Two or three trips like that put the crew on its hands and knees, and then the new crew came in for its shift to do the same. That strike lasted for six weeks.

As many of our deliveries were made in the evening or even at night, we did a lot of running in the dark and got into trouble on a couple of occasions in thick weather. One of these occurred at Funter Island on January 14, 1964. It was an evil night for travelling—some wind, thick cloud, heavy rain and no moon. We were entering Kendrick Arm from Nootka Sound and were preparing to go into Plumper Harbour, steering between the two islands that lie in front of it. We had to make a ninety-degree turn to port to enter this passage and needed to be in just the right position to do it. The radar showed the layout of the landforms around us, but as is normal, when we got very close to the land, the image on the radar screen was lost in the ground wave and clutter, so we had to be steadied up on the right compass course to make the passage. The vessel had a bow light mounted on the stem that would show up the trees on the outside island of the two as the vessel swung in her turn, but on this occasion the weather was so thick that the trees did not show up as expected. We were still swinging around to port when I noticed that the compass course had come to 200 degrees, past the 245 or so that it ought to be. I shouted to the skipper who immediately rang the telegraph to Full Astern, but it was too late and we slid up onto a rock. Fortunately, we had been down to a very slow speed and the surface of the rock was rounded, but I knew there could well be damage anyway.

In the next eight minutes my brother and I uncovered the port lifeboat, lifted it out of its chocks and lowered it to main deck level, while the cook helped the twelve passengers into life jackets. The skipper blew the whistle to alert the people in the logging camp in Plumper Harbour to the fact that we had a problem. On board there was no panic as passengers were readied to disembark.

We had a little time now to have a good look around and found that there was no apparent damage or ingress of water. And the tide was rising so it seemed that we would float off quite soon. A couple of small boats had appeared and they helped to push the bow around once we did float off so we could head into the passage. The situation suddenly looked much brighter as we carried on into the camp. After a better look at the bow, we decided that, even though there was no visible damage, we would have a diver go down in the morning to make sure. It remained then for us to haul the lifeboat up and set it into its chocks again and reassure the passengers that we were back in business.

Throughout this period the two vessels worked alternately; the larger one for the heavier traffic in summer and the smaller for winter traffic. But when a vessel is laid up for half a year, the start-up always presents problems that have to be worked through. Dampness and salt are especially hard on electrical equipment, and wooden vessels have to be kept warm and dry or rot sets in, and we certainly had our share of both those problems. Each vessel had its own redeeming features when brought back onto the run. The No. 3 was more like a ship with its bigger cargo gear, more capacity and broader shoulders, while the No. 2 was warm in winter, had good visibility from the wheelhouse—allowing us to see and avoid floating logs better—and was cheaper to operate. As a result, at the end of the summer or winter seasons, we always looked forward to the coming of the other vessel and its advantages.

When we went into Zeballos, we tied up on the end of the wharf, facing inland where it was shallow enough to ground the forward end of the vessel at low tide. On some days we had to move partway out after unloading at night to make sure we wouldn't be hung up on the mud in the morning at sailing time. We were happy when the Department of Public Works, which was responsible for all the floats and wharves on the coast that had red railings, gave us the job of cleaning out the berth. We turned the *Uchuck II*, with her single screw, around 180 degrees in her berth at almost low tide, set her mooring lines up hard and powered ahead to dredge out the mud from the berth with the propeller wash. Mud and stones and even an old skull came rolling out, but at the end of an hour we had a better place for the vessel to lie.

Wooden wharves wear out with use as vessels rub or thump into them during landings and general working. Grass and moss begin to grow on them as they age and rot, so after a while they are more likely to break when they are hit. Often the damage is small—just a piling here, a plank there—but they add up, so when we saw this beginning to happen to one of the wharves where we regularly tied up, we would call Public Works in Vancouver. The man in charge there was Lou Langston, and we saw him about once a year as he made the rounds to see the condition of his empire. He knew who in each area was capable and had the equipment to do small repairs, such as replacing a fender log, a piling or decking, and he had a discretionary fund that he could use in order to have these repairs done without a lot of bidding and tendering. We could simply phone him in Vancouver and explain a small problem, and he would then ask us to locate the man that we all knew could do the work and ask him to call Lou. If it could be arranged, the local man would get the go-ahead and do the work right away. Serious deterioration begins to set in for wooden wharf structures on the wet West Coast in about eleven years, and then larger portions need to be replaced. Generally, jobs of this size would be too big for the local man, and the job had to go through channels and the time lag for repairs could be months.

Later Public Works got out of the wharf fixing business, turning it over to the Coast Guard, but when a small problem came up at the Gold River wharf, we were told to call it in as we always had. This time the response was different. A helicopter with four men—engineers and such—was dispatched from Victoria to come to Gold River. After looking the problem area over, they decided that nothing was to be done. In our estimation, the cost of those men's salaries and the helicopter time was more than was needed to do the repairs we had called about.

Looking ahead

Even with all the hardships, Esson and George never lost the desire to make a viable business and they were constantly exploring new ideas. Around this time, there were rumours of a possible road going into Zeballos from Woss Lake. This would allow access to Nootka Sound from the eastern side of Vancouver Island from a point much farther up the island than Campbell River. Esson felt that if it were to be a government road, rather than a private logging road, we would then be operating as a link between two government roads, and this would make the company part of the road system and thus more essential in the mind of the government. However, when that road was constructed, it was a private road.

In 1965 Esson wrote a note to George in the journal saying that he felt that they would need the *Uchuck IV* in a year and a half and that it should be a roll-on roll-off vessel. Not only could he see the need, but he also knew that others were thinking of doing the same thing and it would be necessary to get in first. But this meant that they would have to go back and redo some of the conversion work already done on the No. 4. The housework would have to be moved forward again from where it had been put at the beginning of that vessel's conversion, and there would be two hatches in the long, open after deck with a crane installed between them. This configuration would allow trucks and equipment to be rolled on from the stern. They would also change the vessel to single screw, which would still give enough speed and leave them with a spare engine. As always, a lack of money and poor prospects for raising any stopped these ideas from going any further. They could only soldier on and hope for the best.

However, one day it began to be evident that the company was no longer just trying to hang on but was actually moving ahead as there was now enough activity in the area to keep them going. What they needed to do was get the rates up and start repairing and replacing equipment before it collapsed. But it was almost too late for the two partners to enjoy this prosperity, mainly because of the brutal hours they had worked for too many years. On their off-weeks, they needed three or four days just to get back to normal again. By this time I held my master's certificate, but for me to take some of the load from them meant that someone else would have to be hired to take my place as mate, and that would not be possible for a while yet.

We younger men really liked the work but wished we were not so tired so much of the time. Even just running the vessel while bracing against the constant movement was tiring. But one of the saving graces of the whole enterprise was the continual change. No two days were alike. From the cargo to the passengers to the weather, we never knew what would come next so there was no time to get bored. However, I do seem to recall that in the winters of the mid-1960s we always seem to have been running in the dark, always late, always in a southeast gale and always in pouring rain. Our rain gear never dried.

Weather—The Bad and the Good

Today the weather report for the West Coast is broadcast on an endless tape and the forecast is updated every six hours, while local weather reports come from reporting stations every three hours. But back in the 1960s our weather report came just three times a day on the old AM radio telephone from the Coast Radio Stations, and you had better be available to listen if it was important for you to hear. We learned that if we heard of a low pressure system approaching from the southwest toward our coast, we should pay particular attention. If the local conditions at Estevan Point were reported to be, say, southeast forty to forty-five knots and there was a northeast outflow wind at Nootka Light, then the situation when we left Esperanza Inlet to go toward the ocean would likely be passable. If, on the other hand, we heard that at Nootka the wind was also southeast forty to forty-five knots, then we knew that we would have a battle trying to get out of Esperanza Inlet.

One evil night at weather time we were in Hanna Channel on the north side of Bligh Island and about to head out into Nootka Sound when I tuned in to listen to the broadcast because the conditions were already bad and we were not yet clear of the island. The forecast earlier in the day had been for gales (in those days it was not broken down into storm and hurricane force winds), and we really needed to know what the current thinking was. The broadcast came, starting with the forecast of gales followed by the local weathers from the reporting stations: at Estevan Point the reported wind velocity was eighty-five knots and gusting and for Nootka Sound eighty. I had never heard numbers that high before for Nootka Sound.

We rounded San Carlos Point on Bligh Island and began to come into the wind, and already there was a head sea greater than I had ever seen at that position. We came into the full force of the wind as we cleared the Villiverde Islands, halfway across the Sound, and the vessel lay over at a constant fifteen degrees with sheets and then slugs of water flying over us, accompanied by an ungodly roar. The plate glass windows of the wheelhouse facing the wind were visibly flexing, and our ears were pumping with the changing pressure. It was not possible to talk. The passengers sitting down below in the aft lounge were fortunate as the engine sounds partly masked those of the maelstrom outside. They could see nothing out in the black night.

The cabin sides of the *Uchuck II* were built right to the outside of the hull so that the bollards for mooring the vessel were on the deck inside the cabin, and there were eight-inch-long, oblong openings at deck level in the cabin side to pass the lines through. On this night, the wind was forcing gouts of water through these holes and clear across the width of the eighteen-foot-wide deck to drain out the scuppers on the other side, and the passengers were sitting in the booths with their feet up on the opposite seats to keep them out of the swirling water.

We always travelled at night with a bow light mounted on the stem-head to help us avoid wood in the water ahead. It was an ordinary sealed beam that worked quite well on most occasions, but on this night when we dove into the first of the big seas, it went out. Moments later when the vessel rose again, there it was, still shining but now pointed toward the clouds. It survived for the next twenty minutes, which is what we needed before we could turn up into Kendrick Arm and away from the wind on our way to a logging camp at the head of the arm, two miles in. The float landing there was in line with the wind, so we made the approach down-wind and got alongside safely, but we were forced to stay there for the next four hours until the wind had abated somewhat. To back out and turn around would not have been possible with that weight of wind behind us and the beach so close. While we waited, we watched a family of river otters playing and chirping in our lights, happy and unconcerned with the inclement weather.

After the wind had dropped to about forty-five to fifty knots, we were able to proceed, but on the way up Tahsis Inlet we passed multitudes of logs from broken booms, torn loose from all the boom tie-ups. Then from out of the black, there suddenly appeared a white-painted, two-storey building on a log float. Earlier that day this ghostly structure had been towed to Sandpoint from Tahsis, a distance of five miles, and by the next morning it had got itself back to Tahsis. There were a couple of the large deepsea tugs in the Sound sheltering from the weather, and we talked to them about the situation. One of them had recorded gusts of 120 knots, but it could have been higher as that was as high as their anemometer could display. We had suffered no damage but were left with something to talk about for some time.

When the wind was shrieking up or down the inlets, it became difficult to get into the landings at the camps and villages along the way. Sometimes we had to give one or more the go-by for the evening run and try again on the return trip of the next morning. Otherwise, we ran the risk of damaging the floats and structures that often were quite fragile. One night when there was a major wind coming up Tahsis Inlet as part of a southeast gale, we went into Blowhole Bay on Nootka Island halfway up Tahsis Inlet to deliver a ton of groceries for the logging camp cookhouse. We got to the float and were able to get a spring line onto it. We were parallel to it but were hanging straight out at the end of our line because the wind that comes up the inlet bounces off the south-facing hill behind the float, and it was blasting us straight off. If we were to use enough power to spring the vessel in, the float would probably break up, so we held onto the cargo and delivered it on the way back on the next day. That place is called Blowhole for good reason: at times a second set of winds can arrive from the west by finding their way through twelve miles of passes in the hills of Nootka Island to blast out over the bay. Two aircraft have been lost here when these unpredictably strong gusts occurred; each time people have been killed.

Living as we did, we saw close up the effects of violent weather. On one occasion we knew that a storm was at work on the ocean because even in Zeballos where we were tied up the wind was coming through the low gap at the end of the harbour, and that only happens when there is an unusually big storm outside. The gusts came marching up the harbour one after another to heel the ship over slightly in her berth on the end of the wharf. We were tied almost stern to the wind, which was a blessing as we just pulled against our lines instead of crashing against the wharf. The base wind strength was thirty-five to forty knots with much larger gusts. Then above the noise of the wind we heard the sound of an aircraft approaching, though we couldn't see it. When it finally came into view, we could see it was a Beaver flying at a low altitude and preparing to land on the water. This was the scheduled flight but it was arriving a little late. It flew overhead, banked, turned into the wind and landed safely a few hundred feet out in the harbour. It turned again and began taxiing in to the airplane float that was about a hundred feet away from our berth, but it would have to taxi up the harbour a little farther toward the slough in order to have room to make the turn to go alongside, head to wind, at the float. It was almost there when the pilot and those of us watching from the *Uchuck* saw a huge squall rolling up the harbour a half mile away. The water was roiling and smoking, leaping into the air twenty feet or more and looking just like a wide white waterfall. Then over the general uproar we heard the sound of the plane's engine revving up: the pilot, who had not yet got the plane alongside and tied down, had elected to try to take off again. The big radial Pratt and Whitney snarled and roared at full takeoff power. The plane began to make a little headway but was still near the float and on the water when that tangle of wind and water was upon us all. The aircraft, now at full power, simply rose straight up, the wind speed being equal to its takeoff speed, and because the wind was erratic and the aircraft had very little altitude, the inevitable happened. It looked to the four of us aboard the *Uchuck,* standing in a row and watching banjo-eyed out the side windows, as if the starboard pontoon tip caught the water, spinning the aircraft to starboard just beyond the float and then upending it so that the engine went under water and the tail stuck straight up. The whole mess then blew past between the ship and the float, breaking off the jack staff mounted on our stem head and finally coming to a stop on the mud beach just ahead of us.

We set off running up the wharf approach to where the plane had stopped, then had to run back to get a long aluminum ladder when we saw how the situation had developed. In the meantime the two pilots had scrambled out and were hanging onto the aircraft until we could get there with the ladder to get them up onto the wharf. They were uninjured but wet and cold and doused in aviation fuel.

That squall only lasted about five minutes over us before moving on into the village and blowing off metal chimneys and shingles. One porch was torn off and blown right over the roof to smash up on other side of the house. After that, the wind settled down to thirty-five to forty knots for the rest of the afternoon before dying away completely in the evening.

Later the two pilots came down to the ship to get our version of events. One of them was the company's chief pilot doing a routine pilot check-out, and he had been flying on the approach for his own practice. When he saw the situation developing, he swung the controls back to the regular man, thinking he was more used to this place, and perhaps there was a delay during this process. In any event, when we described to them the order of events as we had seen them, it differed with each of their recollections of what had happened, and the chief pilot said that if such a report had come across his desk, he wouldn't have believed it.

That evening when the tide was low and the wind had died, a crew came down and set the aircraft back onto its pontoons and prepared it for towing out to Tahsis the next morning. It was patched up in the company hangar there and later flown back to Vancouver for a full overhaul.

There were, however, quiet and pleasant times as well and we were not always in a rush. On a still, sunny morning we might stop to pick up or deliver something at a float camp and then maybe lie there for a little while and talk to whoever came out to meet us. One day we slid alongside Taylorway Logging's float at Mooyah Bay to pick up Jim Taylor, owner and boss logger. He was fishing off the end of his float, and as we approached, he shouted, "Hold the boat. I got a fish on!"

"No problem," we told him. "We can wait." We all knew you could catch spring salmon there at times.

The crew and dock workers taking a break on a hot summer day in 1959. From left: Pat MacQueen, Helge Urstad, Dave Young, Gunnar Sorensen, Esson Young, Jack Howitt, Sigurd Lea, John Monrufet and Dick McMinn. In front: Harvey McInnis and Robert McCandless.

George had wired the *Uchuck III* for sound and plugged his reel-to-reel tape recorder into the system. There were speakers inside and on deck, including on the front of the wheelhouse, and in good weather we belted out popular songs wherever we went. On one of our trips to Zeballos, our engineer, Dennis Bye, stayed over at the Esperanza Hospital for repairs to one hand after he had lost part of a finger in a V-belt that day. On the following fine summer morning we picked him up before going on to Tahsis, and he told us that, long before he saw us coming around the point, he heard the music playing. That's when we realized we were treating the whole Sound to this every day. It was also this music that woke us up in the morning on board as George was usually first up and his first act was to start the music.

Dennis Bye summed up our lives here with the statement that if there wasn't some fun in this work, it wasn't worth doing. And there was fun, sometimes helped along with a little alcohol. There were lots of laughs with crew, passengers and the regulars we met at all the stops. We might finish up a run and have five hours before we had to get up again so, hell, there was lots of time and we could have a nightcap. An hour later someone would say, "Hell, we still got four hours." It didn't seem to matter, everyone still got up in the morning. Sometimes there might even be passengers who stayed around to talk before going ashore at the end of a run. One night it was an English lady and her daughter who told us, over scotch, about life in a Japanese prison camp after the fall of Hong Kong.

There were parties on board and ashore and interesting people to meet. We in the crews were all healthy animals and needed to balance the hard work with hard play, which certainly happened. Once in awhile on a summer harbour day in Zeballos, we gathered up some townspeople and went out to Catala Island or the Nuchatlitz at the edge of the ocean for the day or perhaps out for an evening run in the moonlight, the tape system blaring music all the way. As we carried nearly everyone living on the sound who was going anywhere, we came to know many people. Some were commuters who travelled regularly, and sometimes I would go to the wheelhouse and find someone else steering with the skipper nowhere around, he having gone off to fix something or other.

For various reasons the skippers switched shifts from time to time, so the crews got to sail with each man. George's crew was known as the party crew and Esson's the more serious crew. George had always been interested in celestial navigation, so we had all the books and sextants on board, and we took sights whenever we had clear space with a horizon that allowed a sight to be taken. This was good practice for some of the younger men who would be going off to sit for certificates at the navigation school in Vancouver.

A passage in good weather left the crew with pleasant memories and a feeling of relaxation that could last a while, especially if it occurred at a time when it was not expected. If it happened in the early spring, we could begin to hope that perhaps the bad weather was coming to an end for this year and soon the softer days would be here.

On such days, when travelling between ports, members of the crew would find a place on deck in the sun and out of the wind to enter into a reverie for a bit, or they would come up into the wheelhouse for a time. If there was any talk, it would get away from the usual stuff about schedules and cargo and move to what we could see outside the ports. Sometimes we would just drink in the scenery. Some of these people had been part of the crew for ten years or more, travelling the same route, but the effect of that scenery on us all never seemed to go away, which is probably one reason why we continued to do this kind of work.

I recall a summer day when we were transiting from Esperanza Inlet to Kyuquot Sound and had just come out of the Rolling Roadstead behind Catala Island, through the rock pile and onto the ocean. We felt no movement in the ship at all, and the tennis ball on the logbook table stayed where I put it. As I looked inland from the sea, I could see rank upon rank of hills and mountains, growing fainter, partly with distance and partly from the ever-present salt mist that hangs in the air—the good weather haze. The air was scented with salt and with that living thing that is the ocean, almost to the extent of having a taste. The few passengers were sitting happily out on the boat deck. All of them were wearing hats, having been warned about the double effect of the sun when it is reflected off the flat sea. Now and then someone would point out a bird or a grey whale in the distance.

In warm weather while we were running at night and were away from the land, the feeling was magical. When there was no moon showing, the stars filled the sky as if there would not be room for any more. Even the regular constellations would be hard to distinguish among the crowd. With my head out the wheelhouse port, I listened to the rush of water as the vessel surged forward in the ocean swell, and I saw the sparkles in the water from the bio-luminescence, outlining the hull and leaving a brightly lit trail for a mile behind the ship. A trip like this stays in your memory and cancels out a whole lot of the other kind.

CHAPTER EIGHT

Changing Times

Refit Struggles

There still was no money available for major restorative work to the *Uchuck III*, and too much time, energy and money was expended dealing with old and worn-out equipment. Many of the problems were caused by the age of the engines. They had been taken, already well used, from another vessel when we did the original conversion from minesweeper to coaster in 1952–55. In Nootka Sound the vessel was in service nearly every day with little maintenance time available for more than a few hours at a time and the crew that ran the vessel also did the repair work. Cylinder heads, pistons, liners and clutches were those parts needing attention most often, but the parts available to replace them were also old and worn so they didn't last as long as they should. The bigger jobs had to be done in the night between runs and, because of the old parts, this had to be done more often. The time needed to change a clutch was still eight hours, even if done by a crew that had done lots of them.

In addition, so much trouble could have been averted if there had been money available to buy new propellers made of Superston 70, a new tough bronze that was available by that time. Constant damage to the vessel's soft brass propellers from hits by logs and other debris gave the vessel vibration and robbed speed and manoeuvrability but it also added premature wear to clutches and reduction gears. We sometimes had to wedge a broom handle between the bulkhead and the writing desk in the purser's office to steady it enough to write on. When it got too bad, the vessel would have to be hauled out to change propellers, and the nearest marine railway for haul-out was at Port Alberni, twelve hours away.

The alternative was to beach the vessel at Zeballos as we had done with the *Uchuck II*. As the job was governed by the tide cycle, it took a full twenty-four hours from start to finish, so we had to fit it in between runs in order to keep to our schedule. However, this came at a cost to the human element as no one got any rest, and when it was done, it was time to go back to regular work.

The government wharf in Zeballos had a long, narrow approach—a one-lane roadway just three pilings wide—over the tidal flat to the two-hundred-foot-wide wharf head, but the sand/mud flats there are firm and level enough that we could beach the vessel safely. To change the propellers—also known in this business as "wheels"—the vessel had to be taken during a high and rising tide around the end of the wharf head, turned, backed in then manoeuvred alongside the approach and held there with a very slight list inward so that, as the tide went out, she would lean gently against the approach. Too much lean and the pressure could push the approach over when the tide receded. Too much lean the other way and the approach could be pulled over in the opposite direction. There was always

Replacing the propellers was tough. Here, in about 1968, George Auld is heating the propeller hub to help the tensioned puller get the propeller loose from the shaft taper.

an anxious wait until the keel touched the bottom and we could see that our calculation was right, while knowing that there was nothing that we could do if it wasn't.

Once the vessel had grounded, we had to wait for the tide to go down another nine feet, which is the draught of that vessel, before we could go to work. In the meantime we lowered the spare props, heavy tools and the oxyacetylene set over the side. We had to do this before the auxiliary engine's sea suction was above the water level and the engine had to be shut down. Then as soon as the depth of the water was below gumboot level, we could begin. We had only about five hours of working time before the tide rose, so we needed to hustle. First, the boss nut had to be taken off and the wheel puller put on and tightened. By heating the propeller hub with a torch, we could expand it enough that the wheel puller, under strain, could pull the wheel off and leave it hanging on the shaft taper. A good thump from a heavy sledge hammer applied to the hub on the forward side would bring it off with a bang, so that the wheel would be hanging loosely on the taper, but it would take three of us to lift it off and set it on the sand. After some maintenance and preparatory work, we would lift the spare wheel onto the taper, and with the shaft key in place, pull it into position with the wheel nut. We would then bolt the nut to the propeller and thread a safety wire through the holes in the heads of the bolts. Everything was then checked before we moved to the other side and repeated the process.

The last thing we did was to put lifting lines on the old wheels in order to get them on board with the vessel's cargo gear before we moved the vessel out.

While we waited for the tide to rise, we rigged lines forward to the wharf head to help heave the vessel off with the windlass in case the tide didn't come back to the same height as it was twenty-four hours earlier. We preferred not to use the engines to assist because the flow of water would tend to dredge out holes in the sea bottom, leaving it uneven for the next beaching—for surely there would be one. But on one occasion in an act of desperation we found it necessary to use power. The tide had not come up to the expected level and the next day's tide was predicted to be lower yet, so we had to get the vessel off. Between pulling with lines to the wharf and propellers churning, we got off to the sound of boulders being drawn into the propellers and clanging off the blades. Once floating, we eased the vessel away and moved around the wharf head to go back to the berth. On the following morning at low tide we saw a huge hole dredged where the vessel had been. And on the day after one of these marathon propeller changes, we hit two major unseen deadheads and undid most of the work that we had just done.

During one of these episodes, we beached the *Uchuck III* on a lovely day in July, leaning her against the wharf approach at just the right angle so that we could swap the bent propellers for good ones after the tide went out. We finished the job around two o'clock in the afternoon. The sun smiled down. There was not a breath of wind. Small children splashed about in the shallow water a hundred yards away. Mothers in swimsuits and sunglasses sat in deck chairs under umbrellas, enjoying the kind of day that really is not all that common on the West Coast.

My job now that the work was done and the tide was rising was to run a headline from the fo'c'sle the 150 feet or so across the incoming water to the outside corner of the wharf head. This was the line that we would use if the water did not come all the way back on this tide. I scrambled over the side of the ship and down into our nine-foot skiff to do this little job. It required some strong pulling on the oars to carry the inch-and-a-quarter-diameter nylon mooring line over the water to the wharf, but when I reached it, the waiting deckhand grappled with his pike pole for the eye in the end of the line and, having caught it, pulled it up onto the wharf and dropped it onto the corner cleat. Good.

I rowed back alongside the ship and prepared to disembark from the skiff by swarming up the side of the vessel like an old-time pirate—without the sword gripped in my teeth—via a convenient line hanging there for just that purpose. But there were three lines hanging there, the one for me to climb, which was tied off to a ring bolt, and two others attached to the bent propellers lying on the sand, waiting to be lifted with the cargo gear later. The ends of these two were just lying loosely on deck, but from where I was, all three lines looked the same. Unknowingly, I selected one of the two attached to the propellers.

I stood up in the boat and reached up to get a good purchase on the line and began to climb. No one was watching, at least at the outset, but that soon changed. I was moving well as I started up the line, hand over hand, but then I began to lose ground while still making the same motions. The line was slipping, slowly at first, as there was enough friction where it passed over the rail, but as more line ran out it came faster and inexorably, although fairly gently, I was let down into the water. This was ocean water into which I was dunked, water that doesn't warm up in summer. The children playing near the beach were all very young, and children don't recognize cold water. They ignore it. But the water on the incoming tide was freezing and I couldn't breathe. I made the appropriate sounds, which got the attention of all on the beach. Everything stopped while they looked to see what all the fuss was about.

I am on my honour at this point, so now grabbing the correct line, I commenced swarming up the side again. This time I arrived on deck, but in order to regain status, I made a show of kicking off my boots and, having had no shirt on anyway, dove off the rail back into the water. Upon regaining the surface, I found that I still couldn't breathe, even while floating on my back, and I began to make the same whooping sounds as before. Defeated, I climbed back up my line and slunk off to hide until the crowd on the beach dispersed, all the while hoping that no one had recognized me. Fat chance.

The Sale of the *Uchuck II*

It was July 13, 1966, the end of a week in which I had been sailing as mate with George McCandless as skipper. We had just berthed the *Uchuck III* in Gold River on crew change day, and on the wharf below stood the relieving crew, but Esson was not with them.

"What's up?" I said.

George Smith, the relieving mate, said, "Sorry, Dave, you can't go home."

We all knew that Esson and George had been negotiating the sale of the *Uchuck II* to the provincial government, and it seems that during the past week the sale had been finalized. Esson had made plans to take her from her summer berth in Port Alberni to Vancouver where she was to be refitted and re-emerge as the *Sointula Queen*, which was to carry school children from Sointula and Alert Bay to a new school at Port McNeil. Apparently he had decided that George should go with him on the trip and I should take over on the *Uchuck III* as skipper. The weather was good and they had a fine time on this their first time sailing together since their early Barkley Sound days.

But this was a good day for me, too, as it was the first day of my next twenty-eight years as skipper. For the first time in all the years I had sailed on the *Uchucks* there would be no one to ask when I was unsure of what to do next.

Esson and his Cars

When the *Uchuck II* was sold in 1966, Esson and George split the $25,000 and each bought a car. George bought a sensible Oldsmobile Delta 88; Esson bought a Jaguar 2.4, the newest sedan model, black with red leather upholstery and walnut dash. He was on a cloud.

In his whole life he owned seven cars. I dimly recall the first one, a black 1928 Chrysler, which looked something like a covered wagon. The end of the war brought the beginning of Barkley Sound Transportation Ltd., and there was no money for a new car until 1951 when a brand new six-cylinder Vauxhall Velox arrived in our driveway. Starting with this car, Esson always had the complete set of manuals and did all the servicing required; it was about as close to a hobby as he ever got. After the '51 came the '53 Vauxhall with different styling and a little more power. Then came that black Jaguar 2.4 in 1966, but when it turned out to be a lemon, he traded it in for a 3.4. This new car was grey, but because he didn't want people to think he was so wealthy he could trade his cars every other year, he had it painted black.

As Esson was a rather skilled driver, he tended to push it a bit. He was particularly fond of the Coombs Stretch of the Island Highway, a mile and a half of road where you could really let a car out—and Esson did. One day my mother was in the car on this stretch. It was nearly up to full speed when an old car eased out from a side road. It was driven by an old fellow with his fedora set squarely down onto his ears. Esson flashed by at 110 mph. He let out a burst of maniacal giggling, but my mother was not amused. Forever after, when she was aboard, that car was driven in a more stately fashion.

Once, after my parents had attended the premier of a film about Nootka Sound at Government House in Victoria—a somewhat gala event—the car refused to start when they were ready to go home. It seems that its 2,000-mile servicing time had come and gone unnoticed. It wasn't very dark, so it was hood up, tools out and jacket off, and Esson worked at it until the car was satisfied that enough attention had been paid to it.

Years later, when a rebuild became necessary, a friend who was also a Jag buff agreed to take the job on and so, for the princely sum of $500 plus parts, the job was done in Duncan. When that car was nine years old, it came time to trade up to a Jaguar 3.8S. This car was slightly different with a longer back deck, but it was still a very handsome car—and still black, red and walnut. Esson was also getting along on the road of life and now fit into his car even better. Wearing his uniform of white shirt and black tie, black leather jacket and his now silver hair, he became a recognizable sight on the road.

Everyone—including the RCMP—knew about Esson's heavy foot on the gas pedal, and he was stopped by the police one time too many and told to walk for the next three months. This presented a good opportunity to do some much needed work on the car. The job was not yet completed when his driving prohibition came to an end, and he suggested that he should probably write to the Superintendent of Motor Vehicles to ask for an extension in order to have time to finish up the job.

When the Jaguar 3.8S got old and needed replacement, Dave Wisk, who was still driving an old 240D Mercedes, convinced Esson that he should buy one, too, and Esson found a new Mercedes 300D at Three Point Motors in Victoria. It was a fine car with a five-cylinder diesel engine, but Esson was essentially a Jag man. After the stroke in 1976 that ended his seagoing career, he used that Mercedes as a truck while he built a fence for his neighbour.

New Arrangement

For a short period after the sale of the *Uchuck II*, we three skippers shared the work equally, each working one week on and two weeks off. That soon changed so that I worked week-on and week-off and Esson and George worked one week on and three off. This meant that the two older men had some time to recover and I was fully employed.

However, the *Uchuck III*, now the company's only vessel, had to run constantly from this time forward, with only a short one- or two-week refit and inspection period in the spring of each year. Time for maintenance became an even greater problem as there was no relief vessel. Sometimes when an engine needed one of its eight cylinder heads changed, the job would have to be done while the vessel was working. This meant running on one engine for a day while the work went on. We could, at best, get nine knots instead of the usual twelve, and we lost time manoeuvring for landings, of which there were as many as seventeen in a single day. At one time there was a major problem with the port engine, which left me with just one engine for a week, but it was all good practice.

We also got a couple of new employees at this time, who really made a difference in the running of the *Uchuck III*. Dennis Bye came to us as engineer in June 1965. He was more than a little gifted in his field with a mind that seemed to work differently to that of other folks. He was also an Australian so brought some of those characteristics with him. When I first became skipper in 1966, he was my engineer and it was a good thing that I am able to adjust easily to a variety of characters.

When Dennis got into the ongoing problems with our machinery, he saw that we hadn't enough pitch in the propellers, and as a result, the engines were running at a higher speed than they needed to. The props were still pitched for the vessel's wartime displacement, which was greater than our present displacement. In her original configuration, there had been a need for a lot of ballast aft in the tiller flat to keep her trimmed properly, but after we moved the housework back during the conversion, the trim of the vessel had been changed and the stern floated too low. As a result, the ballast was no longer required. One day in Zeballos, Dennis and I pulled out from the dock and chucked five tons of ballast overboard; it was made up of dozens of pieces of pig iron. After that, we added four more inches of pitch to the propellers, and the result of those two moves was that we could drive the vessel more efficiently at lower RPMs.

However, there was a legacy from this event at a much later date. During an annual inspection the inspector wanted to sight the permanent ballast, and I had to tell him that we had chucked it overboard many years earlier. Unfortunately, the inspector's request came on the day before we were to leave Victoria to return to Nootka Sound, and it meant that the vessel would have to be put through the inclining experiment again to see if there had been a change in its stability. There is a considerable set-up for this that involves putting some heavy movable weights on board and setting up a plumb bob to measure the change in angle of the vessel as the weights are moved a specific distance across the vessel. This process takes time. The alternative was to put back those five tons of ballast, which was the only thing that we could do in those circumstances, but I was able to have it put in the centre of the vessel where it acted like five tons of cargo—and this was acceptable to the inspector.

Another new employee was Dave Wisk, who joined the company in June 1966 as a replacement engineer. He had worked on the railroad and had been a Finning serviceman working out of Campbell River, so he fit my idea of a good engineer for us—a heavy-duty mechanic who liked boats. As he was a steel man, he was not sure that he wanted to work on a boat made of wood, but he brought all his previous experiences to this job. We had no material and no fancy tools for him to work with but he was a great scrounger and had a way of making something out of nothing. He found a six-volt starter for our 1946 model Towmotor on a wrecked car buried in the dump and an air windshield wiper motor for the centre wheelhouse port on an old Tahsis Company truck that was not going to need it any more. Time and again he invented ways and tools to get us going again. He was just the right man for the times, staying with us for twelve years.

On another occasion we had a problem with the port main engine, and the two engineers, Dennis Bye and Dave Wisk, were puzzled. I was sailing with Dave at the time when that engine broke down as we were manoeuvring out of Mooyah Bay. He considered timing, pistons, injectors and several other things. He tried everything to resolve the problem, and as we were going off shift that day his last word was for Dennis to call him if an answer suddenly came to him. Two days later Esson called me from Port Alberni where he had taken the ship. Dennis had discovered that the problem was in the spring packs on the flywheel that act as a shock absorber between the clutch and the engine. They had sheared off and left the engine totally unable to run, the first time that problem had happened to us. This was a bigger tear-down than we could handle in Gold River so it was to be done in Port Alberni.

Back in 1965 before work began on building the pulp mill in Gold River, there had been a great deal of construction activity on the waterfront there. A problem had become evident the previous year when the tidal wave caused by the Alaskan earthquake (March 27, 1964) had flooded the area on which the mill was to be built, floating pickup trucks and even small buildings. The company's solution was to divert the west arm of the Gold River into the main arm; this would allow them to bring in three suction dredges to pump material from the bottom of the harbour to build up the west side of the delta by seven feet. This strategy made the land high enough to be out of future flood danger while at the same making the harbour deep enough for ocean-going ships.

During the mill construction period, we were moved from one small temporary wharf to another, one of them especially built for the *Uchuck* and Northland Navigation's *Tahsis Prince*. When the mill was finally complete in 1967, the government built a public wharf on the east side of the complex and it remains there to this day. It was made out of materials left over from the construction of the Tahsis Company's deep sea ship wharf and is arguably the best constructed public wharf on the coast. As this brand new wharf gave us a place to lie over between runs, we opted to make Gold River our new home base, changing the schedule so that each run was divided in the middle. Now a complete run took up parts of two days rather than a round trip in one day. It began at Gold River on Tuesday, Thursday and Sunday afternoons and returned on the following days around noon. Overnighting in Gold River between runs also meant that we were more accessible to the outside world, but more important was the unbroken time from mid-Friday to mid-Sunday that became available for maintenance and extra runs.

Changing Freight Delivery Patterns

Back in 1960 all public cargo had been brought to Gold River in the baggage compartments of the Vancouver Island Coach Lines buses. Later some of the rear seats were taken out of one of the buses to make more space for cargo. When the cargo volume rose sufficiently, VICL added a five-ton freight truck on the route and, when that was too small, they started running a single-axle tractor with a trailer. Most of this development occurred while we were working on tiny temporary wharves during the construction of the mill, so the trailer was equipped with a loading deck on the back that accommodated one of our pallets. We loaded directly from it because there was no room for anything else on the wharf while the truck was backed into place. In fact, you could barely walk past it.

When the construction of the mill and the town was complete and the Campbell River–Gold River road was opened to the public, commercial freight lines, beginning with West Coast Freight and Canadian Pacific Transport, added Gold River to their schedules. Others followed and then the various supply houses began to send in their own vehicles, so after a while there was traffic coming and going at all times of the day. As we were the last stop for the public truck lines, there were often times when—for all sorts of reasons—they were late in coming. Any problems back down the line were just added on so that we were often two, three, four or even more hours late in starting out from Gold River. Normally the passengers arrived on the bus at a scheduled 17:30 hours, but they sometimes had to wait until 19:00 or even later before we could load up and leave. As a result, if a passenger was going to Zeballos, he could look forward to another six or more hours between arriving in Gold River and getting to his final destination.

One of the delays was caused by loading automobiles. They had to be held back, then lifted and set on deck after we were sure that all the regular cargo that had to be stowed below had arrived. If there were three vehicles filling up the deck space, one or two would have to be unloaded and reloaded at some stops along the way in order to get cargo out of the hold. All of this was time lost. Car traffic to Tahsis was considerable, so we had a reservation sheet that we had to keep up assiduously as people got very upset if anything got mixed up regarding their cars. As the Tahsis Company would not allow large cars in their company town, we dealt with a lot of small ones. (A Volkswagen Bug was technically too long for Tahsis; one man even took the front bumper off his Bug, but it was still a no-go.) We could carry seven cars in all if four of them were no bigger than a Datsun 510, which would fit down the hatch into the hold.

In 1972 the Tahsis Company decided that all of its cargo coming from the Mainland should arrive via Gold River and then be moved on to Tahsis on the newly opened gravel road between the two settlements. Northland Navigation, which had suffered the loss of the *Tahsis Prince* in March 1968, was already in financial difficulties and this decision by the Tahsis Company meant that Northland would no longer be the company's prime carrier. The policy change also meant that our company would lose much of the cargo that the transport companies had been trucking from the Mainland and depositing at Gold River for us to deliver because that cargo would simply be added to the loads they would be taking directly to Tahsis.

The situation did not look promising, but over time we had lost track of how the volume of cargo we were taking into the logging camps had increased. And while our revenues were down somewhat, we were now able to keep to our schedule better, so we had reduced overtime payments, and except in extraordinary circumstances, we did not need to hire extra workers to help with overflow loads. As well, some of our former passengers who had been finding other ways to travel in order to avoid our long delays came back to us. Then, as Gold River grew, local businesses, such as a new Super Valu store, began to generate cargo for us—groceries, building supplies and industrial supplies to be sent to outlying settlements. Now it actually seemed that the road opening was not going to be a disaster for our company after all.

Unfortunately, we were at the tail end of the supply line, so any problems with the cargo came to us as the last carrier before the consignee took delivery of his order. We had to be very careful that we did not become liable for shortages or damage not of our making, so when the vessel was at the wharf and a freight company was delivering cargo to us, we would carefully check it off the truck and note on the waybill any exceptions regarding condition or amounts before we signed the waybill. At that point we became responsible for the state of the goods as received. The problem for us was that we seldom could get signatures for delivered goods because we often left them in a shed for pickup, or the goods were in containers that were unpacked away from our unloading point, or they were dealt with in a hurry as we worked off small rain-swept floats at night. Should something happen to these goods after they left our hands, then we would just have to trust that the receivers would tell us. Most people understood

Taking a well deserved break after finishing the load, in 1947. Standing left to right, Jack Howitt, George McCandless and Betty Whitlock. Sitting, Frank Bledsoe, Dick McMinn and Esson Young.

how and why it was done this way and most of the time the system worked well.

To keep track of everything, we made up a manifest of all cargo on board from the accompanying waybills, noting the comments on condition, amount and any special instructions regarding handling and delivery. The vessel was loaded on each trip for fifteen to twenty ports and cargo for them could be stowed in several places on board—some in coolers and freezers, some on deck and some in general cargo containers. Upon delivery, we would count off the number of items whenever possible, such as cartons of groceries for individuals, so that at least we knew that we had delivered that which we had received. It was not always possible to check off all deliveries as several orders might be included in a single container that was taken directly up to a camp to be unloaded into a warehouse. We always followed up immediately on any problems arising while people's memories were still fresh because the next day would have a whole lot of new detail in it. Usually things worked out though occasionally not.

Mutual trust between us and our customers was also very important, and without it Nootka Sound Service could not have survived. They trusted that we would do as we advertised and we trusted that we would be paid for our work. Cargo was sometimes delivered to the wharf when the vessel was away on the run, left with simply a note attached saying who it was for and where it was to be taken. One day I found some cargo on the wharf addressed to Slam Bang Logging, and with a name like that, I couldn't help but wonder if we would we get paid for carrying it. But we hauled it anyway and found that it belonged to a very fine fellow who we dealt with for many years afterwards.

However, there were times when theft was a problem. This usually happened in spates, indicating an organized effort, but meat, liquor or tobacco going missing was a clear signal to investigate without delay. Some cases were just one-time opportunistic thefts of a single item, the cost of which we just absorbed while taking precautions so it didn't happen again. But at one time quarters of beef were disappearing from the Canadian Pacific Transport loads, and we came close to being accused—though not quite out loud—of having something to do with it. The CP police even came around to see how our system worked, but eventually they discovered that the problem was back in Vancouver.

The logging camps that we supplied were our major source of work and they were, by the nature of the industry, subject to many problems that affected their bottom lines. Weather, machinery breakdowns and industry conditions all served to interrupt production, but the payments on machinery and general costs went on anyway. These operators would come to us and explain the situation, so we were inclined to allow them leeway. Our thinking was that if we did not carry their cargo, they could not operate and then for sure they could not pay. At the annual audit, done by a firm of chartered accountants, there might be questions about some of these outstanding accounts. Some would be written off as non-recoverable but others were reserved where we trusted that their accounts would eventually be settled. In some cases that took as long as two years but they did pay. We had to be a little careful with some new accounts until we could see that they were really trying and not just playing tricks. But as a percentage, the non-payers made up a very tiny part of those we served.

Trust worked the other way around as well. We were sailing from Kyuquot one morning and had already let the lines go when a lady came hurrying down the wharf to say something to me. As we drifted off the wharf, she reached out and passed some money into my outstretched hand and said to please give it to the Super Valu in Gold River as payment for future groceries. When I looked down, I saw that I was holding a purple one thousand dollar bill.

It is a comforting feeling to know that you can trust others and be trusted in return. The work becomes more satisfying and enjoyable when you have the feeling that you are dealing with friends.

Visiting Friendly Cove

Shortly after arriving in Nootka Sound, we had begun scheduling summer tourist trips to Friendly Cove three times a week, Wednesday, Saturday and Sunday. These runs were inserted into the middle of our regular hold-over time between buses, that is, between noon and 17:00 hours. When we switched to using Gold River as our base, we began to have busloads and small groups of tourists coming on board to go to Tahsis, staying there overnight and coming back with us the following day. The Friendly Cove trips then didn't have to be sandwiched into the middle of a run and that allowed us to spend a little more time to make it a better experience

Friendly Cove in the 1940s. IMAGE NA-41444 COURTESY OF ROYAL BC MUSEUM, BC ARCHIVES.

for our passengers. We could even fit in a little freight work to show how our coaster work was done. Regular commuters who know what it is like to travel in a small vessel under varying weather conditions seem to put up with whatever is happening. Some, having done it many times, even get quite bored by the length of the trip and just go to sleep. Others treat it like a tourist trip and enjoy the ride. These people often come to the wheelhouse, which shortens the trip for them and gives the crew someone else to talk to.

Tourists usually come onto the scene with not much idea of what to expect, as this has become an uncommon form of travel and it doesn't equate to a trip on a cruise ship or even a BC ferry. The scheduled times vary from day to day depending on the weather or where the ship has to go to carry out the day's business.

Some people are surprised at the kind of motion that happens when small vessels move through apparently calm water or even when they are tied up and working cargo. Most soon get used to it but some don't. One calm summer morning a lady travelling from Tahsis to Gold River was out on the after deck as I was collecting fares. She looked a little distressed while I was talking to her, and then she asked, "When will it be over?" It took me a moment to realize that she was referring to a tiny rolling motion of the vessel that I hadn't even noticed. We had emerged from behind Strange Island into Nootka Sound, and I could see Nootka Light Station five miles to the southwest and beyond it the ocean. A small swell from outside was making it this far into the Sound, just enough to move the vessel slightly.

Another time at a place nearby there was a very heavy swell rolling far into the Sound. I was crossing it on a weather course so that I could turn and run off before the swell and not have the vessel roll so much, and I was unaware that I had taken her over a shallower bit until she rolled thirty degrees each way—twice. The heavy ashtray on the steering standard in front of me shot off across the wheelhouse and there was the accompanying crash of crockery from below. I got a really surprised look from the engineer who was up visiting with a cup of tea. I went below a little later to find a deckhand sourly cleaning up the mess in the galley with a mop. Two weeks later in the Fisherman's Pub down-island at Oyster Bay, they were still talking about the rough trip on the *Uchuck*.

As part of the tourist trips, we sometimes went out past Friendly Cove to the sea to give people a feeling for what the ocean is like, but I only did this if the weather seemed settled enough. I learned to ask first if there was anyone who was uncomfortable with the idea and there were some from time to time. On one trip there was a westerly blowing on the ocean out beyond Nootka Island, though not inside, and as we headed out past Nootka Light, we began to feel the swell, which I knew would be quite considerable farther out from land. There were a number of people standing outside in front of the wheelhouse and on the work deck below enjoying the salty wind. The vessel began to lift and fall gently then more and more the farther out we went until after fifteen minutes or so the first little bit of spray came on board and swept over those on the work deck. There was a shout and collective gasp as the six degree Celsius water trickled down necks and then a burst of laughter from those who were not caught. I watched a couple in front of the wheelhouse carefully, and when I saw the man start to look a little concerned, I turned the vessel around and headed back to go up Zuciarte Channel, our regular route back to Gold River. This action brought the wind aft and all of a sudden we were in a world of no wind and very little motion. Everyone had enjoyed the little bonus trip a lot but that could have changed had we gone much farther out.

On another occasion we took a charter trip from Gold River on a warm but rainy day to Friendly Cove. On that trip we also went out to sea a little, and I watched one man standing in the lee of the wheelhouse on the little half deck above and behind. His nose was into the wind, and he was so obviously transported in some sort of personal reverie that he just stood there for a long time, taking it in. It was so gratifying to see people enjoying the experience as that is what we were striving for in the first place.

When the *Uchuck II* first arrived in Nootka Sound in 1960, Friendly Cove or Yuquot—"where the wind blows from all directions"—had been inhabited by the Mowachaht people as their ancestral summer home for at least 4,200 years. However, their traditional way of village life had ended at about the turn of the twentieth century, replaced by a mixture of survival strategies. There had been a large cannery at Nootka, two miles to the north, which employed some of the people, but it closed in the mid-1940s. After that, a number of salmon trollers were based in Yuquot, providing income for a few residents, and some of the men worked in the growing forest industry, but this was not enough to support the village adequately. In spite of this, in 1960 Yuquot was still a living village that functioned independently, and there was still a resident Catholic priest and a teacher for the school.

Our company began its interaction with this village by bringing tourists on a trip into Nootka Sound and stopping for a short while in the cove so they could see the site. While the ship was in the cove, just lying still and rolling gently, some giggling girls in a dugout canoe brought out traditional baskets that had been woven of grasses and cedar fibre by the old ladies of the village. There was a little cheerful bargaining between the girls and the tourists—not a big thing, but fun for all involved. This was the beginning of an interesting relationship with the Mowachaht.

❀ ❀ ❀

In Nootka Sound in 1960 there were several populated Native villages in the outlying areas at Yuquot, Neuchatlitz and Queen Cove, as well as on Aktis Island outside Walter's Island in Kyuquot Sound. However, the government was gradually moving these groups into the more central places of Gold River, Espinosa, Zeballos, Tahsis and Houpsitas, the village site in Walter's Cove, where they were provided with government-built housing. The moves were partly to bring them closer to medical facilities and schools, but the program had its problems when bands that hadn't always been friendly with each other were suddenly stuck together. When these larger villages were formed, some of the people who had moved out to places like Port Alberni also returned after absences of many years.

Over our tenure in the area there was a growing movement to restore some of the Native culture and language before it was lost altogether, and we began to hear the languages being spoken again by younger people. The old people had never lost it, but they were dying out. Still, it was good to hear the dialects being used by old Native fishermen talking to each other over the VHF. Their language has an air of no panic, no hurry.

I remember a day in Gold River when we had just returned from a run and were unloading cargo and passengers in a hurry because we were due out with a full complement of tourists bound for Friendly Cove. There was a lot of movement, talk and noise as this was happening. A few Native teenagers were seated along the foot-wide concrete bullrail on the edge of the wharf, watching it all. It occurred to me to go and sit with them to see what it was that they were seeing, and it was amazing to watch the hurry-up excited world of the white guy in action. My feeling is that their culture looks at this one in just that way and it leaves them shaking their heads, wondering what is going on with us.

One day in Friendly Cove, the Catholic priest walked along the beach and came across an old man sitting on a log looking out over the water. He was about to do something but had not yet started. Later in the day the priest came back along the beach and found the man still sitting there, apparently not having moved. When asked why he was still there, the old man answered, "There is much time. The day is long." Maybe that is not such a bad attitude; they have been there in that place for more than four thousand years so something they've been doing must have been working for them.

In one relocation people from the band at Yuquot or Friendly Cove (down from six hundred in the 1800s) were moved into an expanded government-built village on the home reserve of the Muchalat Band at Gold River. A few of the older people, who really did not want to leave, remained behind. Then gradually, as these old people died, their houses fell into disrepair and were later torn down, allowing the blackberries to take over. One family stayed on to the present day becoming, in effect, the guardians of the property. The light keepers at the Nootka Light Station also remained in their commanding position overlooking the cove and ocean, so there was always someone around to ensure that the place was never totally abandoned. Some of the older people who had moved to Gold River dreamed of one day going home and in summer would go back to stay for awhile. Others came back to the village for brief summer holidays, to do some work about the site and to organize camp-outs for the children of the band and of bands from as far away as Kyuquot or from Hesquiat on the east side of Estevan Point.

In 1966 a proper wharf was built in the cove so that supplies and people could be brought ashore easily, but a problem arose because this improved access was happening at the same time that the band members were beginning the move to Gold River. Visitors came in at all times of any day from other places, some not respecting the fact that this was private property. We, on the other hand, had an understanding that we could land tourists to walk around for the hour that we had available in our schedule if in return we would carry band members and their goods in and out at no cost to them. While this started out as a good idea, the numbers gradually got out of hand, and at times our paying passengers had trouble finding a seat inside. Although many band members made one-way trips as we had arranged, many more just came for the ride and to visit friends for the hour that we were there. Sometimes we had gangs of unescorted children and dogs tearing around the vessel. We tried to set a limit on numbers, but there was no one in authority to regulate the numbers and decide who would go on a given trip. This situation, along with the fact that people began wandering around the village unattended, continued for several years until there was enough friction that the band decided to close the cove to everyone, including the tourists that we carried. This closure lasted for more than a year, but just before this disruption, we had taken part in a major event at Friendly Cove.

On May 26, 1969, the biggest ocean swell that I have ever seen on a day in May rolled past the mouth of Friendly Cove toward Nootka Sound. The *Uchuck III* was lying at the wharf in the cove with extra spring lines rigged to try to stop the vessel from surging back and forth along the face of the wharf. Just outside the cove, the 366-foot destroyer HMCS *Yukon* lay, head to the swell, rising and dipping, putting on a great show. She had brought BC Lieutenant-Governor John Robert Nicholson to the event that was about to take place, the installation of a new council chief of this Nuu Chah Nulth band amid the kind of ceremony not seen in this area for many years. Many Native people had returned from abroad for the event. We had already brought ninety of them to the cove two days earlier, and today we had brought more. As we approached the wharf, a small group of people standing in front of the *Uchuck*'s wheelhouse performed songs and chants, and on the wharf one person accompanied by a single drum responded with a welcoming song. As the passengers disembarked, we tended the gangway carefully, letting them scamper across two or three at a time when the vessel was more or less still. When our passengers were all ashore and had moved up to the village, the lieutenant-governor and his party came over by work boat from the destroyer in a wild ride into the Cove. After they walked up the wharf approach to the village we followed, as our crew had been invited as well. The event was to be held in the basement of the old Catholic Church at the east end of the village.

Three years earlier Parks Canada had carried out an archeological dig called the Yuquot Project in this village, and among other things they had determined that it had been continually in the possession of this same people as an "outside village," inhabited during the summer of each year for at least 4,200 years. As I started up the steep, black-earth path through the blackberries, the deep booming of the surf on the outside beach grew so loud I could even feel it in my feet. Over top of it was the drumming coming from the church as the ceremony got under way. The air was full of a fine mist from the surf, the ocean freshness amplifying the scent of earth and leaves, and I stopped for few moments and thought about where I was. From where I stood among the blackberries, I could not see the village or the church so there was no way to judge time, but the whole environment with its sounds and smells aroused a sense of history, enough to send prickles around the back of my neck. I realized that this day could have been a day in any one of those 4,200 years.

In the church I found the ceremony in progress. Songs and dances were being performed in a revival of old customs that had almost been lost. The dancers were wearing some of the old masks, and duck down fluttered about everywhere, all to the rhythm of drums and chants. The songs that they sang were the property of single families, only given to others as a special honour and after much consideration. As I listened, I imagined the power all of this must have invoked in those earlier years.

At the end of the ceremony I began to worry how we would break the spell and gather up this crowd to go back to the ship for the return trip to Gold River. I needn't have worried. Jerry Jack, the new council chief, brought everyone back into 1969 when he announced, "If you want to go back to Gold River, you better get on the boat because it's leaving in half an hour." The lieutenant-governor and party left at the same time and the village returned to normal, at least for this time in its history.

Forward thinking people among the Mowachaht began to see the possibilities of deriving income from Friendly Cove as a way as to fund the preservation of its history. Three decades or so after the band left the village, the first stages of development began, which if continued may include an interpretive centre and the rebuilding of the village along the old lines, as has been done in other places. A landing fee for tourists was brought in, and a tour was arranged where leaders among the young people took groups around the property explaining what had happened there in the past. The unused Catholic Church received a new roof and other repairs with the intention of having it become a museum for artifacts and copies of carvings. Some small rental cabins were constructed beside Jewitt Lake, which is along a trail a little to the west of the village. This is the lake where the Whalers' Shrine had been located before 1904 when it was taken to the American Museum of Natural History.

Prior to contact with Europeans, the Mowachaht people went out in dugout canoes to hunt grey and humpback whales in spring and summer. The danger must have been enormous: a few men in a dugout canoe armed with spears tipped with mussel shells and attached to long lines made of animal sinew and braided plant fibre trying to kill a fifty-foot-long, forty-ton animal. Once they sank the spear into the whale, the inflated seal hides attached to the line were meant to slow the animal down and to act as flotation after it died. Then it had to be towed home.

The Mowachahts' preparation for whaling was important. Before they headed out, the chief needed to purify himself bodily and mentally for the job. To perform the necessary rituals, he and his wife went to the "washing house" on the small island in nearby Jewitt Lake. The little shelter there contained sixty carvings of men and two of whales, plus the skulls of former whalers and other rather gruesome objects. The chief stayed there with his wife until he was ready, summoning the power of the dead to help with the whaling and to cause the dying whales to come to the beach.

The objects that made up this Nootka Whalers' Washing Shrine were collected for the American Museum of Natural History in 1904 and placed in deep storage where they were only rediscovered by a researcher in 1985. A few years later a movement was started to repatriate the shrine to the West Coast. However, as there was such power associated with this shrine and because it had been hidden on its island and never intended to be seen by the public, not all of the Mowachaht band members were in favour of it coming to light again. In any event, if the shrine were to be brought back there would first have to be a site prepared, a climate-controlled building where it would be protected from the elements.

1978 Bicentennial of Captain Cook's Arrival

In 1978 Simon Fraser University organized a Cook Conference in Vancouver, bringing together experts on Captain Cook's voyages from all around the Pacific Basin. As the final event, the participants travelled to Resolution Cove on Bligh Island, the spot where Cook had moored his vessels in the spring of 1778 to carry out repairs to the rigging. Fittingly, we took these people out at the same time in March and in the same type of weather he had experienced. On board were five admirals, the curator of the London Maritime Museum, the master of the *Queen Elizabeth II* and many other luminaries. It was party time. Raging arguments, fuelled by wine, ensued in my wheelhouse regarding, among other things, the placement of the shore-side observatory that Cook had erected during the month or so he had spent in the cove. "Not there, you bloody fool! Over there!" It seemed a good way to conclude the conference.

Crazy Henry

One morning Johnny Reb, the wharfinger and village handyman at Zeballos, came down to the government wharf in his old green pickup truck, backed up to the ship's side, got out and opened the tailgate, which promptly fell off. On the truck bed was a headstone, which he wrestled off the truck and onto a pallet that was lying handy on the wharf. This was to be cargo for the *Uchuck III* the following day. Upon questioning, Johnny said that he would be taking the Grey Goose, the village's backhoe, up to the graveyard to dig up Crazy Henry and bring him down on the following morning to go with his headstone to Gold River.

Crazy Henry had been a long hole driller in the Zeballos Iron Mine and had died in a rockfall at the entrance to the mine about a year earlier. He had been shipped out to Campbell River for the coroner's inquest and then shipped back for burial. No one had known of any relatives or, if there were any, where they might be, so the men at the mine thought he might as well be buried in Zeballos. That way, they could wave to him on their way to and from the mine. Now he was again being shipped to Campbell River. This seemed very odd.

Then I remembered two strange passengers that we had brought in to Zeballos the night before, one a large expressionless woman and the other a haunted-looking man who seemed to be her husband. Neither had said much and clearly they didn't belong here. It turned out that she was Henry's sister and had come to see her brother's burial place. But when she arrived at the graveyard, she decided that this dark and gloomy place was not a place fitting for him and got permission to have him shifted to Campbell River.

The following morning we loaded the headstone into the cargo hold. Sailors, being a superstitious lot, have trouble with this sort of thing—they just don't like having non-living persons on board. And our sailors were no exception. They didn't want Henry in the cargo hold, so Henry on his pallet was given a place on deck.

We sailed at 06:30 with Henry, his stone and the strange couple, and headed toward Gold River, making stops at ports along the way. At each stop the woman would come out of the cabin and walk up the side deck to check on Henry then float back down the deck and inside, never saying a word.

We arrived in Gold River a little after noon and began unloading cargo, leaving Henry to the last. His pallet was landed on the dock and moved into the freight shed with the forklift and put in the corner by the man-door. He would have to wait till late in the afternoon for the freight truck. The strange couple left the ship and went to sit in a large black car that was backed in, facing out on the far side of the wharf. At one point they drove away for a time and then returned. It was said that they had gone up to the village to get a new shirt for Henry. We don't know; we didn't watch. They went back to waiting in the car. Sometime later the freight truck arrived and Henry and his stone along with laundry bags and bits of machinery, tires, old batteries, etc., were loaded into the truck. Soon after, it departed, followed by the big black car.

Our engineer, who had a little Cree in him courtesy of a grandmother, was a little different to the rest of us. He wouldn't go through the little door into the shed or walk anywhere near where Henry had been, declaring that the puddle that was under Henry's pallet would never dry. Two days later he and I went off shift and drove out to Campbell River to my dad's place on the road to Duncan Bay to discuss the week's events including, of course, the business with Henry. It happens that Dad's property was just across the road from the Campbell River cemetery and while we were visiting him, a stately procession was slowly arriving with headlights on, winding its way into the cemetery. With the procession came the same big black car. Henry was arriving in style to his new home, no freight truck, no pallet, no forklift, no Grey Goose, just a long black hearse and a trail of cars.

Special Trips

In the late 1960s we began running extra passenger trips for special events, such as the shutdown of the logging camps before Christmas. The crews going out tended to leave all at once, so in the week before Christmas there was a grand exodus with hundreds of people moving out to Gold River and beyond. After New Year's Day the order was reversed. Additional large movements of people were determined by industry events: poor log markets, fire season, strikes and extended winter weather, all of which would cause companies to close camps and send people out. On one particular occasion in September 1967 the crown princess of Denmark had the job of cutting the ribbon to open a new pulp mill. Afterwards, she was taken to Tahsis, from where she was scheduled to be flown back to Gold River, then driven out over the Campbell River–Gold River road. We were chartered to go to Tahsis and stand by in case the flight couldn't go; we deadheaded up and later back when it was clear that the flight was on. But another time we were chartered to take a load of visiting company and political VIPs to Tahsis from Gold River since it was a particularly bad winter and none of the local planes could fly. When their bus arrived in Gold River, the man who had organized the trip was there to tell all these people that they would have to carry their own bags down our steep gangway. He told me later that most of them had probably never flown in anything smaller that a 747 and certainly had never hauled their own bags anywhere. The spirit of adventure was alive on that run to the outside edge of the world—helped along with a little libation that came to them courtesy of the organizers.

On a couple of occasions we put on an extra run just before Christmas to bring passengers out to Gold River from Tahsis and the logging camps for a day of shopping. These were riotous affairs that were more like a party. There were runs for fun where local service groups chartered the *Uchuck* for picnics and moonlight cruises. School groups went out for picnics and graduation parties, and twice the Vancouver Island West Teachers Association conducted its annual meeting on board at Friendly Cove. Some groups, if not too big, had functions on board while we were on a scheduled run—one was a wedding and another the scattering of ashes.

Christmas Watch

During the Christmas shutdown many of the small camps hired watch-men—often old loggers in need of a few dollars—to come in to fuel the generator and look out for whatever might happen. We brought them in as the crews were going out and then kept an eye on them to be sure they were all right. One old Swedish gent travelled in with us to a float camp and, without a word to anyone in the whole four hours aboard, got off and faded into the nighttime. When we came by a few days later to check on him and take in a fresh propane tank, he came out to watch, had a word or two to say, and that was all. On the next occasion he started a conversation and was quite pleasant, but on our following visit, after he had been there for three weeks, he began chattering before we even got the ship alongside. Even the loners have to talk to someone sometime.

Crew Accommodations

In our early years in Nootka Sound our crews had travelled in a group on the bus, but after the Campbell River–Gold River road was opened to the public, they could drive themselves at more convenient times for our crew changes. Sometimes a crewman was only needed for a run or two; some-times a man would come early for personal reasons. Another advantage of the newly opened road and basing the company in Gold River was that our cooks could be part of the regular crew, working the same week-for-week schedule. They had to live on board with the men as there was no accom-modation for them in Gold River, but this was now possible since our schedule was settling down and we were slowly improving the living con-ditions on board. But I remember that on one occasion when our run was fouled up by a strike, we found ourselves heading up Tahsis Inlet at 04:00 with Zeballos still to do. Cook Sally Janes, who always enjoyed the coast even though she was buried in the galley for so much of the time, sat with me in the wheelhouse watching the day dawn. She couldn't go to bed as we still had passengers on board and at that time her bed was in the main cabin on a table that converted to a bunk. "Sally in the galley" remained on the job with us for fourteen years, long enough to be around when we built a proper small cabin in that after-corner with a lockable door.

More than seventy-five cooks served in three *Uchucks* between 1946 and 1994. In the fourteen Barkley Sound years they had mostly been long-timers. In the first fifteen years in Nootka Sound there were many short-timers, and it stayed that way until the runs settled down into a steady pattern. With very few exceptions our cooks were women, but the job only suited a certain kind of person. One way to tell she would be a long-timer with us was to see her, sometimes with a camera in hand, taking her few spare moments out on deck happily observing the world going by or watching the men working the cargo. I soon realized that all of our long-timers were also really good cooks and were able to organize ahead of time for almost any emergency. With a good cook on board, the passengers would seem to congregate at the coffee counter, some of them recounting their life stories. As a result, our cooks learned more than they really wanted to know at times, but they never had a chance to get lonely. When there were many passengers on board and we had provided a cook's assistant, the cook sometimes had to hide for a short while in order to relax.

In the first few years after we moved to Nootka Sound, on five days of the week the run started at Zeballos early in the morning and ended there late at night. The men lived on board—sort of—but there was nowhere for the cook to live so, as in Port Alberni, the cook had to be a woman who came on board for each trip. However, the system worked best if there were two cooks alternating, run for run, because our days were so very long and the runs were on consecutive days. Of course, the supply of available women was limited as the village was very small, so we also drew women from a nearby logging camp and even from Tahsis, picking them up on the way through in the morning and dropping them off on the way home. At times women passengers were pressed into service, and any of the crew members' wives who came along for the ride were conscripted as well. But finding cooks was a continuing source of difficulty, and sometimes we were without a cook on board at all and we simply set out the supplies and passengers helped themselves. I don't remember if there was anything charged on those occasions or not. At other times the deckhand could be available to help, depending on what else was happening.

Eventually the *Uchuck III* was fitted with an alternator in addition to the DC generating system, and we were able to install a proper four-ring AC range with an oven, a microwave oven, a big refrigerator, a coffee machine and a bunch of other small equipment. The single cook then began to make more extensive meals for many people, there being the possibility of a hundred passengers on board, although when we had that many, we hired an assistant for her. (The space was so small that two people working in it was the maximum, and even then they really had to be compatible.) The menu was enlarged to include homemade soups and chowders made in the "missionary pot," a huge stainless steel pot that needed special support underneath it so as not to push the element through the top of the stove.

While at an upscale restaurant one evening, I overheard the couple at the next table ordering a prawn dinner—she would have the smaller dinner that featured four prawns and he would have the full dinner with six prawns, thank you. This reminded me of the day when our crew was given a feed of prawns by a fisherman friend. They were very much alive and jumping about in the bottom of a five-gallon bucket when they came on board. The whole bucketful was in motion, the inhabitants squeaking and fluttering feelers in this new environment.

Immediately the missionary pot, so dubbed because of its size, was set on the stove, filled to the three-quarter mark with salt water and then an extra fistful of coarse salt added. While the pot was coming to the boil, we fell on the prawns and ripped off the heads, being careful not to be stabbed by their spikes. The beheaded prawns were dumped into the pot as soon as it boiled. Two minutes after the water had returned to the boil, the prawns turned a bright pink and floated to the top. Done. Then they had to be doused in cold seawater to stop any further cooking. After test driving a few, we decided that they didn't get better than that.

The four of us enjoyed a feast as we stood in a circle on the main hatch around the drained bucket of prawns and a box of beer. We got to the bottom of the bucket and the box and then lost any further interest in prawns for that day. I do remember having a night full of very strange dreams.

Once the *Uchuck II* had moved to Nootka Sound, the crew lived on board so they had to be provided with all their meals. At first, as the cooks only came aboard in the morning, the crew fended for themselves for breakfast, usually eating soon after we left Zeballos, while the cook was busy opening up the coffee shop and getting her day started. At lunch and dinnertime she would close the coffee shop long enough to make the crew's lunch and then dinner, but the men always cleaned up after their meals. On harbour days the crew looked after themselves.

During refits at Gold River in our later years, the galley would be open to feed the crew and our hired workforce with full meals and snacks. This was always a difficult time for the cooks, especially if there was work happening inside the cabin. Kay Lowery, another of our long-serving cooks, survived in the job while her whole galley was torn apart and rebuilt around her. The range was moved out and set up farther down the cabin, and the entire structure of the coffee shop was torn apart in a welter of dust, noise and confusion. Supper still showed up at 18:00 precisely.

After we moved the ship's base to Gold River in 1967, the cooks began working the same schedule as the rest of the crew, coming and going once a week, and the average length of employment for each woman went up sharply. By now we had concluded that it was better to have mature women on the week-for-week schedule for some fairly obvious reasons. After one particular set of problems, Esson and I decided that we would only hire women over age forty-five. Fortunately, most younger women don't want this work schedule, especially if they have young children at home.

When travelling on our scheduled runs, we could generally count on enough time—twenty minutes or so—to sit down for a meal between stops. But in bad weather or when there was an engine problem, the mate or the engineer or the oiler would sometimes not be able to get off as usual for a meal. Then the skipper also had to remember to warn the cook so she could adjust the menu to something that could be kept hot for a longer period without destroying it. It was also a good idea to warn the cook when we were about to load cargo that would require a heavy lift that would heel the vessel; a ten or fifteen degree change in angle could cause a real clatter in the galley. (Some skippers were better than others at remembering to issue a warning!) And if we were leaving the shelter of the Sound and heading out onto the ocean, the cook needed to know so she could secure the galley; none of our vessels' galleys had been set up for operations in open coastal water as that was such a small part of our passenger-carrying schedule, which was mostly between settlements in the inlets.

Winter Weather

Some years in the depths of winter, there is a blast of real winter conditions on the West Coast. The deep freeze comes first, followed by the snow when the low pressure weather systems come in off the ocean to replace the cold air. These systems can lay deep snow everywhere and create up to six inches of ice at the heads of the inlets. There are stories of float camps in these inlets being cut off by ice so that no supplies could get in and the people could not get out. In the freeze of 1949–50, a large tug was sent to the head of Muchalet Inlet from Mooyah Bay with crossed logs attached to the bow in order to break the ice so that supplies could be brought in to an isolated float camp there. Because modern logging is nearly all truck logging, nowadays if the weather shuts down an operation for more than a day or two and the forecasts show that there's no relief in sight, the crews will be sent home. Even if they could find the felled timber for the yarders to assemble, it could be impossible to take the logs out because the roads might well be impassable. So everything stops.

Aboard the *Uchuck III,* when we had one of these wintry blasts, our

Very pretty, but not the sight we want to see first thing in the morning due to the extra work it will entail. This picture was taken in Tahsis.

first job was to clear the vessel of snow and then clear the wharf. It is a frustrating experience to shovel the deck of a vessel off; the shovel only moves six inches before it comes to a stop against something. Then there's the walk to the side to throw the snow overboard and back again to shovel more snow. If we were lucky, the roads had been ploughed enough to allow the freight trucks to arrive in Gold River, but at each stop along our delivery route we had to shovel off the landing places, a time-consuming and treacherous job. The only pleasant thing about these occasions was that travelling at night in the inlets could often be quite delightful as the snow on the beaches made the land more visible, especially if there was a moon.

The *Uchuck III* was not designed for sustained cold winter work, so we had to be careful not to let the water lines that ran through the vessel freeze up, especially those in the hatch area. In ordinary weather we would stow groceries and small freight intended for delivery to side ports out on deck in order to have it easily accessible when the main hatch was covered with vehicles or larger items, but in very cold weather it had to be all stowed in the hold to prevent it from freezing.

The winter of 1973–74 was a bad year for snow. On one occasion I was on the incoming crew and left Campbell River around midday with Dave Wisk, the engineer, in his old Mercedes 240D. Light snow was falling, which became heavy snow once we went up General Hill, just out of town, and even heavier snow the deeper we went into the mountains. The old car had no trouble with it, so the journey, although interesting, was not a white-knuckle affair, and in due course we arrived at the wharf for crew change. Changing crews usually took an hour or so as the incoming crew was brought up to speed on what had been happening, but this time we hurried it up in order to let the other crew get going in case the road became impassable, and so they could avoid travelling in darkness.

After we finished lunch we got busy clearing snow, necessary because our Towmotor forklift trucks with their hard rubber tires had trouble in even a small amount of snow. Then quite late in the afternoon the phone rang. On the other end was my mother reporting that Esson had not yet arrived at home in Campbell River. Even with current conditions the journey should not have taken him more than a couple of hours. This was worrisome as he was driving his Jaguar, which was not a good vehicle in snow. It was low slung and the front wheels were set wider apart than the rear ones, so it would not stay in any ruts on the road. When I checked with mother again an hour later, I learned that the Jag had still not arrived, and as it was getting dark, Dave and I decided to go and find out what might have happened.

While we gathered up boots, coats, blankets and shovels, our cook, Kay, put hot soup in a thermos and packed us some sandwiches. We set off with Dave driving the old Mercedes up the road and through the canyon to the village of Gold River. There was still heavy snow falling, but as the ploughs had been making regular passes, we made good headway. Once through the village and headed into the mountains, we found a greater accumulation of snow. When we caught up to a plough heading east, I expected Dave to settle back and follow him. Not so. He pulled out around him and went on. Fortunately, we could just make out more tracks in the snow showing that somewhere up ahead was another plough. In a while we caught up to him also, and again I thought that we would just follow. Once again, not so. Dave pulled out around this one, too, so now we were in virgin snow almost up to the head lights, but still moving at twenty to thirty miles per hour. We all knew this road well, having made the trip so many times. We knew where the curves and bends were supposed to be so I knew that as long as we didn't stop we would be fine. We saw no other traffic, just snow and more snow, until we came to the Buttle Lake bridge, and found a ploughed road on the other side. This was the divide between Highways Department jurisdictions; the ploughs from Campbell River had turned around here and gone back, leaving everything to the west for the Gold River units. The road climbs from the bridge up through a rock cut, and we could see there had been a small rockfall and slide. It was obvious that the traffic heading east, including Esson in his Jag, had come to this point and stopped, waiting a few hours for ploughs to come through to open it up. There had been no real problem, just a long wait. We still had to keep moving in the same direction as there was nowhere to turn around, so it wasn't until we got to Strathcona Park Lodge that we found a spot wide enough in which to do this. We had come about thirty-five miles.

Once we were turned around and headed back, the snow began to ease up, and by the time we got back to the bridge, it had stopped falling altogether. The Gold River ploughs had cleared to the bridge, the sky had cleared and suddenly we were driving on a fifty-mile-an-hour-road in starlight. When we got back to the village we had to take down the barriers that had been erected to keep traffic off the now-closed road.

Once back to the ship, I learned that five minutes after we had left, my mother had phoned to say that the Jag had finally arrived. It was the right outcome and just fine with Dave and me.

CHAPTER NINE

A Brighter Future

The Princesa Pass Rock

In December 1971 the *Uchuck III* hit the rock opposite the light in Princesa Pass when she was on a scheduled run from Gold River to Tahsis and making the turn from Kendrick Arm into Tahsis Inlet. This place was always difficult for us because the rock is submerged and so placed that, no matter which way we approached the pass, we had to make a forty-five-degree turn to go around the Green Pass light sitting on its little rock. But we could never know what the current direction or strength would be when we arrived at that spot, and on this day while the No. 3 was in her turn, she was swept over the rock by a strong north-setting current. She was caught well aft, severely damaging the port shaft, propeller and rudder and totally disabling half the propulsion power.

The vessel had to be hauled out immediately, but we couldn't take her to Port Alberni where we normally hauled out because we would need bigger than average tides to get her up on the ways, and that month there were none big enough. That is when we learned that Yarrows Shipyard in Esquimalt, which had built merchant ships and warships in World War II, had space in its schedule and was able to handle her. This would be the first time that the *Uchuck III* was to go anywhere other than Alberni Engineering for a haul-out. My crew and I came aboard at Gold River the next day and set off to limp to Victoria on one engine at a speed of little more than eight knots, but the weather was relatively settled and we got

The *Uchuck III* on the cradle at Yarrows, waiting to be launched.

there in twenty-three hours. Once the work commenced, we saw how fast a big yard can work when all the equipment needed is available at hand. There wasn't a problem that the workers in that yard had not seen or a repair they had not done before.

When the job was finished and the *Uchuck III* had returned to work, we talked to Bill Lore, a local road builder, who figured that he could, without too much difficulty and expense, blow enough of the nipple off the top of that rock to make a passable channel for traffic on all but the lowest of tides. This would be wonderful for us because we used that pass twice and sometimes four times a day, and this was the second time the vessel had run afoul of that one rock. In retrospect, I realize that it would have been best to just keep quiet and let him do the job, telling everyone later, but someone mentioned what we were planning to do to someone in government, who then came up with a list of all the steps necessary for formal approval. In the end the government decided that it would be too expensive for the gain achieved. So there the rock still sits, waiting for its next victim.

The Pivotal Year

Although 1971 had ended with the grounding in Princesa Pass, taking the company to a low point again, the year 1972 was pivotal for Nootka Sound Service. It marked the point of change between the very hard times of the past ten years and a brighter future for the company in the coming decade And while the completion of roads had chased Barkley Sound Transportation out of Barkley Sound and Alberni Inlet, it was the construction of roads around Nootka Sound that was making it possible for the company to reinvent itself and prosper here. We had known that the roads were coming, but we didn't think it would kill the trade, and this proved to be true. In 1969 the Tahsis Company moved its logging division headquarters from Fair Harbour in Kyuquot Sound down to Zeballos, and the twelve-mile road connection between these two points joined Kyuquot Sound to the outside edge of Nootka Sound. Then in 1970 the road between Zeballos and Woss Lake was opened, so now Kyuquot Sound was joined to Zeballos and to Woss Lake and from there to Gold River via logging roads and so out to Campbell River via Highway 28. In 1972 a link between Gold River and Tahsis, which had both been incorporated as villages, was completed, giving about two thousand people a way out overland, but this road remained rough and hard on equipment for another two years. A local company, Tahsis Transport, ran from Tahsis to Vancouver on a regular schedule, hauling most of the Tahsis Company's incoming freight but struggling with road conditions. Trucks belonging to Dairyland, Pacific Brewers and various furniture carriers also used that road as an extension to their delivery trips to Gold River, but it was hard on their vehicles. At the same time a link was being constructed from Zeballos to Tahsis, although this one was only roughly done and never properly completed. All of these roads began as active private logging roads where public access was restricted. As they were built with trucks in mind, not cars, they were narrow, and as the road builders often routed them around obstacles rather than going to the work and expense of blasting them out of the way, they were also winding.

The *Uchuck III* was now busy most of the year because the Tahsis Company's logging camps and contractors were generally increasing their output. They supplied logs to the Tahsis sawmill and a new cedar mill called Nootka Cedar Products, which was also at Tahsis, as well as fibre for the pulp mill at Gold River. Other forest companies were shipping logs out by barge to processing units elsewhere. All of this resulted in more people moving into the area. Most of the logging camps, manned by twenty to a hundred workers, provided married quarters, and two camps even had schools. Therefore, when the *Uchuck III* wasn't carrying the logging crews and all of their equipment, it was carrying their families and their belongings back and forth.

The "just-in-time" system of inventory had not been introduced into the logging camps at this time (that came after 1980), so all of the camps in the Sound carried large inventories of parts and supplies, and we were kept busy maintaining these stores. Some years earlier the Tahsis Company had established a boom gear depot at Herring Bay, across Tahsis Inlet from Santiago Creek, that handled the boom chains and swifter wires for all of their camps and contractors. We brought in new gear from the outside and, after the booms were stripped of their gear at the mill, the *Uchuck* and various tugs took it back to Herring Bay. There it was sorted and culled if necessary before we took it back out to the camps with their new gear. This resulted in a huge and constant movement of logging gear.

The Tahsis Sawmill supplied the logging camps with bridge timbers because they were constantly extending their roads as they moved into new cut blocks. We often carried 20,000 foot board measures per week of four-by-twelve and twelve-by-twelve rough and random length wet hemlock from Tahsis to all their own camps, as well as to those belonging to other forest companies. I can remember using binoculars to look up Tahsis Inlet from five miles away to see if there were carrier loads of lumber lined up on the approach to the wharf. On a busy day we hoped that there would not be much lumber waiting because carriers of lumber meant that we would be working well into the night wrestling with the heavy lifts, often at a low tide. If we had a car on deck for Zeballos, it would have to be unloaded and reloaded later on top of the lumber. The mate's instruction on these occasions was to stop loading lumber when the pile was getting too high for the skipper to see over it from the wheelhouse. We were very fortunate that the *Uchuck III* had a lot of positive stability. (In the late 1980s logging companies changed to using metal culverts instead of bridges over creeks. Although we carried these culverts, that traffic was much less than the lumber traffic.)

With the increase in general traffic, on many of the *Uchuck's* trips the carriage of cars made it difficult to fit everything else on board, and the problem was compounded by the fact that the space they occupied was not reflected in the revenue they returned. And their drivers complained when faced with $21 for small cars and $26 for full-sized cars on our run—our rates for cars increased exponentially over time—because they were accustomed to paying just $5 per car when travelling on BC Ferries. Gradually we instituted a policy of encouraging drivers headed for Tahsis to drive there from Gold River, though in the beginning that road was very hard on the undercarriage and tires of passenger cars. We always accepted cars and trucks destined for the logging camps as they had no other way to get there.

Our company's progress after 1972 was also indicated by the fact that we now had telephone service from the outside world to the dock and a post office box in the village of Gold River. What we really needed now was an Arvid Petri, as in Port Alberni, to be in a small office on the wharf, receiving freight and answering questions while the vessel was out on her runs. Unfortunately, it was not yet financially possible to hire such a person to do this, but it would have been good. Another office person would have allowed the cargo to be prepared for loading and cut the working time for the ship's crews. But this would come later.

The vessel was still running with a bare minimum crew—four men and a cook. The master also acted as the purser and walked around collecting passenger fares as soon as we got underway. When he finished that job, he became the freight clerk, writing up the cargo manifest from the trucking lines' waybills. In winter this meant an hour or two of paperwork while the vessel moved on in the blackness with only one man on watch in the wheelhouse, although the master was just three steps away and through a door. Ideally, a cargo manifest should have been put on board at sailing time, but that was just not possible. The positive aspect of writing it up ourselves on board was that it gave us a proper count of what we had to deliver. We could keep the details of the load in mind for the duration of that run and even afterwards.

By this time the Gold River wharf had come to be generally known as the "*Uchuck* wharf," although it was actually a government installation and was shared with anyone who needed it. It is where fishing vessels met the trucks that carried their catches to market, and where small freight was transshipped to camp work boats. None of this was a problem for us, but it did require some cooperation. The one difficulty at this wharf was the location of a barge ramp directly behind our berth. When a tug and equipment barge needed to move up to the ramp, there was not enough room between the *Uchuck* and the log booms, so our vessel would have to be moved out to let them in and then out again when they were finished. This could happen night or day. The tugs tried to give us advance warning but that was not always possible, and we sustained some hard hits from barges when we didn't move out because we were in the midst of loading or when we had been lulled by good weather into thinking there was enough room to allow a safe barge movement past us.

This problem was the result of log storage taking up most of the general space on the waterfront. When the log dump was operating, the bundles of logs were tipped into the water here and corralled in loose bag booms, which were then pushed to the outside edge of the storage area, ready to be towed away at the end of the day or the next morning. However, the anchor system for the buoys that held the booms was not adequate because the depth of the water increased suddenly at the outside edge of the booming ground, limiting where the anchors could be placed. We would come in from our run to find that a strong westerly inflow wind had wrapped the bag boom around the opening to the berth and even over to the floats where the planes and small boats tied up. We would have to burrow our way in by pushing the boom out of the way while turning the vessel around 180 degrees and then darting in before the door closed on us again. At other times the boom trapped us alongside so that we had to push our way out. Always we had to take care not to break one of the boom chains because that would have caused logs to scatter everywhere.

By this time refit periods for the *Uchuck III* were becoming more like real refits where work was done to improve her. In 1974 we took her to Yarrows in Esquimalt to do extensive work on the fore deck area, work that included taking out the mast and derricks and repairing the deck area directly under it. During the following year's refit, which took place in Seaspan International's yard at Point Hope in Victoria, two men—Higgs and Jones—made an attempt to buy the company, but in the end their research indicated that the price Esson and George quoted was too high, so there was no deal.

It was also at this time that we needed a new engineer, and Walter Winkler's name was put forward by our bookkeeper, Florence Kapchinsky, and her son Bob. Walter was then working at Ackland's in Port Alberni where he was in charge of the engine rebuilding shop. He had come to this country from Austria, where he had been an apprentice with Mercedes, to join his older brother in Ontario. It was there he had finished his apprenticeship before coming west. He had no marine experience but agreed to have a look at the situation with our company, but as we were still recovering from the past difficult years and the *Uchuck III* looked like it, he had a hard decision to make.

In the end Walt decided to risk it and he started the job on August 29, 1974, which was also the day I came back from a two-month leave of absence, and we sailed together off and on for the next twenty years. Right from the beginning he left his mark by the way he performed every job. If it was necessary to fabricate a part, he finished it completely and then painted it. This signature style became more and more evident the longer that he was with the company.

The Russian Ship and the Boom Boat

By 1975 Tahsis had become a village of about eighteen hundred people, not yet at its peak but big enough to support several private businesses. The two with which we became involved were the Tahsis Co-op, which began an outport business in groceries, and a building supply company that shipped construction materials and later propane around the Sound to the camps and to Kyuquot. As this port could be very busy, whenever the government wharf was occupied, we would be shunted to the main deep sea lumber shipping wharves. This meant that we had to go right up into the mill site to No. 2 dock to pick up our cargo and passengers for the day.

That is how it happened that we were alongside the No. 2 dock in Tahsis one morning at our 08:00 sailing time. I was idly leaning out the wheelhouse port, waiting for a couple of last minute items be put on board and for a six-hundred-foot-long Russian ship to move past us into the berth ahead at No. 1 dock. She was moving slowly, attended alongside by a twenty-two-foot steel boom boat with a single operator on board. His purpose was to take the ends of the mooring lines from the ship and carry

A view of Tahsis from the 1950s or 1960s, a well-protected village at the head of Tahsis Inlet. A sawmill is located in the centre and to the right, a log boom is in the foreground and the A-frame building on the left is the United Church. ALBERNI VALLEY MUSEUM PHOTOGRAPH COLLECTION.

them, one at a time, to the wharf. There, the waiting longshore crew would pull them up and drop the eyes onto the wharf cleats. The ship could then be warped in alongside.

All was going smoothly as the boom boat drifted back along the hull of the ship. The operator, clad in his orange life jacket, was on the after deck with his pike pole in hand, ready to grapple for the dangling line from the stern of the ship, twenty-five feet above him. The ship was in light condition, which meant that the propeller was half out of the water. It turned very slowly, at about eight to ten rpm, just enough to give the ship a little forward movement. It was also creating a tiny current along the ship's side as it pulled water from forward, and the boom boat was moving in this current. I could see the man judging whether he had time to grapple for the line before he would have to move his boat away from where the propeller was turning. It turned out that he didn't.

I stood transfixed as I could see what was about to happen, inexorably and in slow motion. The propeller slowly turned, and when it was right in line with the boom boat, the next blade came around and caught the steel edge of the boat and pushed it under the surface.

Everything happened fast now: the boat was spun on its longitudinal axis through one complete revolution then was spit out to the side, right side up with its engine still running and a cloud of steam coming out of the open cabin door. Then the operator in his life jacket bobbed to the surface, and even from where I was standing, I could see that his face was ashen. He was quickly picked up by another boat and, except for a dislocated shoulder, was uninjured. But the outcome of this event was that the existing rule that there should always be two men on the boom boat for that job would be strictly enforced in the future.

Changing Inter-port Traffic

For many years one of our regular jobs for the Tahsis Sawmill was returning the boom gear that had been stripped from incoming log booms, but after the mid-1970s there were changes to the system. By this time the company's boom gear depot at Herring Bay had been shut down, so the gear was now loaded aboard a float and towed out to us so that we could lift it off, load it aboard and take it to a depot at Gold River. The chains and swifter wire were left on the wharf there until we received our weekly orders from the company telling us where to deliver it. The tangled half-ton lifts of bundling wire were trucked away to a site where they were straightened, rewound onto spools and returned to Gold River to be sent out to the camps again. We knew from what the men working at the beach sorting grounds in the camps told us that they did not like this used stuff much. They explained that all the splices in it made it hard to pass around the logs that were put into the cradles above the water, and the wires sometimes broke when the bundles were released from the cradles to slide down the skids into the water.

There was some other inter-port work beginning at this time as well, generated mainly because we were already available there with a scheduled service. Some of this traffic came from tree planting and falling contractors who often had operations in more than one camp at a time and sometimes needed to ship vehicles, tools, supplies and men between sites within the Sound. Cedar shake block cutting operations also provided us with business. This was salvage work on cut-over forest land where tall cedar snags still stood or lay on the ground, taken down by fallers in the original logging operations to get them out of the way. This wood was bucked into bolt lengths to be sent off to the shake plant in Campbell River. We also carried some of the products generated by a few entrepreneurs living in the camps, loggers who augmented their main employment by splitting shakes in their spare time or running small portable sawmills.

About this time a privately held island in the Nuchatlitz Inlet area was divided up into twelve five-acre lots and sold to people wanting to build houses there. We carried some lumber from Tahsis for them and dropped it into the water in the protected bay close to the island. From this land development enterprise an oyster growing enterprise was also started up. At the same time a few Gold River people were building summer getaways on log floats, positioning them here and there in the coves and bays of Nootka Sound. Commercial sport fishing lodges also began to appear to take advantage of the excellent salmon fishing in this area. Even today there is a considerable traffic in fuel and supplies for these fishing camps in season. A few small clam digging enterprises were started up, but these never grew into industrial-sized operations. A custom cutting sawmill was established at Ceepeecee, southwest of Tahsis, and from it we got some of the lumber that we needed in our ongoing refitting of the *Uchuck III*.

Business continued to rise in a gradual fashion during these years. The camps were all busy, only shutting down for extreme winter weather or fire season or for an occasional strike or some other business disruption. Sometimes when this happened, we shortened our schedule to one run per week, leaving the vessel idle at the dock in Gold River for the rest of the week. Esson and George and others would take turns as watchmen, staying on board to look after the vessel and answer the phone. But most of the time there was boom gear moving back and forth and large amounts of groceries and supplies to deliver to the camps. The married quarters of the camps were full and now there were schools operating at Kendrick Arm, Port Eliza, Esperanza, Zeballos and Tahsis. At Frank Beban Logging's camp at Port Eliza one student eventually went from grade one right through his grade twelve graduation. The long-serving teacher, Mr. Barton, tutored him through his senior years.

Passengers moved in and out from the camps and the towns. We would see more of them in winter when roads were likely to be poor and travel by small boat unsafe. On New Year's Day 1976 four buses arrived at Gold River with people destined for every port in the Sound. Suddenly there were about a 120 people standing on the wharf, as well as people who had arrived by car and on foot. With help from the superintendent at the Gold River Logging Division, we were able to persuade two of the bus drivers to drive through to Tahsis, something Vancouver Island Coach Lines was not doing at that time. The roads had beaten up their equipment in the beginning when they were the only public carrier allowed on the rough private Campbell River to Gold River road, and when the road was improved and opened to public travel, they had lost much of the traffic they had worked to build up. They did not want a repeat of that situation. For this trip we also arranged to have a local work boat take the crew heading to one camp back home, and we managed to handle the rest of the bus traffic and those people who came by car.

Tourism was also generally increasing at this time, helped by writers who travelled with us and then published stories on the area. KOMO-TV sent up a team to film a segment for the series *Exploration Northwest*, and later the Knowledge Network, makers of *BC Moments*, made a segment for their series. That one aired for years afterwards. The word was getting out. And having a telephone made a big difference because people who became aware of the service through these media presentations could phone for immediate information and to make reservations.

The issue of a subsidy was always present. Originally the hope was that at some time it would not be necessary to have one, but we never seemed to get to that point. In order to extend service to all places in the Sound on a fixed schedule, it was inevitable that on some runs there was not enough revenue to offset the costs, but people had to be able to depend on our schedule. However, whenever a subsidy period—usually five years—ended and was up for renewal, the company asked its customers and the village councils to write letters to government in support of the company by saying that they needed the service. This support was always forthcoming.

Big Changes

In May 1976 when Esson was sixty-five, his seagoing days ended. That day I had relieved him as usual to begin my shift, and he had gone to the freight shed to get his car out to drive home to Campbell River. I went down to the galley to have lunch and was surprised when, a half hour later, he reappeared in the galley looking confused and wanting a cup of coffee. He made a mess of getting cream and sugar into the cup, spreading it around on the coffee counter. My initial thought was that he had suffered a stroke and that turned out to be what had happened. But because he was stubborn, nothing would stop him from driving home as he had intended. None of us could talk him out of it or even get him to agree to let someone accompany him home. As soon as he left, I phoned my mother to warn her that something had happened and to watch him carefully as I was sure that he would not mention it at all.

It took him longer than usual to drive to Campbell River as at one point in the trip he drove off the road and into a rock wall, puncturing a tire and losing a hubcap. It took him some time to change the tire and find the hubcap, but as he did so his condition improved. When he arrived home, he didn't tell my mother any of this.

When I finished my shift a week later, I stopped to see him at his home in Campbell River, but finding no one at home, I went into town where I saw his car parked by his doctor's office. They would not tell me anything in the doctor's office, so I went to the hospital where I saw my mother's orange Volkswagen in the lot. She was in the waiting room. It seems Esson had finally gone to the doctor and had demonstrated his problem right in the middle of the waiting room floor. Had he seen his doctor when he came home a week earlier, it is probable that this would not have happened. As it was, he spent three weeks in hospital and a year recovering at home. It was a frightening experience for him in hospital when he found that he couldn't even form full thoughts. I looked at him and saw a man who had suddenly become old.

During his recovery, Esson took on the job of building a fence across a field for the neighbour on the farm next door, digging the post holes by hand and stringing the wire while being watched intently by one of the cows. He said he thought she was watching to see where the weak points might be. Having worked hard all his life, he enjoyed this job as a means of keeping busy and doing something useful, and one day when I visited him, I observed that he was much improved and told him I thought he could go on like this for a long time. He replied that a couple more years of this would be enough.

After Esson's stroke George and I worked week-about, but with Esson gone he was disheartened and fast tiring out, so it was clear we needed another solution. The answer came one day when Neil Watson walked into our office looking for a skipper's berth. He was qualified and became my opposite number. George went ashore for good after his last run on July 12, 1976, so from that time on I was effectively in charge. By the end of that year, Esson had recovered considerably and wanted to be kept up to date on company events since he was remaining as president of the company. In the meantime, when it came to instructing the new skipper on the day-to-day business, I had become aware of how much of the company's business was done by the master on board. I had grown from a boy with the company, had sailed as deckhand, mate and skipper, and had been involved over a long period of time with all the ins and outs of the day-to-day work. But more than that, I was imbued with the philosophy of the company, which entailed more than just running the vessel. It involved business practices and how we dealt with the public. Our public.

In the spring of 1977 engineer Walter Winkler and skipper Neil Watson went through the exercise of determining the value of the company with the object of making an offer for the shares. It was timely, as both Esson and George wanted to sell, but when they made their offer,

Esson deemed it too low. One day he came to my house and said that he wasn't dead yet, and if I would continue to run the company, he and George would keep it. I agreed and again we went on.

On November 22, 1977, a year and a half after his stroke, Esson died suddenly of an aneurysm. It was a shock, but not a complete surprise. He had lived hard as many of his generation had and was worn out in spite of his relatively young age, although aneurysms are not governed by age.

George McCandless was profoundly affected by Esson's death, and though for a time things went on as before, in mid-1978 he let me know that he wanted to be out of the company altogether. This time Walter Winkler and I enlisted Roy Friis to go through the numbers exercise with us, along with our accountant, Ted Cowan, the object being to make an offer for the company. Ironically, we came up with a set of figures that was very close to what Walter and Neil Watson had arrived at previously. George was not satisfied with this so for another half-year nothing more happened. At last we raised the amount of our offer, taking it above what the figures showed was reasonable, and after long and unpleasant negotiations we reached a deal. The three of us—Walter Winkler, Roy Friis and I—became the new owners on January 19, 1979, and after a time we realized that, yes, it would be possible to make a go of it. Meanwhile, Roy had been thoroughly bitten by the possibilities in the oil business, so after another year Walter and I bought his shares.

Roy Friis had come to the company in 1965 as my young deckhand when I was the mate, and

A happy Esson Young just after the commissioning of the *Uchuck III*, in 1955.

after I became skipper he was mate. Later we were opposite numbers as skippers although he would be gone for periods of time while he sat for examinations or worked in the oil exploration industry. He served in rig support vessels on the West Coast when the Sedco 135 was drilling holes from Victoria to Hecate Strait in 1968–69. Then he was involved directly with oil companies in the Beaufort Sea and would come with us during the down season for them.

Facing Steamship Inspection

Then came the bombshell. Less than six months after buying the company, Harry Mitchell, senior surveyor of Steamship Inspection at Nanaimo, informed us in a letter that he was not sure that he could continue to pass the *Uchuck III* for further service and that we had better be looking for another vessel. The years of never having enough money for real refitting had caught up with us, but as we had just put ourselves into serious debt, this development was a real blow. We began looking around for a replacement vessel in Canada and the US and even in Europe. Then Roy Friis called one day from North Carolina to say that he may have found a possibility down there, but it was not to be. It became evident that it was not going to be possible to find a vessel that could simply be dropped into place for service on the West Coast. It would have to be just exactly like the one we had, and if it was found outside of Canada, it would have to be modified to satisfy Canadian inspection rules. And to provide capital for a replacement vessel, we would have to sell the *Uchuck III* and that would be difficult. Meanwhile, there was no money for extensive refits of the ship or many months before the next inspection time rolled around.

CHAPTER TEN

The Refit Years

In the years between 1946 and 1960, refit and repair work to all three vessels had been done as the work was needed. This had been possible because the company was operating out of Port Alberni and could get work done in the local shipyard between runs or while one of the other vessels covered for a run or two. There were annual inspections as well, but even these didn't cause much delay because again the other vessels were available.

However, neither refits nor inspections were as simple in the first ten years after the move to Nootka Sound because company funds were in short supply and it was a twelve-hour run to Port Alberni. The aim during that period was to get the job done in the shortest time and least expensive way possible.

The problem was exacerbated after 1966 when we were down to a single vessel. We would warn our customers well in advance of our refit date that we would be leaving for a given period, so that the run before we left Nootka Sound was always very busy as customers stocked up on everything that they might need until we got back. In spite of this, loggers usually found that the transmission failed or the grapple broke just after we had sailed away. On departure day for Port Alberni, we left Zeballos at 06:30 on our regular run and went through the day doing our usual work. As there was such heavy traffic on that day, we were often quite late leaving Gold River on our return run, and on one of these occasions, we finished unloading at 04:00 the next morning in Zeballos. We needed to leave immediately for Port Alberni in order to catch the tide for haul-out, and I remember asking the crew if they were all right with that. When they said yes, away we went for the twelve-hour run down the outside. In our normal day-to-day work, it was not possible to use a watch system; instead there was really only one watch because there were only four men aboard and every one of us was required for cargo loading at each port. On the run to Port Alberni there was a chance for crew members to be spelled off for a time to get a little sleep, though in foul weather there was not much rest in that.

The necessary Department of Transport annual inspection was always carried out in May in Port Alberni where the vessel was hauled out for hull inspection, bottom maintenance, painting and propeller changes. Later, back in the water, all the deck inspection requirements were fulfilled. Every four years there was a major inspection called the quadrennial, where all through-hull fittings had to be removed, dismantled and serviced. Propellers were taken off and shafts pulled out to check for wear on the bearing surfaces and then engines had to be totally pulled down and the parts viewed. This last requirement was highly annoying as it takes weeks for an engine to settle in again and to correct all the little fuel and water leaks. During one quadrennial inspection, after the engines in the *Uchuck III* had been dismantled, the engineer came up on deck to report that he was ready for the inspector. The inspector, in the meantime, had gone down the other ladder to the engine room, had seen the engines and arrived on deck shortly after the engineer to announce that, okay, they could be put back together again.

The engines in the *Uchuck III* are GM medium-speed types, more like the so-called package power and not the old slow-turning, heavy engines of the past. The problems for each kind are quite different. In these smaller machines, cylinder heads, liners and pistons are constantly being changed as necessary. Thus, it finally evolved that, if we kept a complete record of all work done during the year and showed this to the inspector, it would be sufficient to pass inspection. All that dismantling and rebuilding had been costly and time-consuming, leaving less time and money for improvements.

Mast and Derricks

During this early period of major refits, one job on the *Uchuck III* had been beyond simple repair work—but it had to be done. This was to replace the wooden mast and derricks that had come from Canadian Pacific's *Princess Mary* as they had begun to show signs of rot. We had known for a few years that the mast was rotting under the hounds band two-thirds of the way up its length. This fitting, that in the old days had been made of wooden blocks bolted to the mast in a circle, is nowadays an iron ring that is bolted or welded to the mast, and it has eyes to take the shackled ends of the rigging. It was originally designed to prevent the hemp standing rigging from slipping down. As a stopgap after we discovered the rot, I had gone aloft to drill two small holes in the mast at that location in order to inject a little diesel fuel and let it soak into the wood and stop the rot. For a whole summer I had climbed up that mast twice a day to do this in an attempt to arrest the rot, but we finally realized that the time had come to find new gear.

In Victoria Esson had discovered a good second-hand galvanized steel mast. It had come from the *Princess of Alberni,* which had come to an abrupt stop against Gore Island in Nootka Sound. The mast, however, had tried to keep going with the result that it was badly kinked not far from the heel, but Esson could see that if it was bucked off at the kink, it would suit our purpose nicely. Carrying on to Seattle, he found two forty-four-foot steel derricks that had come from a 10,000-ton cargo ship. Back in Port Alberni, we used logging equipment to remove the ship's old mast and derricks and replace them with Esson's finds, afterwards adjusting the fifty-year-old wire rigging to fit. However, as time went on, the rigging stretched until there was no more adjustment left in the rigging screws, so during a refit at Yarrows in Esquimalt, the mast was lifted a little and a steel fabrication put under the heel to raise it up a foot. This adjustment allowed us to tighten the rigging again. At the same time, we put wire clamps on the splices at the top ends of the stays and shrouds to stop the splices from pulling. The bottom ends had babbitted sockets fitted where the wire had been shortened from the length needed for the *Princess Mary*.

In the mid-1980s one last thing was done to this mast. It was taken out again in order that the wooden topmast could be removed and a steel plate welded across the top where the topmast socket had been. This was to be a platform for a new powerful searchlight that could be operated from the wheelhouse. As the mast was lifted and rotated to the horizontal, the unstayed topmast broke off and dropped into the harbour, but the new light turned out to be a great boon as it could almost set the trees alight from a quarter of a mile away.

Even after the company moved to Nootka Sound, all our refit work was still done in Port Alberni, partly because that was where it had always been done and partly because our company had a good rapport with the shipyard and machine shop people. There was distance to consider, too—it was a twelve-hour run from Gold River to Port Alberni and an eighteen-hour run to the next closest haul-out in Victoria. However, the facilities at Port Alberni were marginal at best, the marine railway being just big enough to handle the vessel. The refit period had to be set for May as we did not want to break into the running schedule in the busy summer season and we didn't want to do it in winter as we wanted at least half decent weather in which to do the outside work. However, the vessel could only be hauled out on the bigger tides of the year, and in May these tides were in the middle of the night and barely high enough for us to get onto the cradle. To complicate matters, the yard's hauling winch with its old flathead V-8 engine was just barely adequate to pull up the cradle with the *Uchuck III* on it, and on one occasion, the hauling wire wasn't up to the job and broke when we were nearly up. The ship rumbled back down, came off the cradle and shot across the harbour. Luckily, the engineer was still below and he was able to start up again in time to keep us from piling into the trollers tied up at the floats behind us. To make matters worse, on the days that the vessel was out of the water, work had to stop when the next high tide flooded the cradle for an hour or two in the middle of the day.

We all knew about the little holder that sat on a post beside the railway, a holder that contained a box of Cow Brand bicarbonate of soda that was meant to be added to Portland cement to speed up the setting time of the small quantities that were mixed for caulking underwater seams in hull planking. More importantly, it was used by the shipyard foreman, Roy Williamson, whenever he knew that the *Uchuck* was going to be hauled soon. He was an anxious sort of man, and he became even more anxious when the *Uchuck III* was coming in as it was the largest vessel that they hauled, and he worried about something going wrong.

The Upgrades Begin

It wasn't until 1977 that some funds became available to put into upgrades rather than just the necessary repairs to equipment and structure, and we decided to extend the *Uchuck III*'s boat deck toward the stern by about ten feet to provide more seating for tourists. This was not a very ambitious project and, as we were re-covering that deck anyway, it made sense. Although it caused consternation in some quarters as being an unnecessary expense, it was a good start on improvements.

At this point we had begun to rethink our future refits. Labour rates were rising so we had to think about this in the context of the Port Alberni yard where so much of the work was labour-intensive. For instance, when we had to pull shafts, we had to call on several shop men to do the job manually, and this was done at the shop rate. On the other hand, at Yarrows in Esquimalt the cradle the ship lay in was decked over, allowing mobile equipment to drive right up to it so one man on a machine with a hooker was all that was needed to remove a shaft and take it to the machine shop. Quicker and cheaper. On the negative side, there was much more overhead to pay for at Yarrows, and it seemed to us that there was some featherbedding going on. I know that this was probably not the case, but the yard was so big that all the people needed for each job had to be committed and on hand or the job could get stalled. None of them were allowed to cross trades barriers to do someone else's job, even very small acts. All this was irksome when nothing could happen till the right man got there or we watched someone just standing around waiting to do his part of the job. There was, of course, sense to all this but still it was hard to watch. We had hand-stowed a lot of other people's groceries to earn the money to come there to watch these guys stand around.

The Mid-Life Refit for the *Uchuck III*

With our purchase of the company in January 1979 followed so closely by the letter from Harry Mitchell of Steamship Inspection informing us that he was not sure that he could continue to pass the *Uchuck III* for further service, we had some rethinking to do. We had quickly ruled out the possibility of replacing the vessel and had come to the conclusion that, if the company was to survive, we would have to find a way to keep the vessel that we had. As a result, in February 1980 I sent a letter to Harry asking

John Friis planing hull planks in 1982 when the major hull rebuilding was in progress. Under his direction, we got the *Uchuck III* seaworthy again.

that he send a surveyor up to Gold River to go over the whole situation with us before inspection time in May. We wanted to see what it would take to save the *Uchuck*. Harry sent us Captain Frank Johnson, who turned out to be our saviour. Frank had been a master in British ships before he came to this country and joined the Ministry of Transport as a steamship inspector. Among his other postings, he had served as an inspector in Newfoundland where he had dealt with lots of old wooden vessels, trying to find ways that would allow them to stay in operation while at the same time satisfying the ministry's rules.

For two days Frank went over the *Uchuck*, looking at every place he could get to, inside and out. At the end of it he came to me and said, "Hell, Dave, she's not so bad." He then laid out a number of things that would have to be dealt with immediately and said that, if we did those, we would get her through the next inspection. We drew up a program to deal with these critical items and presented it to Harry Mitchell. This was the beginning of a twelve-year program during which we totally rebuilt the vessel, bringing her to a point far beyond her original conversion.

To get us started, Roy Friis brought his father, John, a retired shipwright living in Port Alberni, to look over what we had to do. Roy and John paddled around the hull in our twelve-foot aluminum boat, poking at the hull planks above the waterline to get an idea of their condition. John was not a young man and would not be able to take part in the heavy work, so the plan was that he would be the boss shipwright and would hire some construction carpenters that he knew and turn them into shipwrights. He got four men—all of them named John—who became the crew to do the heavy hull reconstruction work over the next five years. At the same time we worked with Alberni Engineering on other projects.

For the initial big refits we tied the vessel up at the Pacific Towing Company's floats in Port Alberni for three weeks each May. We organized all the tools, borrowing John Friis's heavy old band saw and table saw, and on Walter's say-so I bought a thickness planer. In time we gathered a full complement of all the necessary equipment. We were to be our own contractor, hiring tradesmen as required for all the work over the next many refits. The exception was when we were on the cradle in the shipyard because the yard was responsible for what happened while the vessel was out of the water. They needed full control of all that transpired there.

On the first morning of the first major refit period, I was sitting at my desk in my cabin at 08:15, when I heard a chainsaw start up. This was it. There wasn't going to be any fooling around with hammers and chisels pecking at little pieces of wood. The chainsaw cut between two frames in the hull below the sheer plank, slicing down about five plank widths to a position about a foot above the waterline. That cut was repeated in the next frame space and so on for fifteen feet. The butts in the planking were staggered beyond the opening for a number of feet in each direction. The cut pieces were all knocked out leaving spaces between the frames, letting the sun shine in there for the first time since 1942. This was the pattern for the next three weeks. While this was happening, planking was being prepared on deck to go back into these spaces. For ten hours a day, seven days a week, with minimal stops, the work forged ahead.

In all, we used thousands of board feet of three-inch edge-grain fir planking. This material is very expensive and not easily available, so we found our own logs and had them custom cut to our specifications at small private sawmills where they were then stored and dried for a minimum of two years. The wood had to be without knots for up to twenty feet, which was no small thing, but the real trick was to judge from the outside of a log what the inside looked like. Fortunately we found people who could make those judgments. Cutting this way is wasteful but the offcuts could be used for other purposes.

The refits did not all go smoothly. On one haul-out, when the ship went up on the marine railway at Port Alberni, the track collapsed behind her, but we didn't know this had happened until we tried to get the ship off ten days later. The carriage would not go down beyond the problem area, so she was stuck there. I had already informed our customers that we would be back on the run by a certain date so that they could order their groceries and parts and have them sent out to Gold River ready for us to pick up. Now I had to phone everyone and cancel. We tried for three days in a row to get off the ways, each time with no luck. Finally we knew that there would be only one more chance before the tides would be too small to float us off for another month, which would have left us as nothing more than a coffee shop for the yard crew. I phoned all our customers to say that we would be back the next day, fervently hoping that would be the case. Again we were let down the ways and again got stuck, not quite floating, even after divers had twice worked to make temporary repairs to the rails. But it was our last chance so we were pulled partway up again, the carriage was released and this time, when we got into the water with the engines running, I rang up half astern both. The propellers bit in and we rumbled off, rocking and rolling into the harbour.

We half expected to see twisted track poking up into the engine room, but we were lucky. The next morning at low tide, the wreckage of the rail-bed was visible above the water's surface, and we realized that it was a wonder that we had got off at all. We were very lucky. No more delays now. As fast as possible, we finished up our deck inspection and went back to work.

Every year there was some crisis because we were always trying to fit in twice as much work as was reasonably possible. All hands, ours and the extras, got into the spirit of events and made it happen. For all the hard work, it was fun, especially as we were making progress in the overall plan, and each person could see the contribution he had made.

One year after two weeks of frantic effort, we had just finished a refit at Alberni Engineering and were finally loading our lifeboats back on board at 04:00 on sailing day. The boats had been in the water for days as part of the inspection as well as to make room for work being done around the area where they were stowed. The crew was giddy with fatigue but we had to go. They heaved up the heavy and now partially waterlogged boats by their lifting tackles in stages, one end at a time, whooping and hollering in the night. Then we sailed. Four hours later we were headed out of Carolina Channel onto the ocean near Amphitrite Point and felt the old girl lifting to the moderate southwesterly swell that was rolling in. Shortly, the vessel was diving into the swell enough to put the raised fo'c'sle well into the water as we rounded Amphitrite and headed west toward Estevan Point.

It was quite a pleasant May morning and I was settling in for a bit of a lumpy ride. The crisp salted air of the ocean was doing its magic of erasing the memory of the dust and confusion of refit. With a fresh coffee in hand, I leaned out of the open port on the lee side of the wheelhouse. It was then that I looked forward on deck and noticed that a big plastic garbage can was sliding around from its position behind the washboard just inside the open heavy steel starboard door of the fo'c'sle. This seemed odd as we were not moving about all that much. Then I saw that there was water in there as well. This was alarming. When I went down to look, I saw lots of water there and more coming in, and there was daylight in a place that had been dark since the vessel was built. I knew there was no danger as this area was above the main deck, so there was no water getting into the hull at that time. The deckhand and I went down and closed the big hatch that leads to the crew's quarters on the other side of the fo'c'sle to keep the water from going down there. Next we explored the forepeak and found that some of the hull planking had been stove in by the pressure of the water as she dipped her head into the swells. The two-inch-thick planks there had rotted in their centres although both skins were still hard, showing no signs of rot at all. The way to check would have been to give it a good thumping with a hammer, listening and feeling for the dull sound that indicated soft wood. We did this regularly on the three-inch hull planking below the main deck for just that reason, but this came as a real surprise. Right then, we turned around and went back to Port Alberni for another few days of work to take out and replace planks, teaching us yet one more lesson and creating confusion back in Nootka Sound where everyone had been prepared for our scheduled return.

In the 1983 refit, we scheduled repairs to the cargo hatch coamings because we had been observing the progression of rot there for some time, and this was to be the year to address it. It would be done while the vessel

A refit at Gold River, showing Mark Appleyard and Dan Prain hard at work.

To protect these old, wooden ships from ice, a layer of gumwood sheathing was placed over the softer hull planking. It was a real pain, though, to remove the gumwood, as these workers are doing here, so that the hull could be recaulked.

was hauled on the ways at Port Alberni for the annual inspection. We had decided to replace the wood with steel and had the prefabricated sections and heavy I-beams all ready to go in. The old coamings were torn out, and at the same time thirty pieces of deck planking beside the hatch were removed. As well, in the same part of the vessel, some starboard hull planking below the main deck but above the waterline was selected for replacement.

But there was a problem lying in wait for us although it was not as yet recognized. The railbed under the ship was not quite true, having a slight hump in it at the top end where the carriage rested when it was hauled up. That hump was transmitted to the carriage and so to the vessel on top. We had always been aware of some distortion of the vessel when she was on the ways because various doors and other tightly fitting parts would bind but, when back in the water, everything had always returned to normal. But this time, as the ship sat on the carriage, she conformed to this shape because of all the wood that had been removed. As a result, when those sections were replaced, that hump was built into her. The first clue that something was wrong came when we started back to Nootka Sound. The mate was doing his rounds of the vessel as she worked in a seaway and, while standing in the hold, became aware of sounds coming from the hull and deck. The new planking was complaining about the unnatural strains imposed on it, caused by the changed shape that was now built-in. Upon arrival in Gold River we saw that most of the new caulking had worked its way out of the new planking seams above the waterline. The refit had left the vessel with a built-in hog (hump in the middle).

During the reconfiguration of the vessel at the original conversion, the weights of structure and equipment had become concentrated over the narrow and therefore less buoyant areas of the fore and aft sections. As the main buoyancy of a vessel is in the middle, the tendency is for the ends to bend down over time, creating a natural hog. With the *Uchuck*, the interference with original design through moving the housework around and the addition of an eight-foot by twelve-foot hatchway plus our current changes to the hull and deck planking around the hatch coamings had only increased those natural tendencies. If the vessel had been built in its present configuration, there would have been design principles factored in by the naval architect to counter this hogging tendency.

In mid-1983 we decided that the main engines were about worn out. They had served the vessel for nearly thirty years and were not new when we had installed them. Some had called them worn-out even then. Over the years we had used a mix of used and new parts to sustain them, but now it was not reasonable to try to extend their lives any further, so Walter went looking. Coast Ferries Ltd. of Vancouver happened to have two World War II yard freighters that they had recently bought from the US government. They had converted one to become the MV *Tyee Princess* for use on their mid-coast run; the other was so far surplus. These vessels were 130 feet long and powered with exactly the same type of engines as those in the *Uchuck III*. They had been completed near the war's end, and though they were now forty years old, they had been run less than a hundred hours before being mothballed, a process designed to preserve machinery forever by having all the parts covered in a thick waxy material. As a result, there is great deal of work necessary to clean the pieces and reassemble them to become running engines again.

We made a deal for the engines, and one day Walter took a five-ton flatbed truck to Vancouver to pick up the two engine blocks and a container full of all the parts belonging to them. He took all this to his home in Port Alberni and then for six months worked at preparing them for installation in the *Uchuck III*. They were inspected at each stage of the rebuilding by Steamship Inspection and at the end were certified for use.

As the reassembled engines weighed close to six tons each, Walter had looked ahead when it came to how they were to be moved down to the waterfront, equipping them with running gear from a pickup truck, steerable front wheels and a trailer tongue in front. As in all things that he does, this assembly was very complete. To set it off, he fashioned a driver's seat and mock steering wheel. At this point the rig looked like an eight-cylinder Bugatti about to enter a race, chromed cylinder head covers and all.

He hooked his truck up to the hitch and started out of his driveway on the down slope and discovered right away that this thing was going to take charge. The whole works was about to go over the bank into the neighbour's yard below, so a re-think was in order. Soupy Campbell was then brought in with his mobile crane and flatbed truck to load the engines at one end and then go down to the wharf and lower them into the ship at the other end. This worked just fine.

In the refit period of 1984 we sailed into Port Alberni, the old engines were taken out, all the plumbing and wiring replaced in and around the

Another engine replacement for the *Uchuck III*, this time in 1984. Doesn't it look like a Bugatti starting off for a race?

beds, and the new engines installed. It was a very smooth operation. In the meantime all the other items slated for that refit went on around this job and at the end of the three weeks we went back to work. Some of the run-in procedure was done on that trip back and involved running the engines up to a high rpm for specified periods of time. Whenever we did this, it seemed as if the lighthouses were going by like the pickets of a fence.

Over the next several years more and more of the refitting was done in Gold River, while the out-of-water work was done in Victoria. We owned most of the tools to do all of the work scheduled for Gold River by then, so, prior to the refit dates, we gathered up the materials we would need, sharpened our tools and found the tradesmen needed for that year's work. One of these men was Dan Prain of Comox, a building contractor who had approached me at the marina there and asked if we ever had need of a shipwright for temporary work. I remembered this and contacted him before we started on that year's work, beginning an association that endured for years, in which he and a partner, Mark Appleyard, came to Gold River and worked on the planking jobs and other shipwright work.

At times we rented or borrowed travel trailers to house our workforce and borrowed log floats to bring alongside so that hull planking work

And here they are installed: the two Cleveland GM 8-268A engines, just like new.

could be done. We were not totally alone out there because the pulp mill, known to us as the Marshall Wells by the Sea, was right next door. We were able to buy supplies there and could have some machine shop work done on an emergency basis. Sometimes in the middle of it all we would down tools and make a run up the line to take supplies to the camps and villages and then go back at it. The *Uchuck* was a strange looking vessel on some of those trips.

At the beginning or end of these periods, we would have to go to Victoria for the out-of-water work and steamship inspection, but sometimes we took both Dan and Mark along to continue the work there while we were in the yard. For the trip south we imported old friends so it took on a holiday atmosphere. They either arrived in Gold River the day before for the short, seventeen or so hours of the passage, or came earlier in order to make a run or two with us before we were to leave. Each year the core group who travelled with us consisted of Rick McCandless, youngest son of my father's old partner, George, and Ted Cowan, accountant to the company, plus one or two of Rick's friends. They all knew the drill and became part of the crew during the trip, some to steer or handle the cargo gear, others to cook, and there was usually a bottle of scotch somewhere in the mix for the evenings.

In the later years the Victoria part of the refit was mainly carried out at the Point Hope Holdings shipyard. It was a good fit for us, that yard being smaller than Yarrows, which was coming to an end anyway, and at Point Hope there was still a large, efficient carriage on the marine railway for the ship to lie on. The hauling procedure there began with building blocks on the carriage to fit the profile of the keel of the vessel about to be hauled in order to raise the vessel for easier access to the keel area. If the keel profile was not completely straight, there had to be a plan made to enable the building of the blocks to the right heights.

Before going to Victoria we needed to make up such a plan, so Walter made special brackets, one for each end of the keel. A thin wire was attached to the one on the forward end and then stretched to the after one where it was redirected and led up to the deck level to be pulled tight with a come-along. A diver marked the keel at six-foot intervals and then measured up from the wire to each of the marks in turn, recording the values as he went. Not only did we get a profile of the keel shape to

On the cradle at Point Hope Shipyard, 1990. Kitty McCandless and I are standing in front of the *Uchuck III*. HENRY MCCANDLESS PHOTO.

give to the yard for building the blocks, but we also now had a gauge to note the changes in the hog year by year. We found in succeeding years that there was virtually no change, which meant that the hog had been mainly produced in that one event in Port Alberni. However, we continued to monitor the situation, aware that as the ship aged she would weaken, especially given the radical changes in configuration that were made in the original conversion.

The human eye is a very discerning organ and can pick up the smallest of irregularities, and this hog, being measured in inches, was more than just evident. There was a one-foot-wide white line painted on the black hull and bulwarks that followed the deck line, having been put there to break up the expanse of black hull and hopefully to reduce the slab-sided look of the vessel. As that line really showed up the problem, at one time I tried to have the line painted as a fair curve to hide the obvious hog, but after once or twice we put it back to the old way. Later we had it painted out altogether.

The refits of 1985 and 1986 made the greatest changes to the look of the vessel. When the *Uchuck III* was commissioned, she had been fitted with much the same life-saving gear as the first two ships. We had discovered the first of the inadequacies of this system one day in the late 1950s when two men fell into the ocean. They were part of a group of four who had been sitting outside the rail, feet over the side, outboard of the stern of one of the lifeboats. When one tried to stand, he came up against the curve of the hull of the lifeboat, and this toppled him over the side. The man next to him tried to prevent him falling and he was pulled off, too. We turned quickly back to where they were in the water, but we had no rescue boat or even a gate in the rail at that time, so the engineer dove over the side, and pushing a life ring ahead of him, swam to where one of the men was treading water. He was holding up his friend by the hair, but the man's face was a foot or so underwater. When the engineer managed to get them alongside, we somehow manhandled them up the steep side of the vessel. The one who had been underwater was revived on deck by a doctor who happened to be on the passenger list.

After that we stowed a nine-foot Davidson rowboat on edge on the main deck and cut a proper gate into the solid bulwarks amidships on either side. We made a ladder of just the right size to be able to get into or out of a small boat, using it also at our regular passenger stops at camp floats as well. When a man jumped two years later, we were better prepared, but we still didn't have the procedure right, which created a delay getting him back aboard. Fortunately, he had changed his mind once he hit the cold ocean water and cooperated in the rescue. It wasn't until 1974 when a woman jumped at night that we were fully prepared and effected a rescue in good order.

In those early days the boat-deck space had been taken up with the two twenty-one-foot, clinker-built, double-ended wooden lifeboats, formerly belonging to the Canadian Pacific's *Princess Mary*, and the four luffing davits that were there to handle them. The unfortunate thing about these boats was that they were iron, rather than copper, fastened. The iron rivets eventually failed and caused the wood around them to rot, so that we were forced to replace one of the boats in 1976 with a new fibreglass twenty-foot Davidson lifeboat built in Vancouver. Meanwhile, John Friis replaced the four planks on either side of the keel on the other one, thus extending its life until 1985. It was necessary to have a little water in this one in summer to keep the wood swollen so it would not leak when put into the water. We did launch it at one annual inspection in Victoria and found that we almost couldn't lower it as fast as it filled with water. The inspector observed that it might be difficult to ask a little old lady to climb down a jacob's ladder and get into such a thing. Both lifeboats did, of course, have copper flotation tanks in them that were supposed to keep them afloat with a full complement of passengers even if totally flooded. However, it is probably a good thing that they were not put to the test in a real situation as it was difficult enough to handle them in practice.

From the beginning the boat lifting gear in the *Uchuck III* had been a little more modern than that in the two earlier ships. Instead of radial davits, there were luffing davits, which had an arm that, when the boat was lifted off the chocks, was cranked out rather than rotated to suspend the boat over the water for lowering. There was still the problem of controlling a one-ton boat in a seaway, so we had tricing lines to help keep the boat from swinging around, but it would be necessary to the get the boat down as fast as possible. We never even considered having people in it for that evolution. Once in the water, two men would jump into the boat to let go

Walter Winkler inspecting the funnel, which was sent to Port Alberni for sheet metal work.

the falls and, with help from on deck, they would move the boat up to the gate in the main deck bulwark to embark passengers.

As well as our cumbersome lifeboats, in the past there had been a stack of four buoyant apparatuses right in the middle of the deck space. These antiquated things were four-foot by four-foot wooden platforms with looped lines around the outside for people in the water to hang onto. For each of these rafts the flotation was provided by four copper tanks, which had to be taken out and tested every four years, taking an inordinate amount to time. Just the act of taking them apart each time helped to wear them out. Often repairs to the tanks were needed, leading us to believe that if we had had to use them in a real lifesaving situation, they may have been disappointing. With much smaller crews in modern times, all this type of equipment is hard to handle; two or three men trying to control a one-ton boat swinging in the air in darkness and lumpy seas would be, to say the least, difficult.

In the 1985 refit, because the regulations had changed for ships operating mostly in inshore waters and because new equipment had become available, we changed over from boats to rescue platforms, donut-shaped inflatable rafts that could be used either way up and could carry sixty-five persons. These platforms, housed in canisters, would self-inflate in the water when someone yanked on the lanyard, then they could be pulled up to the gate in the rail for loading. Our new rescue boat was a twelve-foot Davidson lifeboat with a twenty-horsepower outboard engine. This boat could to be used to collect the rafts once they were launched and then keep them together. As well, it could work independently at other times on other tasks, and even provided fun times for the crew. After the old lifeboats were gone, we installed the much smaller rafts and platforms on each side of the boat deck and the Davidson boat with its small davit on the starboard side. Now there was lots of space for more seating in an area where people could see all around.

At the same time that we changed all the emergency equipment, the whole boat deck was torn off, repaired and covered with a new urethane coating of a type used on the flight decks of aircraft carriers. Had these coatings been around when really good wood was commonly available, there would perhaps be many more old wooden vessels about. Certainly in our own company, much money had been spent doing and redoing these types of jobs in the past. The funnel and the engine room cowling ventilators were also removed during this refit and taken to Port Alberni in Walter's truck for repairs at a sheet metal shop, an event that left the vessel looking very strange indeed.

A slightly different formulation of the deck covering was used on the vertical steel of the wheelhouse, which required it to be sandblasted down to its grey metal. The eleven glass ports in their frames had to be unbolted and taken out and the spaces covered with plywood. As well, all the equipment on the top of the wheelhouse had to be removed and stored. We sailed on one of our periodic runs during this refit, with no ports in the wheelhouse, just open holes and nothing on the boat deck except two tons of black sand that was lying around from the blasting job. This was just about too much for me and I nearly lost my sense of humour. But it has been said that if you can't take a joke, you shouldn't be doing this stuff.

In the shipyard part of that refit, the vessel was put on three-foot-high blocks that were removed, a few at a time, in order to replace the wooden keel shoe. This shoe was made from twenty-foot lengths of four-inch by eleven-inch Australian gum wood and held on with big spikes. The job was done at night when the other work had stopped, and the crew, lying in our bunks, were treated to a thumping that shook the vessel for hours. It was good to have it done, though, because it made it possible to seal up the wooden keel to keep out the teredos.

During these years, the galley, wheelhouse, cook's cabin and master's cabin/office had also been gutted out, redesigned and rebuilt. The total rewiring of the vessel, which had been going on for three years, was also coming to completion. In 1987 the cargo winches were replaced with new (though twenty-year-old) units, still DC powered but much better than those we had before. In the hold we installed a walk-in cooler for perishable cargoes and an updated electric forklift truck, and we put in an electric pallet jack on deck.

In 1988 Point Hope had problems with its marine railway and needed time to repair the tracks and rollers under the carriage. One option open to us was to go to the Government Graving Dock but the cost would have been $17,000 for just the drying out. Besides, that facility had handled the *Queen Mary* during the last war, and we would have been lost in there, so in the end we went back to Yarrows.

At the end of all these refits we had a vessel in good condition that was reasonably well equipped for the work that we were doing, and she looked good. From almost losing the *Uchuck III,* we now had an asset that would take us into the future with only a regular maintenance schedule and elected upgrades. In addition, this vessel had become interesting in her own way by being an example of how water transportation had been done on this coast for more than a century. She had lived to become one of two surviving coasters of that style on the West Coast of Canada.

CHAPTER ELEVEN

Expanding Routes

Recession

In the late 1970s the forest industry had been in a major upswing on the western slopes of Vancouver Island so our company was very busy, and the resulting income allowed us to keep on track with our vessel refits. But cracks in the economy began to show by late 1981 and by early the next year the coastal forest industry had fallen into a serious recession, creating the need for major restructuring. The cost of running camps with crews living on site had become too much for most of the companies to fund, especially as more and more often the logging shutdowns were for market problems rather than the old problems of strikes, fire season and snow season. Wherever possible, they began closing bunkhouses and cookhouses and bringing workers in on a daily basis. This move was helped by the recent advent of the aluminum crew boat, which provided a means for transporting crews at whatever time the individual camps needed them. We could not adapt the *Uchuck*'s scheduling to the new conditions so these fundamental changes had the effect of reducing our cargoes and passenger lists and seriously reducing our revenues.

Subsidy Renewal

Then in 1982 our subsidy contract came up for renewal. We had been one of three companies on the West Coast of Vancouver Island receiving subsidies from the federal government, first directly from the Water Transport

Board in Ottawa and then from Ottawa via the provincial government. This meant that all our subsidies were taken from a single fund determined by the federal government. But that year a new arrangement was instituted: from now on, the British Columbia Ferry Corporation (BCFC) would be the issuer of contracts and be responsible for the amounts paid to the four original West Coast transportation companies and to the companies operating the smaller marine and inland lake routes formerly run by the Department of Highways. The federal government would have no more direct involvement.

The BCFC put out tenders to be returned on April 23, 1982, on three West Coast of Vancouver Island routes. The tender documents for our area echoed exactly the routes and services that the *Uchuck* was already performing. The contract was to be in effect for five years and then come up again in the same way, so we filled in the forms and sent them off, wondering what sort of changes to expect. At the time we were beginning that year's refit in Port Alberni and had just removed the old cargo winches for rebuilding at Alberni Engineering when we got word from BCFC that we had been underbid. This was a scary moment. We had no idea what would come next for us. Fortunately, the tender documents did state that the lowest bid would not necessarily be accepted, and it turned out that

The boat may be in refit at Point Hope but Walter Winkler and I are off to talk contract renewal with BC Ferries.

the other bidder had no equipment ready to put into service, so their bid was rejected.

We now learned that the BCFC wanted to combine two of the subsidized runs on the West Coast of the island under one contract. We were asked if we could handle the routes in Kyuquot Sound that were currently being served out of Fair Harbour by the *Patsco*, owned by Kyuquot Freight Services Ltd., as well as the routes we already served in Nootka Sound. With a little study we realized that we would need to make very little adjustment to fulfill this request. In fact, our running time would be increased by only two and a half hours to take the *Uchuck* from the last stop in Nootka Sound to the village inside Walter's Cove in Kyuquot Sound, and because of the slowdown in the forest industry, we would have sufficient time to fit in the extra running at not much more cost. So yes, we could do this as a two-day trip. The subsidy payment would now be a little more, and the revenue from the extra volume of cargo would help with the cost of the ongoing major refits that we had just undertaken. The BCFC was a winner as well because the new subsidy amount was less than the sum of the two previous amounts.

Kyuquot History

Kyuquot Sound is the traditional territory of the Kyuquot First Nation of the Nuu-Chah-Nulth people, and before Europeans arrived, these people occupied villages in Kyuquot Sound proper and in Checleset Bay, a little to the west but just short of Brooks Peninsula. The Kyuquots' principal village was Houpsitas, which lies on the mainland near the northern entrance to the Sound, while another group lived on nearby Aktis Island in the Mission Group. In the 1960s most of them were moved to live in government-built houses in the expanded Houpsitas village site.

After Captain Cook made contact with the Native people at Resolution Cove on Bligh Island in 1778 and learned about sea otter fur, the people from both Nootka and Kyuquot sounds were enlisted to catch them, and a lucrative trade in furs was established with China. The sea otters were depleted by the middle of the nineteenth century, and by the 1870s local people were hiring on to work in the northern fur seal hunt. In 1907 the Pacific Whaling Company set up a station in Cachalot Inlet, a small waterway extending southeastward on the south side of Kyuquot Channel;

A motorboat coming out to meet the *Uchuck III* at Kyuquot. ANDREW SCOTT PHOTO.

the station was closed in 1925 and Wallace Brothers converted it into a pilchard reduction plant that they ran from 1927 to 1937. Meanwhile, many of the Scandinavian workers from the whaling station had settled in Walter's Cove on Walter's Island, opposite Houpsitas, and used it as a base for commercial salmon fishing. The Red Cross established an outpost hospital there in 1937, and as there was soon a store, a school, a fish camp and boatways, it became the business centre for the Sound. The combined communities of Walter's Cove and the Native village of Houpsitas are usually referred to as Kyuquot.

When Nootka Sound Service arrived in Kyuquot Sound in 1982, there was a robust economy based on troll fishing and forestry, and because we were replacing an earlier freight service, our the company did not have to face the start-up difficulties it found in Nootka Sound in 1960.

Preparing for the New Route

Once we knew that we would be adding Kyuquot Sound to our schedule, the refit in May 1982 was expanded to include the installation of some extra navigational equipment. We would now be dealing with ocean conditions as we passed out through one rock pile at the seaward end of Esperanza Inlet to the ocean and then moving in through another

Most of the two crews plus office gal and one temporary deckhand. From left: Dave Holm, Dave Young, Kay Lowery, Eileen Erb, Keith Machin, Dan Newman, Evan Borovica, Walter Winkler, Angie O'Keeffe and Gary McDonald.

rock pile at the other end of a twelve-mile run as we entered Kyuquot Sound. There was no room for error here so we always needed to know without any doubt where we were at every moment while travelling in all seasons, night or day. To this end we fitted a Furuno 16 radar as back-up for our primary Decca radar, a Loran C navigator and a flasher sounder. This was still not a lot of equipment but was adequate for what we wanted to do.

We also reorganized our dock equipment at this time. Back in Port Alberni in 1958 we had bought a three-wheeled Mobilift forklift truck, an excellent machine, but when we first came to Nootka Sound, we couldn't use it at all because of the nature of the landing places, so it was parked in a corner in the after hold where it stayed for years. Once we had a wharf base, we traded it for an old 1946 Towmotor four-wheeled forklift truck owned by R and M Trucking of Campbell River. It was a better type for us, while they were in need of a short turning-circle machine to use in their warehouse. When we were in the market for a second one, we found it in Tahsis being used by the local freight company. This one was a 1956 Towmotor, which we could just barely lift with our ship's gear, so after we rebuilt it, it was confined to the Gold River wharf. It was purple and named Daphne. We thought we might mate it with old Huff, Suck and Blow, our first Towmotor, and maybe get a litter of pallet jacks. Didn't happen.

While we had always had a forklift in the hold to handle everything except coolers and freezers, we began to carry a second motor-driven fork-lift on deck to be put onto wharves or floats to take pallets and containers away from the ship's side and over to where trucks were waiting for them. When in Gold River, where we also kept a forklift, in one afternoon we could load a whole wharf-full of cargo with our crew of four. (In 2005, I was at a light industrial shop in Courtenay where I spotted a Mobilift fork-lift parked in the yard and, sure enough, it was the same machine we had bought in 1958, identifiable by the lifting lugs that we had welded onto it so that we could carry it around with us.).

When we first went to Kyuquot in 1982, we discovered a contraption in the government shed there that we thought we could use. It was a pair of forks attached to a metal frame; forks like those of a forklift truck. As they were not doing anything useful and had been there for a long time, we thought we could make a flying fork by adding an arm to the frame that projected over the forks. A slider was welded on to the arm so that a shackle could move up and down the length of the arm and fit into notches at each end. The cargo hook was hooked into the shackle and the forks slid into a pallet of any description to make the lift. When the forks were empty, the shackle was in the notch near the frame end so that the forks would fly level, and when loaded, the shackle was in the other notch, counterbalancing the load so it would stay level in flight. This was a neater way of moving pallets when we were working in tight quarters and was used as much as the pallet transporter system.

We knew that the start-up in Kyuquot Sound would not be the same struggle as had been the case in Nootka Sound. There were already large and busy logging camps in several places so we could count on a certain volume of cargo to be moved from the outset. The first trip on June 3, 1982, was busy with food, supplies and logging gear orders for people, stores and camps, none of whom we had dealt with before. It was a sudden immersion and we had to start swimming right away.

The First Kyuquot Run

My opposite number in the skipper's job, David Holm, came with us on the first run to Kyuquot so that we could establish a way of doing business in the sound that would be the same for both crews. David had first joined us in September 1976 as a deckhand/acting mate, and had worked his way up to skipper after getting a Watchkeeping Mate's certificate with a command endorsement and then serving as an alternate master. He served with the company until 1991.

Going to Kyuquot, the two of us recorded compass courses for running in fog and named unnamed points and islands so we would be working from the same logbook. As our crews did from time to time get shuffled about for various reasons, we did not want them to have to learn two ways for doing everything.

On that first run there was a good load of groceries on board for everyone including the Kyuquot Market, which was the general store in Walter's Cove, so we unloaded our big old 7,000-pound Towmotor forklift onto the government wharf in the Cove to move the containers around. But as soon as the forklift started to move, there was an ominous mushing sound as its hard rubber wheels started to go through the tired old two-inch deck planking. We put it back on board immediately. Instead, from then on we used the Kyuquot Market's small garden tractor with its four-wheeled trailer, which had been the longstanding way for transporting goods to the store at the head of the wharf. (It often carried a load of kids for the ride back.) The tractor was already old then but it had not been used often, so it was still in good condition. A few weeks after that run, we carried the new deck planking for repairs to the wharf and its approach, cut in the small custom mill at Ceepeecee in Tahsis Narrows.

The logging camp floats in Kyuquot Sound had been set up to accommodate the *Patsco*, which had been operating there before we arrived. She was a side-loading vessel, too, though half the size of the *Uchuck*, but our ship was more manoeuvrable because of her twin screws, so little change to the float systems was required beyond shifting the tie-up points. The comment of the logging camp superintendent at Chamis Bay was simply, "Oh well, something else to get used to."

When we were preparing for this new route, we had to take into account that we would be receiving perishable goods for these ports days in advance of sailing, so we acquired four cast-off portable cooler/freezer units from Coast Ferries in Vancouver and had them rebuilt. We could load one or more as needed for any given trip, leave them in the wharf shed in Gold River plugged in until sailing day, and then plug them in again once they were on board. In addition, we still had our old built-in cooler in the hold so we were reasonably well equipped to handle whatever came, although occasionally the hot summer weather did create a problem. (We installed a walk-in cooler in the hold in 1987.)

In our most recent refit we had also built some four by four by three-foot-deep open-topped stackable containers that made the stowage of cargo a one-time handling event and helped keep the cargo separated. Cargo for Kyuquot that came days before sailing could be stored in these containers and left in the wharf shed until loading time and still not interfere with our Nootka Sound cargoes.

We began our regular service to Kyuquot by leaving Gold River on Saturdays at 07:00 loaded for Port Eliza and all the Kyuquot Sound ports. We were usually clear of Port Eliza between 13:00 and 15:00, and if the weather was passable, we would arrive at Walter's Cove sometime in the late afternoon. There would be a flurry of activity in Kyuquot as we unloaded, loaded the outgoing cargo and then left for the International Forest Products camp at Chamis Bay farther up in the Sound. If the weather was truly wild, I would head the ship the long way around Union Island rather than chance the short way up the trickier Crowther Channel. After unloading at Chamis Bay, we went to Freil Lake Logging at Janis Bay, the next bay over, to unload and then called it a day. The camp there had a tiny float that was tucked around the point of land at the entrance to the bay. Once we were within a hundred feet of this float, even if there was a strong southeast wind blowing, it passed over top of us, giving us good shelter for the night. In the morning we went over to Hankin Cove across the Sound with the last of our cargo, and by noon we were usually ready to start back toward Gold River. Along the way we did any extra inter-port work.

To leave the Sound, we ran down Kyuquot Channel toward the ocean to see what changes had occurred in the weather overnight. On one trip while we were doing this, we found that the wind had risen to storm force southeast. The hinged lids on the chained-down garbage dumpsters we were carrying on deck blew open, revealing a mass of magazines and books minus their covers that the store in Kyuquot was throwing out. The wind happily plucked them out and sent them off to leeward like batches of confetti at a wedding.

We had much to learn about what conditions were suitable to travel in on the new route, and we experienced some weather where it would have been better to wait a while before travelling between the sounds. We had never cancelled a run within Nootka Sound and the inlets because of weather, but at times we had to make the decision not to go on the ocean leg of the Kyuquot run at the scheduled time if it seemed that we were near the height of a major gale. Even then, we never delayed until after we had tried to go out, in case things were not as bad out there as forecast. We tried because people were expecting to travel or to receive the cargo that we had on board, but if we pushed too hard, we ran the risk of damaging the cargo, frightening our passengers, doing damage to the vessel or worse. Often the situation would change in a few hours so we could just hang out and patiently wait until conditions improved. If we were unlucky, usually in the depth of winter, we would get gales back-to-back with no chance to move in between. Then the wait would get longer or, if we ran out of time, the trip would have to be cancelled. The trick was to find out how far we could push it before we would actually be working against ourselves. I am pleased to say that in the twelve years up to 1994 that we covered both sounds, we only had to cancel two runs and delay a few more.

One of the reasons for our difficulties with weather in this area had to do with water depth. The near shore route that we followed between the sounds is only ten to twelve fathoms deep, so storm seas there are shorter and steeper, more than is the case farther out to sea. On one trip near the beginning of these runs, it took me five hours to go from Kyuquot to Esperanza Inlet, normally a one-hour run. We had started out in a rising gale that gave us a royal beating even after we moved ten miles offshore to try to find easier travelling. Apart from the wild ride, the difficult bit was turning to enter Esperanza Inlet, which left us beam-on to the wind and sea and barely able to control the direction of travel. Even with full power applied, the helmsman had to keep the helm nearly hard-to-port to steer the course that was needed. The configuration of the vessel's superstructure was such that she weather-cocked and was trying to round up into the wind. Any more wind than that and we would have had to heave-to or run back to where we came from.

On a later run we learned something new about the *Uchuck*'s behaviour in these waters. The previous day the weather had been too vicious for us to leave Port Eliza in Esperanza Inlet to go up the outside to Kyuquot Sound, so we had lain over there for the night, hoping that this major southeast gale would subside. It did, and the wind veered into the southwest, indicating the backside of the storm, and that allowed us to go on about our business. When our schedule was interrupted like this, we often reversed the order of events in Kyuquot Sound, delivering to the ports in the Sound proper before going to Walter's Cove. This meant that we travelled westward in Crowther Channel. On this occasion we were almost to the ocean, headed out past Amos Island to go around and into Walter's Cove, and we could see that although the gale had subsided, the huge southwesterly swells had not. They needed a lot more time to go down, but they looked spectacular as they bashed up on rocks and islands close around us.

That was when the old girl poked her nose skyward, paused and then fell. She stopped cold with a crash and shudder that ran through the entire vessel, as if she had struck some part of Canada. In the wheelhouse Glen and I stepped back together and said in unison, "Oh, shit!"

Out on the ocean, a ship simply toils up one side of a swell and slides down the other, but in shallowing water the dynamics change. When the swells smell the bottom, they slow down through friction, but since all that energy has to go somewhere, it goes up. The swells get higher and, more importantly, closer together. Unless the vessel slows down, it has no time to recover after plunging into one trough before the next crest comes. We had simply not been paying attention to our speed. Had we been going the other way in this channel in these conditions, we would have had an exhilarating surfing experience, and I would have been taking pictures and having a good time. But here, we were making our usual twelve knots as we approached the western end of the channel where the swells were marching toward us at fifteen knots, giving a closing speed of twenty-seven knots.

We were lucky that the engineer had not stopped the engines when he felt the hit, maybe thinking that we had hit something real, and it would have been understandable for him to think that. But if he had stopped the machinery, it could have been disastrous. We were in a narrow section of the channel that shoals to become almost a bar with a set of fangs that we call Nicolaye Reef close aboard to port, so we needed to keep going. Fortunately, similar although lesser situations had occurred before, and it had been decided after internal discussions that it was better for the engineer to always wait to be told to stop, regardless of how the situation looked to him down below. As it was, on this occasion the old vessel gathered way again and we carried on, made the various turns and went safely into Walter's Cove.

I thought it prudent to have a good look around to see if there were any problems resulting from this incident, and I discovered that the ship had flexed so much that there was a crippled metal stanchion in the cargo hold and all the nails holding the ceiling—the light inner planking on top of the frames on both sides in the forward part of the hold—had popped out, leaving the nail heads sticking out a quarter of an inch. She was not making any water, but right away a note went onto the refit list to be sure to inspect the hull closely when she was next on the cradle at the shipyard.

The question then became: "Why did this flexing happen?" With a little thought, the answer was evident. The vessel had been designed and built as a mine sweeper. In that role she had to be fast and strong, so the beam was less than if she had been designed to maximize carrying capability. When converted to a small coaster, she would carry cargo, which was best carried in the fattest part of the ship—the middle. As a mine sweeper the work deck had run from the middle of the vessel to the after end, but to make the vessel useful to us, we had disconnected then jacked up all the housework in one piece and rolled it aft thirty feet. To do this, all the hold-down bolts that went from the top of the cabin edges, down through the main deck to strong points in the space below had to be cut. These bolts through the housework, when it was in its original position, provided stiffening for the whole ship structure. Adding to the problem was the eight-foot by sixteen-foot hatch cut into the deck where the housework had been. As the breadth of the vessel at this point is only twenty-two feet, it was no wonder she flexed when she fell off that one big swell.

One could argue that you shouldn't fool with a ship's design, but this vessel had operated in this configuration for over half a century. We owed her longevity to her original heavy scantlings. When doing the ongoing repairs, we never went back to original specifications as the cost would have been prohibitive, yet we still had lots of reserve strength for our purposes. Repairs had been made as wood rotted with time and as damage was done from the endless landings and the handling and carriage of many thousands of tons of cargo. Over the years 90 percent of the deck and hull planks above the waterline had been replaced, many of them several times, all adding credence to the idea that a wooden vessel is a living thing. As with a DC 3 aircraft, after a number of years the only thing original is the name and number.

It had simply been a few moments of not thinking that created the situation that we had found ourselves in that day. We should have been going more slowly at the time.

A Winter's Passage to Kyuquot

Some customers in Kyuquot Sound were initially doubtful that we would be able to keep to our sailing schedule in the winter months. However, in designing it, we had taken into account the fact that there would be periods of heavier business activity where more time would be needed to

There's nothing like taking the groceries home and anticipating that next big meal. Here a pallet of groceries from town is picked up by a herring punt and taken across the bay in Walter's Cove, Kyuquot.

get the work done, so we had made our overall schedule slack enough that even with a weather delay, we could always be back in Gold River in time for the next scheduled run. In order to put together a combined schedule for both sounds, we had dropped one of our three round trips in Nootka Sound, but that still left the option of making deliveries within the Sound, if necessary, while on the run to Kyuquot as we had to pass through the whole of Nootka Sound when heading for Kyuquot.

I remember one winter trip in particular. Heavy rain was falling at 07:00 on that dark morning in December. I topped up my coffee cup in the galley and headed for the wheelhouse to wind the clock, open the log book for the day, turn on the four radios, the radar and the running lights. When all was ready, I rang up standby on the engine room telegraph and got the answering bells in response. The lines were let go, brought in and we were on our way. There was a gale warning posted, but within the inlets of the Sound, we were sheltered from the ocean swells though not the wind, which in itself could give us interesting times as we went in and out of the places that we visited. All going well, we would end the day at Kyuquot.

We worked our way from port to port discharging cargo—a truck here, a lift of lumber there and a couple of pallets of groceries for a small logging operation—until we had delivered several tons of cargo of all descriptions to ports in Nootka Sound. Then we started out of Esperanza Inlet toward Port Eliza and the logging camp where we would finish delivering our Nootka Sound cargo. We had a preview of the current ocean conditions by looking to seaward as we turned into Port Eliza from the Inlet. Not good.

At this last stop we delivered a week's supply of everything for a large logging camp, a job that took more than two hours. It was 13:30 when discharging was complete, and it was time to secure the vessel for the offshore portion of the journey. In settled weather, it would only take three hours from Port Eliza to reach Kyuquot, but it could take much longer if we had to struggle with bad weather and sea conditions. Naturally we always hoped for a decent day, but when it wasn't, we went to extra effort in the lashing and stowing of everything on the vessel.

On our way out of the camp and before we got beyond the end of Esperanza Inlet, I checked for the latest weather forecast and especially the latest local weathers, both of which are broadcast at 13:50. One by one the crew joined me in the wheelhouse, which they always did on a day like this in order, I suspect, to see what the old guy was going to decide to do this time. When we heard that the sea conditions for our area were "combined wind wave and swell height of two to three metres," they would just shrug and shuffle off to do something else, but if the word was for five to seven metres or greater, their faces would grow more thoughtful because they knew that this would be something more to deal with.

In recent years I had found that weather forecasting on the West Coast was about 80 percent correct, especially in winter, partly because the weather we encountered out there had not been modified by landforms yet, so it was pretty much as dictated by the pressure systems. We could read between the lines of the forecast and local conditions as reported by the light keepers and apply it to our particular area. In any event, we would go out and have a look at it. During a discussion with a local friend on how we did our job, he paid us the compliment of saying, "You always say that you'll go out and have a look at it and then we never see you again." The other thing I had learned about the weather on the West Coast was that if you waited six hours, odds were that you would be looking at something quite different.

On one delayed run, I had decided that we would stay overnight tied to the camp float in the shelter of Port Eliza. Before early darkness set in with its low clouds and heavy rain, we readied the vessel for the move early the next morning and rigged extra mooring lines for the night. Then we put tomorrow out of mind.

Since I had decided that we were to stay, the next couple of hours were my own so, before full darkness, I went for a walk up the logging road toward the camp five miles away. I went far enough to get to a place where I could see out over the water. The exercise felt good as it helped to bleed off the tension that had built up over the previous hours. When I walked back to the warm, dry and brightly lit vessel, supper was about ready and the crew was gathered in the mess room. After dinner there was time to talk and play a hand of cards, but no one stayed up late because we knew that tomorrow would start early.

On this current trip, the forecast seemed reasonable so I decided to carry on. We left the camp in Port Eliza to return to the entrance of the inlet before hauling around for Gillam Channel and the ocean. The swell was large even this far into Esperanza Inlet. Once clear of the nearby small islands, we looked for the two channel buoys, five and six miles out. When it was not raining, we knew we should see them, and if we did, then we watched to see if they dipped out of sight behind the swells. If they did that, then we looked to see how long they were gone from sight. On this day they disappeared for a longer time than they were visible, which indicated a very large swell. The farther we went, the more the vessel lifted and fell. Water came over the fo'c'sle in driven sheets and piled up on the face of the wheelhouse, shutting off visibility for ten seconds or more at a time. Then the fo'c'sle started to go right into the odd swell, throwing up large slugs of water, and we were glad to have the three-quarter-inch-thick tempered glass in the round ports.

As we approached the Middle Reef buoy, which is actually sitting over a bar and partly accounts for the short steep sea there, the outgoing tidal current only added to the fun. But it leveled off a bit beyond this point and as we got to the channel entrance buoy, we made the ninety degree turn that headed us off to the west. We were out through the rock pile by now and had the wind well aft. From here we had a true picture of conditions, which now seemed quite passable. We had a heavy southwest ground swell more or less on the nose, a rough southeast sea on top that had been generated by the wind, and a leftover southerly sea from somewhere far out on the ocean. The vessel didn't know what to do with all these wave trains so she bucked, jumped and rolled all over the place. (The *Uchuck* can easily roll through an arc of seventy degrees.)

When we were clear of the mouth of Esperanza Inlet, the effect of the outgoing tide lessened and things settled down a bit. I jammed myself into the corner of the wheelhouse, and since the wind was more aft, I opened one of the ports and stuck an elbow out. The mate and I talked over what we had to do at the next port of call, raising our voices to be heard over the roaring of the wind and the moaning and thrumming it made in the several antennae on top of the wheelhouse. At least the rain and spray were now blowing past us from astern.

An hour and a half later we approached the Kyuquot channel buoy, which until now we'd had difficulty seeing either by eye or radar. We altered course to enter the Sound, bringing the swell onto the port beam and causing some prodigious rolls. Gradually they eased off as we passed through the Barrier Islands and turned up into the passage between them and Union Island, toward the settlements at Kyuquot. Walter's Cove lies sheltered in the middle of a group of islands, the shelter provided in part by a stand of huge old spruce trees.

Suddenly, having threaded our way between the islands, we were out of the weather, and we had only the rain to contend with as we went alongside the wharf to secure. The crew went into action, knocking out the wedges that held the hatch battens in place, taking off the hatch tarp and boards, letting go lashings and digging out equipment to begin discharging cargo. The cook in the meantime had resurfaced, reassembled her galley and begun to make a whole mess of spaghetti, homemade clam sauce and garlic bread—a hot and fast supper.

Work done and supper finished, it was only 21:30 but everyone headed off to burrow into their bunks. The wind continued to roar in the spruce trees but not across the wharf. We were content to deal with tomorrow when tomorrow came.

It was not all ugly winter weather. Some runs on the ocean were totally delightful and benign, even in the winter months. The sea was dark blue, foaming brightly on the rocks, the hills capped with snow, and the air sharp and clear, more so than in summer. On days like this it was good to see everything in technicolour to remind us of what it could be like.

Passengers

In the 1980s tourism was gaining in importance to the company so we paid more attention to it. We ran more day tours as well as two overnight cruises that required bed and breakfast arrangements at Tahsis and Kyuquot. This meant more effort and time on our part to make sure that there would be no problems with scheduling and reservations. The overnight runs started early in the day, so most people liked to come into the area the day before and stay overnight on the day that we returned. Thus, we had to be ready to direct people to B & Bs, motels, hotels, restaurants and any other services that they might need in the Gold River area. Soon the villages of Tahsis and Gold River became interested in tourist travel and, in their attempts to foster economic diversification, they hired economic development officers. Tourists had been coming through Gold

River since 1960 to come specifically to the ship, but as the villages grew, there began to be services for the travelling tourist. As well as accommodation and restaurants, they began offering fishing charters and caving adventures, which gave reasons for tourists to spend more time in the area. Once a week the Chamber of Commerce in Tahsis sponsored a one-hour bus tour of the village and mill site for the passengers booked on our day trip to Tahsis, and we would call in as we approached to say how many we had for the tour and were met by a van and guide. In Kyuquot the over-nighters sometimes had offers from the local people to take them out for short tours in the evening to the islands and beaches outside of the Cove. This sort of thing helped our mini-cruise have the feel of being much longer as it started early in the morning, ended twelve or more hours later, then began again early the following day.

In the beginning we understood that we were not licensed to carry passengers on the ocean part of the new run, but it wasn't long before we discovered that we could carry some passengers by making a few changes to the *Uchuck*'s lifesaving gear. That done, we could carry twelve persons, although this capacity was not much used because a regular water link to Nootka Sound had never been available in the past so most people in the Sound kept cars at Fair Harbour and went in and out that way. Then a few tourists began

Ready to sail, but where are the passengers? Here we are waiting at Walter's Cove.

to book passage with us. They needed overnight accommodation in Walter's Cove so the Kyra family opened a bed and breakfast, and as it is a great run with lots of variety in the scenery, it soon attracted more and more people. The numbers that we were able to carry increased later, although I was always nervous about having passengers on board in rough weather, even just the stiff westerlies of summer. As many of the people interested in booking for this run were middle-aged or older, I worried that some might be too fragile to be tossed about by the ocean in our active little coaster.

The overnight trip to Kyuquot involved two hours of open water on the way there and the same on the way back, so if the weatherman had served up some wind and swell, the passengers would just have to endure it. Most were fine with this, but even in summer there can be a sharp westerly with action enough to make people sick. When that happened there was often a chain reaction, which then gave the crew something to do—passing buckets and cleaning up. When the motion stopped, most people recovered quickly and soon were hungry again.

For some people the run was memorable, far beyond what they had imagined. On one such trip five couples came on board, all of them quiet by nature and all unknown to each other. This was the two-day trip where they would stay overnight in the bed and breakfast in Kyuquot. But it was a proper summer day so they moved around the vessel, watching the action at the various ports, and they soon began to talk to each other and the crew as they figured out what was happening. As one would understand something new about the activity on the dock or in the water, he would pass it on to his neighbour and then they discuss what should happen next. They got along with each other very well so by the end of the trip, back in Gold River, they were all friends. On leaving, they stood around on the wharf for the next half hour exchanging addresses and talking about a reunion next year before separating, climbing into their cars and leaving.

We discovered that there are a few people who really like to travel in winter, but I would always caution them to make sure they knew what they might experience. One winter a lady really wanted to go to Kyuquot, so after I was satisfied that she knew what was possible and I had explained that the bed and breakfast there would be closed, I told her to get her sleeping bag out of her truck because I wasn't sure that we would return on the day that we were supposed to as the weather forecast was not good.

She was fine with that and happily spent a night on one of the tables that knocked down to become a bunk.

By this time kayaking on the West Coast was becoming very popular. People would drive to the heads of the inlets at Port Alberni, Gold River, Fair Harbour and anywhere else that would bring them to salt water. They would launch there in order to paddle to unpopulated areas with lots of islands and protected waterways, places where they could camp on sand and shell beaches. To reach good kayaking areas in Kyuquot Sound, they had the choice of driving into Fair Harbour and paddling twenty miles to the Bunsby Islands, a mecca for kayakers, or coming with us from Gold River to Walter's Cove and then having only eight miles to paddle to their destination. Starting at the Cove gave them an advantage as it provided a good staging point and a place to come and wait for us on their way out. There was even one young woman who appeared with a kayak between Christmas and the New Year wanting to go to Kyuquot and camp out in the islands for a week. She was obviously well equipped and able, so she came and everything worked out well.

The first kayaks we saw on the West Coast had been made of canvas

The Kyuquot Inn in Walter's Cove, popular with kayakers and ready for guests at the end of the *Uchuck III*'s run from Gold River. PATRICIA STEEB PHOTO.

Being hoisted over the side for a wet launch proved popular with kayakers. ANDREW SCOTT PHOTO.

over a wood frame or were wooden planked and usually built by those who paddled them. But in the 1960s there was a production explosion of fibreglass vessels of all types, kayaks included, and because they were less expensive and simple and tough, the sport flourished all over the coast. In Nootka Sound the islands off the west end of Bligh Island and in the Nuchatlitz area across to Catala Island in Esperanza Inlet were ideal for kayaking, and in Kyuquot Sound it was the Bunsbys. We began to carry these small vessels around and deposit them at the logging camp nearest to where people wanted to paddle. They unloaded all their gear onto the logging company's float, got organized and shoved off for a week or for whatever time we arranged with them. At the end of the time we came back and reloaded them for the return trip.

Soon we came up with the idea that we might be able to wet-launch kayaks almost any place. We devised a way to lash the cargo-lifting bars to a substantial four-by-six-foot freight pallet, adding two ex-grader blades as ballast to the underside, so that when the pallet was lifted over the side and put into the water, it would sink. A half hour before the vessel arrived at the launch point, the kayak was placed on deck and loaded with all its gear, food and water. When the vessel stopped, the kayaker—or two if it was a double kayak—got in and put on splash skirts, then the kayak was lowered into the water by the cargo winches. The pallet dropped out from under the kayak and was retrieved. In this way, within a few minutes six or more kayaks could be afloat and ready to set off on an adventure. At an agreed time and place we would meet them and reverse the process. Some kayakers even said that they came with us just for the experience of loading and unloading. At times there were as many as twenty of these units on board, coming and going from different places. On their return we had to make sure the galley was well supplied with chili and especially Nanaimo bars, as these people had good appetites.

Dangerous Cargo

One problem for which we never found a proper solution concerned dangerous cargo, a term that covers a multitude of goods but really came down to two—explosives and propane—and we carried lots of both of these. In the past we had carried explosives for all destinations on the run to the Port Eliza logging camp, which we made every two weeks from Gold River. But after the Kyuquot run became popular with tourists, we no longer had any passenger-free runs, so we couldn't carry dangerous cargo there, although we might take a propane tank to Friendly Cove or one of the tourist fishing camps out that way. We just had to be fully aware of what we had on board and make sure no one was leaning on a propane tank with a cigarette in hand or doing some other dumb thing. We never made carrying propane tanks a secretive activity; it was just a fact of life that we had to supply what people needed in that part of the world.

We had begun delivering bulk diesel fuel in the 1970s. We were not at all equipped for this work although we had always carried fuel, both gasoline and diesel, in drums as regular deck cargo. Most of the bulk fuel for the region came in tankers and then barges from refineries on the mainland, but occasionally a camp would run out of fuel between barge deliveries. At that point, unless they knew that the barge would be arriving in the next day or so, they would have to send their workers home, a costly move. One day when we stopped at Mooyah Bay, the camp superintendent asked if there was any way we could help before their supply ran out. The fuel barge was on its way but had been held up, waiting for the weather to improve in the Strait of Juan de Fuca. We were not a tanker in any way, but we did have a fuel capacity of twenty-two thousand litres in our own tanks when they were full up, so we just needed to find a way to transfer some of it to the camp's tanks. We had a small portable electric transfer pump that we could employ and with the addition of a few pipe fittings, we used it to pump—with some difficulty—from our own tanks into theirs and saved the day for that camp. If this had been anywhere near a large centre, we could not have got away with doing this, but out on the coast it was considered a business emergency.

After this event at Mooyah Bay, the situation arose again from time to time and then more and more often. In the meantime, on instruction from Canadian Safety Inspections, we had acquired a motorized Honda trash pump as an emergency fire pump and mounted it in a semi-permanent enclosure on the after deck. We began to use this as a transfer pump for fuelling jobs, but while it was better than the portable electric pump, gasoline and hot exhaust are not what you want around a fuel pumping station. As time went on, supplying fuel became more of a regular event, especially as the intervals between barge deliveries became longer. In addition, some of the logging operations were very small and ran for such a short duration that they never set up a tank farm, relying instead on a fuel tank or two on a float. In these cases the volume of fuel required was too small to have the fuel barge come in, so we began to serve them as well.

The answer to our pumping problem came from the fuel agent in Gold River. Cliff Craig was enterprising and wanted to increase his business, so with his help we worked out better ways of moving fuel safely and accurately. He supplied us with a proper fuel meter and good hoses so it became a simple and safe operation to move fuel in these small quantities. The meter was plumbed into our own on-board fuel transferring system in the engine room. It was then just a matter of taking the end of the hose below and connecting it to a fuel fitting so that the engineer could start pumping and also monitor the flow. We could only move twenty thousand litres at a time, after which we would be in danger of running ourselves out of fuel to get home. In those days the average logging camp had a tank farm capacity of approximately four hundred thousand litres of diesel as well as a small amount of gasoline, so what we brought to them provided only a temporary fix, but it was still useful for keeping the camp operating.

As log quotas grew smaller and log market problems occurred more often, the logging camps in the sounds faced longer shutdown periods, which made the scheduling of fuel deliveries by barge uncertain. And because the barge needed to start out from the refinery with a full load to make the trip worthwhile, there were more and more times when camps went short. Occasionally the bulk plant operator in Gold River had to charter the local equipment barge to take his fuel truck on board to deliver truckloads of fuel to nearby camps. At the same time the area's marine fuel stations, which were also supplied by the barges, experienced less traffic as the commercial fishing fleet was reduced in size. Then, with the virtual demise of the troll fishery, traffic decreased so much for the bulk fuel distributor in Kyuquot that his business was no longer viable, so he shut down his fuel station and dismantled his tank farm. From that time on, local vessels needing fuel had to get it while they were outside the area or else have fuel drums sent in with us. These mini-shipments increased the expense to the customers, but there was no alternative.

Returnables

About this time environmentalists were raising the alarm about what was happening to British Columbia's land and water, and one area of concern was the disposition of used oil, which was simply dumped on the ground in the logging camps or sometimes used as a form of dust control on roads. Now there was pressure to do better. There had always been some re-refining of used oil, but since it was a cheap commodity, it had not been economical to gather it up and send it back. But the rise in price added to the growing environmental concern changed this, so that we began to see a traffic in containers that were dedicated to bringing back used oil. These "lube cubes," which held four barrels of product, became one more regular item on our cargo manifests.

One other type of traffic relating to fuel was the one-way transport of fuel drums: we brought them to the camps full, and when they were empty, they were most often just kicked aside. There had always been a deposit on the empties, but it was so low that it was not worth going to the effort of gathering them up to be sent back, so they piled up. In the 1980s that deposit was raised significantly, and as the fuel company representatives made their rounds of the camps, they began to talk up the idea of recycling them. Now there began to be a greater traffic in empties going back, but there was a huge backlog to clean up. One day as we went up Zeballos Arm, we saw a curious large red blotch on the hillside at Barr Creek. It turned out to be the red ends of about five hundred empty barrels, which had been gathered up to be shipped out. The *Uchuck* could only carry two hundred at a time in the hold, enough to fill one forty-foot trailer to the doors. Over a half year or so we caught up with the backlog everywhere and thereafter got a few at a time from each camp, keeping the situation sane.

Two other types of returnables that still have not found their way back to their sources in any numbers are empty pallets and empty wire reels. So much cargo is carried on pallets for ease of handling by forklift trucks that there are millions of pallets in transit at any one time. In the sounds the ones that were returned included those that carried oil products in cases and pails, explosives, fish feed and wholesale groceries. Those industries want them back as they have been constructed specially to size and design for their products, and they charge the consignee a deposit if they are not returned. In the logging camps some pallets were used to send out machinery parts or anything else that would fit on them, but most went onto the burn pile. (We learned that one small pallet, smashed up and burned in the barbeque, was enough to cook four steaks.) The wire reels, with a few exceptions, were never sent back, even though the big ones were very strongly built of hardwoods and steel and cost into the hundreds of dollars to construct. They had to be strong as a reel with steel wire rope wound around it weighed up to five tons. But these things are scattered about the coast wherever there has been a logging operation, and you can find them used as tables and work surfaces all over BC.

There always has been a bounty on empty beer cans and bottles in this province, and because we operated on the frontier, we transported multitudes of them. We found they were best handled in containers as their cardboard cartons had usually been torn; if they came to us on pallets, we could be sure that we would be cleaning up a mess. In any case, the sailors always looked them over carefully because once in a while they would find an unopened full bottle that had been overlooked.

Garbage

I was sitting in the crew's messroom aboard the *Uchuck III* having a mug-up and a bit of a rest as we travelled along when Ruth Masters, environmentalist extraordinaire, marched around the end of the coffee counter and plunked herself down on a stool beside me. "David," she said, "you can't do that anymore."

"Huh?"

She pointed to the five-gallon bucket on the floor in the coffee shop, the bucket for food scraps, opened tins, styrofoam cups and anything else that was being thrown out. The next deckhand on the way through would grab it and dump it over the side.

When man first ventured out onto the water, anything he didn't want he tipped over the edge and it was gone. In Nootka Sound this practice carried on unchanged almost to that day in 1969 when Ruth boarded the *Uchuck III* with a group from the Historical Society of Comox, headed out on a day trip to Friendly Cove. On that day the change in how garbage was handled in Nootka Sound began. I thought about what she had said, made some enquiries at the village office in Gold River and, yes, it would be possible to have a dumpster set on the wharf and to have the village garbage truck come by to empty it once a week for a small fee.

Up until the 1960s even ports like Vancouver and New York had garbage scows that were towed out each night and dumped at designated sites. The military had sites for dumping old ordnance, those places being marked on the hydrographic charts so that fishermen would not trawl over them and snag the old shells. Raw sewage was dumped by cities and towns directly into the ocean. When crossing from Vancouver to Nanaimo or Victoria on CPR ships and then on BC Ferries, one always saw a cloud of gulls following the ships, waiting for the scraps to be tossed, and they weren't disappointed. The slogan on the sides of buses even said, "Follow the Birds to Victoria!" Then legislation was passed that cities had to build sewage plants to render the output harmless. And then it became mandatory that larger ships—and now vessels down to the smallest—must have a system built in to either treat and release or hold the material for disposal ashore or at the very least dump it out in deep water.

Possibly the single biggest factor in bringing awareness of the problem to the forefront was the advent of the plastic container. Before plastic, most throwaways broke down and returned to their elemental form and didn't cause damage unless in great concentrations. But plastic doesn't break down in the environment, and because it floats, it piles up on the beaches.

There began a local movement to halt this dumping when there was a high-tide line of white Styrofoam cups beginning to form on the shores of Washington state and Vancouver Island. This was probably a little before the day that Ruth came with us to Friendly Cove, but not by much.

In the logging camps, garbage had been either dumped into shallow pits in the ground or chucked into the water where it floated away. I remember a dump truck coming regularly to the wharf in Port McNeil back in 1960 and simply dumping camp garbage into the harbour. We berthed the *Uchuck III* at the other end of that wharf when we came in with cargo because it was too slippery to walk around at the dump end. Sometimes on our way into Kyuquot, we would pass bagged garbage coming out on the ebb tide. It would end up on the nearby beaches where it would sit until the birds and animals got into it for what they wanted, leaving the rest scattered about. In some camps garbage was burned on the beach at low tide; later they switched to burning it in a barrel ashore, then went high-tech with an oil-fired incinerator that consumed everything. But some of those materials being burned contained a lot of noxious substances that were best not put into the atmosphere, so another solution was needed.

This problem existed in all the remote places that we served until we began hauling empty dumpsters from Gold River to the camps and villages. Once filled and back in Gold River, the material was taken to the town's sophisticated waste management centre where it was sorted for recyclables, with the remainder going to the landfill and compost areas. That mountain of compost was sold to the people of the town as soil for an area that did not have much.

In the 1960s it had become mandatory for companies closing down logging and mining camps and other work sites to take everything away that had been brought in. The ground had to be levelled and the whole site returned to a condition as close to original as was possible. This included planting trees and grass and deactivating old logging roads. As well as getting rid of stuff left over from their own operations, they had to deal with the rubbish from previous operations at the same sites. Old bone yards of defunct machinery had to be dug up and removed, and the government gave contracts to salvage companies to go around the coast to clean up the very old sites. At last it became a natural way of thinking for companies and individuals to automatically do the right things. I once saw one of my crew, as he walked down the deck, take the last cigarette out of a pack and, instead of tossing the empty pack over the side, as I probably would have done at his age, take it inside and put it in the waste bucket.

From the beginning with that one dumpster for the *Uchuck III*'s garbage on the Gold River wharf, the movement has multiplied. Today the ship carries many of these to villages, fish farms, logging camps and anywhere else where people gather and make garbage. We are advancing. The younger generations take the new behaviour as normal while we dinosaurs from earlier generations slowly die out.

Tree Planting

As in Nootka Sound there was tree planting in Kyuquot Sound. Some contractors moved their people and equipment through Fair Harbour, while others came up the outside from Nootka Sound and then moved from place to place within Kyuquot Sound. On one occasion we made a special arrangement to go into Fair Harbour, pick up people, gear and trucks, and move the whole lot to one of the camps. We always tried to hurry with special jobs of this kind because they really altered the scheduled run back to Gold River, although in winter, if there were no passengers for the run

All aboard at Mooyah Bay, this tree planting crew catches a ride to the nearest road aboard the *Uchuck III* in September 2011. JAYA SURJADINATA PHOTO.

back, we sometimes stopped for the night somewhere along the route before getting to Gold River.

Fish Farming

In the middle of 1987 we began to get the first enquiries about prices to haul fish feed for proposed fish farms in the Kyuquot area. It was only talk at that time but was something for us to keep in mind. However, we didn't know if we would become involved at all as their needs seemed to be beyond what we could do for them. However, by 1989 Envirocon was farming Atlantic salmon at Centre Cove on Whitely Island in Kyuquot Channel. One day Keith Machin, who had come to us as a deckhand/ acting mate in August 1976 and had by this time worked his way up to relieving master, took the *Uchuck* into the farm site to see if we could be of service to them. The upshot of that visit was the transportation of a trial load of fish feed. As the farms don't need much feed at the beginning when the smolts are tiny, this was a good introduction. From that trial we developed a regular service to provide feed for this company.

Fish farms are located at sites where there is a good flushing current so that the water near the pens stays clean, but we had to learn to watch those currents while manoeuvring the vessel alongside the feed sheds. We also had to dodge the lines running from the pens and buoys to the anchors that were all over the place, holding everything together. I soon learned to call ahead on the VHF to ask for the current direction at the feed shed as it could easily be different to what I was experiencing out in the channel. (Vessels dedicated to this work have powerful side thrusters fore and aft to help them in and out.)

The Envirocon farm was a standard-sized operation with several hundred thousand small fish being fed. When the fish were young, the farm required twenty-two metric tons of feed per week, but that number grew as the fish grew. The feed came in bags loaded onto pallets, with one ton of feed per pallet, and these arrived on forty-foot freight trailers. At times there were two and occasionally three of these trailers waiting for us on the dock; on one occasion we could not accommodate it all and our regular cargo and had to make a special trip. All the feed made the vessel look full, but the freight rate was only one quarter of the regular rate and even that was almost too expensive for the farms. On the east side of Vancouver

Island where there were many farm sites by this time, the feed could be moved in bulk at a lower rate, but we had to treat it as regular cargo and fit all the rest of our cargo around it. This was sometimes very difficult, but the crew got pretty crafty about fitting everything on. We often ended up with the hold full of feed right to the hatch covers, on top of the hatch and on the forward side decks. This extra weight forward put her head down three feet, which coincidentally gave us much better visibility forward from the wheelhouse. It didn't affect the speed much but it did make our stopping times longer and manoeuvring a little more difficult. All this activity with fish farm feed worked the equipment hard, raising the cost of maintenance significantly.

In the meantime, as the fish farming industry was new to us, we were still unsure if it would prove viable here, and our accounts receivable kept growing as we became more and more involved in bringing in loads of feed to Centre Cove. But Nootka Sound Service always ran too close to the edge to let receivables get too big. In fact, at the beginning of our time in Nootka Sound, Esson had to ask the Tahsis Company to settle its account every two weeks rather than every two months; they complied and that had helped us to survive in that early period. We had also been burned by a few outfits in the past, such as cedar shake cutting businesses, where we had hauled their gear and people around before there was any production returns. Some of them never paid on their accounts as their companies failed before they really got started. In the case of a capital-intensive operation like Envirocon, I could see they were going to be paying out money for years before there were any returns. I was very relieved when I learned that the farm was well capitalized and could stand the lengthy start-up time.

As well as carrying feed for Envirocon, in time we began to transport the harvested product in small quantities from Centre Cove to the Fair Harbour roadhead. We could not do this on a large scale because they harvested the fish in small batches and at odd times that did not necessarily fit our schedule. The trick was that as soon as the fish were killed, they had to be on the move to the processing plant in Campbell River and from there rushed to market in the US. The product could be in the mid-western states within two and a half to three days. Thus, the fish had to be ready when we came by on our weekly run.

The *Uchuck III* alongside at Walter's Cove, Kyuquot Sound.

Later the farmers solved the problem of fish transport by buying an old car ferry to move their own product and supplies. We were a little concerned that it would begin to cut into our business if they started transporting other goods as well but that never happened. It did promote some business of moving vehicles around, but it was new business so we did not see any reduction in traffic.

Other Inter-port Work

At this time we also developed a little inter-port work between the logging camps, Walter's Cove and Fair Harbour. Like most of the roads across the island from east to west, the road into Fair Harbour was made up of old and active logging roads and followed a route from Fair Harbour to Zeballos to Woss Lake, near Port McNeil, and on down to Campbell River on Highway 19, which had been completed in 1978, connecting Port Hardy to Campbell River. As this road went by Woss Lake, the traffic from Zeballos and Kyuquot no longer had to travel down to Gold River but could go directly down Highway 19 from Woss Lake. (There was a strong move in 1985 to have a road from Tahsis northward to Woss Lake, which would complete a circle route from Campbell River to Gold River to Tahsis to Woss and back to Campbell River via Highway 19. By this time, however, a recession had set in hard; the idea has never been revived as the most easily accessed and best timber was depleted in this area, and logging was in decline.)

When the local fish packer was not available during the short salmon trolling season, we moved some wild salmon from the fish buyer at Walter's Cove to trucks at Fair Harbour and took some to Gold River as well. One season we did try to make the Gold River delivery on a semi-regular schedule, but the flake ice in the open totes tended to melt too soon and all the travelling and waiting time affected the quality of the product. It didn't help that there was usually a delay in Gold River as we waited for trucks, which then had to drive to the ferries at Nanaimo then on to Vancouver and the processing plants. This work dried up altogether over the next few years as the troll fishing industry collapsed.

There were also side jobs that came up from time to time. Once we went to Fair Harbour to lift a boom boat from a lowbed trailer into the water, a diversion of an hour or so. We billed the boat owner according to the extra time needed to go there to do the job as it was away from our regular route. We based this on the hourly cost of operating our vessel and applied that as a basis for a charter minimum. This kind of thing was all very informal because often the arrangements were made on the spot by the skipper, so it was deemed best that there not be a complicated tariff for him to interpret for each situation.

Sometimes a job would involve just lying at our berth in Gold River to transfer goods from the wharf to a float or boat or the other way around. This procedure might mean lifting broken logging truck or skidder parts from a camp crew boat to a waiting truck or the reverse when the camp couldn't wait for our regularly scheduled run. If the broken machine was critical to the logging operation, it was worth it to the operator to call us in as the whole camp could be idled while they waited, and that could become very expensive.

We often lifted gear that had been stripped from booms and left at the Gold River pulp mill onto the wharf for later carriage back to the camps. If we happened to be loading anyway or if the crew was handy to do it, a little job like this would often be done at no charge. But unloading fish totes from a series of boats onto waiting trucks wasn't a small job, so it was done at an hourly rate. This job was charged at a lower rate than when the ship was away on the run, because it could be done using less than the full crew with no main engine time and therefore little fuel cost.

In the fall when the chum salmon gill net season opened, there would be a fleet of gillnet boats working in Nootka Sound. When the opening ended, the catch was transferred to trucks on the Gold River wharf with a combination of our winches, the winch on the end of the wharf and a number of crane trucks. We also rented out our forklift trucks complete with drivers at these times, and the work often went on well into the night until it was all cleaned up.

Sometimes when the job would take too long or have to be done at a time that did not fit in our schedule or was off in a direction away from our regular routes, we would have to make special runs. During one saw-mill upgrade at Tahsis, we were asked to take a "bull edger end feed table" from Gold River to Tahsis. This thing was thirty feet by fifteen feet by four feet and weighed fifteen tons. As we knew that just getting it loaded was going to take several hours, we used a harbour day for the job. To carry it, we built up the side decks and hatch coaming with empty pallets to the level of the bulwark rail, and then with the help of a mobile crane on the wharf, tried to lay the thing across the width of the vessel. It turned out to be even too heavy for the crane, and in the end we had to help with the ship's winches. Then with this thing looking like a wing across our twenty-two-foot width and carrying some extra parts for it in the hold, we headed off to Tahsis. Once there, I took the vessel a little past the wharf and then backed in along the face as far as the protruding unit would allow. There on the corner of the wharf another mobile crane was waiting and it successfully plucked the feed table off our deck.

On three occasions we carried broken aircraft from where they were damaged to where they could be worked on or shipped out for repairs. We discovered that once the wings were removed from a Cessna 180 on floats, it could stand on the hatch with the tailplane through the gate in the rail on top of the deckhouse in front of the wheelhouse or be left athwartship, standing on the hatch cover with its tail hanging out over the side. We would put the wings on edge on the work deck and lash them to the rail. These planes are fitted with lifting eyes around the point of balance on the top of the fuselage, so a simple set of four hooks was all that was needed to move them.

Once we were asked to remove a marine pilot from a freighter heading offshore. Today when a pilot is on a ship leaving port, he joins the ship before she sails and is taken off at a designated station by a pilot boat or helicopter. In this case, the ship was leaving from Gold River with a pilot who wanted to get off as soon as the vessel cleared the Sound because it would not be going near the pilot boarding station at the mouth of Barkley Sound. The pilot would be going offshore, too, if we didn't help him to get off the ship, so on our run to Friendly Cove with a full complement of passengers on board, we went alongside the ship off Mooyah Bay. She was still slowly moving ahead, and I well remember that wall of black steel punctuated by hundreds of rivets and the people looking down at us from the decks far above. It is really difficult to manoeuvre away once alongside when vessels are moving, and I had to worry about all our curious passengers who might get some part of themselves between the two vessels. It worked out all right, but I hoped that we wouldn't be needed too often again for this little operation.

Unique Jobs

There was an old Native village site in the bay next to Graveyard Bay, which lies in Esperanza Inlet between Zeballos Arm and Espinosa Inlet. This old village had been long abandoned—we had never seen any buildings

Float planes are subject to hitting driftwood too, and sometimes need a lift.

there—but one totem pole remained standing alone in a patch of long grass. One nice day in 1963 we had stopped just off the beach and let the vessel drift for a short time while George and a couple of others went ashore in a skiff. George had his old bellows camera with him and a plan to photograph the pole from different angles close up. By the following Christmas he had carved six nine-inch replicas from cottonwood sticks found on the beach, and he gave them to Esson and others.

For the next couple of decades nothing changed at that village site, and when we went by one day in the summer of 1985, I noticed that the area around the pole had been cleared. We soon learned that this pole was to be taken down and we were to take it to Gold River. People from the provincial museum came and organized the move. They hired a local company, Seabreeze Ventures of CeePeeCee, to take it down carefully, move it onto a log float and tow it to CeePeeCee where we could load it aboard in calm water. The pole was a little more than forty feet long and was brought alongside us with the parts wrapped in blankets where the lifting slings were to be placed. We handled it carefully as it was very fragile, weighing practically nothing, and we certainly didn't want pieces of it lying on deck afterwards. We loaded it on our starboard work deck, took it to Gold River and there set it carefully on a forty-foot flat-deck trailer for the trip to Victoria. It had been arranged that the carver Tim Paul would receive the pole in the carving shed beside the Royal BC Museum and make a copy of it. When completed, the plan was to truck the copy to Gold River and from there we would carry it back to the original site.

Months later I saw that tools and cement were at the site waiting for the return of the pole but at that point there was a change in plans. One day shortly afterwards, the brightly painted replica, instead of coming to us, was taken by road to Zeballos where the family who owned it now lived. That is where it was raised but sadly, in the following winter, a major gale blew through the valley, blowing the pole down and destroying it.

Occasionally we were asked to set anchors for floats or booms. This involved setting up the concrete block on the rail with all its gear attached and then cutting a lashing at the precisely correct moment to send it down in a predetermined spot. The anchor created a prodigious splash as it hit the water.

One morning we were asked to raise a car from the water at Zeballos. It had raced down the wharf approach in the middle of the night and had not stopped at the end. Luckily, we had not been tied up on the face of the wharf under that spot on that particular night or else we would have been wearing that car. The driver and his passenger got out all right, but the car was resting in forty-five feet of water. In the morning a diver went down and tied a long wire to the front axle assembly and then brought the end of the wire to the surface. We then lay alongside the face of the wharf and fastened our cargo hook to the eye at the end of the wire, lifted the hook to our derrick head and stopped the wire off at deck level. When the front of the car was at the surface, we attached a short wire for the lift to the wharf, but as the car came out of the water, we had to stop it partway to let it drain in order to reduce the weight so we could lift it clear of the water. Then we carried it, dangling from the end of the wire, across the ship and landed it on the wharf upside down. Next we rigged a line to parbuckle it over onto its wheels so that the owner and his friend could push it away off the wharf.

We also dealt with mystery underwater lifts. We were asked to lift a boat that had sunk at a logging camp, and I had in my mind a standard little steel boom boat, which I already knew would weigh four to five tons. We had lifted lots of those. But what was in my mind was not what was underwater: this was a little steel towboat and much heavier. We found that we had hold of something too heavy to lift, but we couldn't let go of it because it had shifted with our first effort. The only solution was to try to wiggle it up the underwater slope into shallower water, so we secured it to a mooring line bollard and hours passed as we used the ship to hump the towboat along the bottom. Finally we had dragged it close enough to shore that we could disengage our lines. As far as I know it is still there.

On a number of occasions we were asked to lift engines out of tugs or fishing vessels when they were to be repaired or replaced. This was a simple operation once the owners had done the preparatory work of cutting through the deckhouse top and the main deck to expose the engine and had towed the vessel alongside. The *Uchuck*'s cargo gear is precise, so this kind of work could be done without damage to either engine or structure.

Once the engine was out, we would arrange a time for the reverse operation, putting the new or repaired engine back into the boat.

In time the Kyuquot run became a favourite for the crews because of the variety it gave and the feeling that the vessel was actually going to sea for a little while. Cargo and gear had to be secured as if going on an ocean voyage, whereas before we had just propped things up temporarily for short periods. We installed a number of eyebolts and other lashing points as the problem areas became evident. However, at times in winter the trip could seem like a little too much of a good thing.

Rats

Last of all, I really should say something about rats. Every waterfront has them. They live above the tide line and under the wharves or whatever structures line the waterfront. A nice warm place with a chance of something to eat is ideal for them, so we had to think about that in our business as we were handling food products in relatively unsecured containers and, latterly, fish feed pellets in enormous quantities.

One of the coziest places on board for rats to take up residence is the outside lifebelt locker. The style of jacket on board in our time had kapok, a cotton-like fibre mass, as flotation. The mother rats discovered that once they could get through the canvas and plastic on the outside of the life jacket, they had found the motherlode of nest building material. And the surrounding piles of life jackets in the locker created a secure fortification in which to bear and raise young.

One day when we were on a scheduled run and aware that we had again developed a rat problem, the boys began digging into the lifebelt locker located on the after deck, going through the jackets one by one as they looked for critters. I was in the wheelhouse two decks up and half a ship forward when, over the sound of engines running at full rpm, I heard a scream followed by the sound of pounding feet. The boys had indeed dug down far enough and had come to the nest in the last jacket in the corner. The rats were at home. Walter, with his big boots, kicked a lot of young rats over the side and generally gave the rest a bad day. This happened on more than one occasion, but less frequently than one would think, given the circumstances of the food we carried and the spaces available for rats to hide.

CHAPTER TWELVE

Dealing with Danger

Rescues

Over all the years we worked in Nootka and Kyuquot sounds we were not called on very often to make medical runs, but once in a while when the weather was too bad for a plane to land or a faster means of travel was not available, we did make a special run to move a sick person, usually during the night. However, we did rescue the owners of countless small boats. Usually the boat had hit something and damaged the outboard leg. A few had run out of fuel; others had suffered engine failures. We would come across them while on our regular route and, by using some dedicated wide nylon straps, simply pick them up with our cargo gear, land them on the hatch cover and carry on. These rescues were seldom dramatic, but if the distressed boaters had not been seen by someone, they could have been in a bad situation as night fell or the weather turned sour. Occasionally we would get a request to be on the lookout for a specific vessel that had radioed for help. At other times we saw something that just looked odd and decided to investigate.

One night while crossing Nootka Sound, I saw a light where there should not have been one among the Villeverde Islands on the northwest side of Bligh Island. We went to investigate but found nothing. It was probably someone clam digging on the beach who had decided to flash their lamp at us for fun. The reason for our extra caution on that occasion was that there had been a tragic accident in the same area just a few weeks earlier. A man and his wife were travelling back to Tahsis in an inboard/outboard boat when they hit some object in the water, tearing off the outboard leg. They made it to the beach from their sinking boat, but as they were some distance from any habitation, they started to struggle along the beach toward where they knew a camp was located. Meanwhile, the temperature had dropped below freezing, and they were wet. They came to the end of a logging road and started along it toward the camp, but by that time they were so cold that when they came to a log blocking the way, they just could not go any farther and perished there, one on either side of the log. The sad part of it was that we must have passed that position at about that time on our way to Tahsis, but there was no way we could have known their plight.

Since man is a creature of the land, when he ventures out to sea, he must take precautions if he is to survive. He has to think of and address all that might go wrong before he goes, and the two most important are staying afloat and not having the vessel burn. All other problems are secondary.

Weaknesses on board will likely show up when the vessel is working hard and being flung about in a seaway. In those conditions, everything must work all of the time—the structure, the machinery, the steering and all the other interdependent parts as well as the people—or you can end up with a cascading of effects, even if each one may not be cataclysmic in itself. In all my years as skipper I had to feel in my bones that everything had been done that reasonably could be done to make us ready to do the work safely.

There were a few places that we travelled past where, if there had been any hesitation in the machinery or steering, we would only have had thirty seconds to react before we could have been in serious difficulties.

I checked regularly for wear on the five-eighth-inch-diameter steering wire where it changes direction ninety degrees on the sheaves in the upper after corners of the tiller flat as it is redirected toward the rudder quadrants. Wear shows up there as broken wires that appear as jaggers. These cables lasted in our application for an average of eight years, and one day I asked Harry Mitchell, the surveyor at that time, how long they should last. "Oh," he replied, "about eight years."

Many of the inspection requirements for ships hang on empirical evidence derived from problems occurring in different vessels over a period of time. Inspection rules may also change as new types of gear made of new materials appear, but all of these rules have to be interpreted to apply to each individual vessel. Each inspector will have some of his own prejudices based on his experience so the details may vary a little, but the overall result is the same. Some operators think that inspectors are looking for ways to shut them down, but at the end of an inspection the inspector has to sign the certificate, so he has to feel that the vessel will comply for at least one more year. We always worked well with the inspection people and built a level of trust. They knew that we would do as we had agreed to do and often suggested simpler ways of doing things that would still satisfy the regulations.

The rules are constantly changing as new equipment comes into use or as the result of an investigation into accidents. In the late 1950s polypropylene cordage appeared. It seemed magical: it did not rot, it floated, it didn't freeze, it was strong and it was light. We all began to use it for many applications, including lifeboat falls. What we didn't know was that it would be attacked by the sun's ultraviolet radiation and would fail over time if not covered. There were some accidents in the industry before the problem was recognized, and then we could not use it for that purpose. Later, the deterioration was slowed by an additive, so we could again use it, provided that it was changed out on a regular basis.

Many earlier small vessels such as the *Uchuck II*, which was built in 1925, had few bulkheads in the hull below the main deck, and they were usually just on either side of the engine room. Some of these vessels were lost when the hull was breached in a collision, which resulted in the flooding of much of the ship's length. When there had been enough such cases, the subdivision rules were changed to require collision bulkheads at each end of the vessel, not just forward, where most vessels have some protection. In one refit we were told to put a collision bulkhead aft in the *Uchuck II*, isolating the last twenty feet. Two years later the vessel backed into Funter Island in Plumper Harbour and did enough damage to flood that space.

Metals fatigue so shafts can break suddenly and for no apparent reason. The broken crankshaft in the Atlas Imperial engine in the *Uchuck II* was an example; that engine had been periodically opened up for inspection and there appeared to be no problem. The danger can also lie in where these events take place. Northland Navigation's *Tahsis Prince* had an intermediate shaft break while sailing past Victoria. She was easily towed in there and repaired, but that break could have happened anywhere on the West Coast where no help was available. Afterwards, when asked about that, the skipper said that if you were too bothered by the prospect of such an event, you would never go out to sea in the first place. In spite of all precautions, accidents and breakdowns will happen, so it remains for crews to always be aware.

Another source of trouble was the electrical system. The marine environment is hard on electrical equipment in ships because of the violent motion, heat, vibration, moisture and salt, and as a result, grounds and shorts in the wiring are more likely to occur than they would in a shore-side installation. The early electrical systems on ships all supplied DC electric power where a dead short in any of the wiring could create a lot of heat, certainly enough to set adjacent material alight. One morning while the ship was tied to the wharf, I woke up to see solid smoke two feet above my bunk. I was wide awake instantly, but there was no sign of flames. I called out the engineer and oiler, and together we laid out our firefighting gear, then went looking for the source. We saw nothing in the cabin and nothing in the wheelhouse until we lifted the hatch cover to the quartermaster's stores, which is located in the deck behind the wheel. It is an enclosed space about two feet high and the width of the wheelhouse. A gout of smoke rolled out and with it with a lot of heat but still no flames. However, when I dropped down into the space, I found the problem: a roll of charts and a canvas stretcher, both smouldering. I grabbed them and, since the wheelhouse door was open, tossed them into the sea. Then we looked again for the source and found a point where two armoured cables crossed: one was arcing to the other. Over the years water had seeped into the wire casing from the light fixture on the outside of the wheelhouse until finally the insulation had failed.

On another morning I woke to hear a frying sound. That noise turned out to be a heater switch on the cabin wall; it had failed for no apparent reason, and it continued to fizzle until one wire behind the plywood surface burned off the switch. I could only stand there in my gaunch looking stupidly at it until it stopped.

All our crew members were very conscious of the smell of woodsmoke, especially because they were working on a wooden vessel. One day I caught the slight smell of woodsmoke while I was in the wheelhouse. I immediately went on the hunt for the source, going to the main deck and then below into the forward end of the hold where I met Walter Winkler, who had entered the hold from the engine room. It turned out that we had both picked up a faint smell on the wind coming from the burn pile at a logging camp's dry sorting ground. But it was "better to be safe than sorry," and I remembered George McCandless cautioning us to "Remember the *Noronic*." She was a 362-foot cruise ship that burned at the wharf in Toronto in September 1949 because of a fire that started by spontaneous combustion in a linen closet. She was completely destroyed in fifteen minutes; 118 people died.

Some cargo items—compressed flammable gases, explosives and corrosive agents—are potentially dangerous and must be handled properly. Blasting caps must not be stowed near bagged explosives, so in the early days we stowed them in our lifeboats. Some goods that one would never expect to cause problems do. Ice cream was shipped in large cardboard cartons with blocks of dry ice (solid carbon dioxide) as the refrigerant, and the flaps of the cartons were sealed with tape to prevent any leakage of air. But one day at Sarita River, I was in the hold of the *Uchuck I* loading boxes onto trays, when I noticed that I was having difficulty breathing and I was starting to feel woozy. Fortunately I was able to climb the ladder to the fresh air. It turned out that one of the ice cream cartons had leaked, and carbon dioxide was filling the hold in the same way that a fire smothering system would work. To finish loading, Esson and I took turns working down there until the air cleared.

We came very close to a real disaster involving cargo in June 1987. It came about because, when loggers finish with a cutblock, they burn the slash, partly as a way to get rid of what could become a fire hazard but also to make way for replanting. A time is chosen when the slash is dry enough to burn but not so dry that the fire will spread into nearby standing timber. If an accelerant is used, it is laid out in a preselected pattern in the slashed area to produce a tailored burn. One type of accelerant consisted of two chemicals that when mixed resulted in a delayed action but a very hot fire. From time to time we were asked to carry these materials to the logging camps, along with other tools and supplies that the crew would need for the job. Later we hauled the tools and leftover chemical supplies back again.

On one outbound trip to Kyuquot, we stopped at Kendrick Arm to pick up one of our covered cargo containers that was full of the remains from such a job. As the vessel was fully loaded, the master decided to free up work space by dropping the container off temporarily at Tahsis, knowing he could pick it up on the return trip. So at Tahsis it was landed on the wharf and trundled into the government freight shed. Fifteen minutes later the container burst into flame, creating a torch of fire that rose to the rafters, burning right through the roof and gutting the shed in a very short time. Apparently, while in transit some of the chemicals had spilled from some partly used but not properly resealed containers, and in the shed they had managed to find each other and do what they were designed to do. This incident brought home to us that we really needed to know exactly what was in our cargo, in order to know what hazards we would have to guard against. In this case, it had been a simple mistake in how the container had been loaded in the logging camp, but it was nearly a deadly mistake for us.

As with the lifesaving gear we had on board, when the company started out, the firefighting gear on the *Uchucks* was old technology. The equipment consisted of one-and-a-half-inch canvas hoses in fifty-foot lengths arranged in racks at three hydrants around the deck so that we were able to bring two hoses to bear at any site on deck. They were fitted with brass tapered nozzles, which produced a solid stream of pressurized water. There were three types of fire extinguishers on board as well. The first was a two-and-a-half-gallon soda-acid extinguisher, which when inverted, released sulphuric acid into a solution of sodium bicarbonate to cause a reaction that built up pressure and sent a stream of water out a short hose. This type was effective enough but it contained only two-and-a-half gallons of water. The second was a foam producer, which was intended to fight an oil fire, and it also worked with two chemicals in a two-and-a-half-gallon tank. The third was a small handheld pyrene pump cylinder containing carbon tetrachloride, which, when it vaporized, was effective on electrical and oil fires. It was in use until the 1950s when it was discovered that this chemical was poisonous and, in heavy concentrations, could kill people. The third basic element in the ship's equipment list was the fire bucket; each ship had six that were stored in two racks of three. They were painted red and had rounded bottoms so that they would not be useful for any other purpose. The lanyards attached to them were long enough to allow one to dip seawater from the height of the upper decks. This equipment and three fire axes stowed in brackets on bulkheads was the extent of what we had. The axes, especially the one that was mounted inside the cabin, caused problems when fights broke out between passengers. Fuelled by alcohol, some of the young guys figured on settling their differences with it.

From about 1970 onward, improvements in equipment and procedures began to be available. The old soda-acid extinguishers were replaced by plain air-pressured water tanks of the same size. As well, there were several new types of dry chemical extinguishers to deal with different types of fires, replacing the pyrene and foam extinguishers. New firehose nozzles appeared that were adjustable so that a spray or fog could be created as well as the stream, and another type was introduced that allowed a canister of foam material to be attached to the nozzle that mixed the foam with the water flow. We did not have this latter type because we would not be dealing with large oil fires; besides, we were able to buy effective dry chemical extinguishers plus inert gas smothering systems for the situations that we might actually be dealing with. The government also offered proper training programs in conjunction with certificates of competency for deck and engine room officers. Hands-on firefighting courses, a part of the Marine Emergency Duties training, showed trainees that, with just the equipment found on the average vessel, they could do a lot toward saving a bad situation. We began sending crew members for some of this training, even if they were not at that time preparing to sit for certificates.

The engine room was the one place that a substantial fuel fire might be possible. To counter that, we installed a halon gas flooding system, which would release the inert gas to smother a fire in the enclosed space of the engine room and tank spaces after everyone was out of those spaces. Later, although not dangerous to human health, halon gas was found to be one of the contributing gases affecting the ozone layer above the Earth; new installations went back to using carbon dioxide. We acquired two used sets of breathing apparatus for entering smoke-filled spaces. Fire hoses made of different materials, stronger and rot resistant, became available. But the fire buckets remained because they are basic and effective. With knowledge, these tools can be enough to save a ship.

Special Problems when Carrying Passengers

The annual steamship inspection is the time for all the safety gear on board a ship to be serviced, thoroughly inspected and exercised, and those vessels that carry the travelling public are the most carefully scrutinized. The crews of these ships have to think about the special problems that passengers can cause for themselves, the ship or the crew. On the *Uchuck III* there was a second engine room telegraph at an upper control station outside of and behind the wheelhouse. Esson and George had installed it there so they could manoeuvre the vessel from where they could see clearly. One day after we had gone alongside at Gold River and tied up but not yet shut down the main engines, a little girl who had seen the handles of the telegraph moving thought it might be fun to climb the ladder and do it herself. That telegraph was connected directly to its mate in the wheelhouse, so all of a sudden she was controlling the engines. She rang up "half ahead" and the vessel began moving. The gangway was already rigged and people were walking across it when it started skidding along the wharf edge. Fortunately, the vessel stopped when the mooring lines came up tight. When I realized what was happening, I scrambled back to the wheelhouse and rang the telegraph back to "Finished with Engines" before there was a serious accident. We took those handles off and put them away.

Children love to run on board boats. They like to climb railings and ladders, anything that presents a challenge. As they charge about, sooner or later one of them comes to grief as there are any number of things to trip over or into and very heavy doors in which to get fingers caught. We would just follow the wailing to find the problem. We never lost a child but we considered that a small miracle.

We carried logging crews when the camps were about to open for the season or when a regular shift was coming back to work, and at times there would be more than one of these crews on board. They virtually always carried liquor with them; some were already well on their way to being blotto when they boarded and they always consumed more while on the ship. Since they were generally with us for several hours as we took them from Gold River to their various camps, there was a good chance for trouble within one crew or between different crews. On a couple of occasions when things got out of hand and stuff started to get thrown about, I had to separate women and kids from the general mass and move them to the safety of the crew's quarters in the fo'c'sle. Our crew of four could not have quelled a real disturbance with any certitude so we pretty well had to let them have at each other. On two occasions, one in Barkley Sound and the other in Nootka Sound, we refused to take one certain camp's crew with us until there was a way to police the action. In each case that state existed for two weeks because we had become fed up with the damage and the possible injury to themselves and us. For awhile we separated them from their booze as soon as they arrived in Gold River, stowing it in the cargo hold till we reached their camps. This measure was moderately successful but not the real answer.

I was not on board when a bunch of them got really out of hand. The master had made the mistake of detouring to make a small delivery to Friendly Cove, an hour and a half out of our usual way, while there was a logging crew on board. That extra hour and a half on top of the three and a half hours it normally took to get to their camp was just too much. They began tearing the place up. Thinking about it afterwards, I decided that it would have been nice to take that lot out to sea a few miles past Friendly Cove and then just stop the vessel and let her roll around in the swell with the lights off for half an hour. Trouble was, there would have been one hell of a mess to clean up later. Apparently the local airline sometimes had a similar problem when an inebriated soul wanted to help drive. The pilots found that taking the plane up to 10,000 feet and turning on the cabin heat soon quieted things down.

Toward the end of the big logging era in the sounds the problem of wild crews eased up. They had been keeping up the historical image of loggers, but now more of them were doing very responsible jobs and running some very expensive equipment. Besides, the camps were in a tighter financial environment and couldn't afford to lose time while drunks were healing up, so their crews became more civilized. In addition, they began to commute in different ways, coming in at more frequent intervals and in smaller groups.

On the *Uchuck III* there were chains across each side deck with "No Passengers" signs attached to them but for some people that was not enough, and from time to time we would find someone wandering around the work deck. When we were making heavy lifts with the cargo gear, the vessel heeled appreciably, a movement that could throw people off balance anywhere on board, but if they happened to be near the open cargo hatch, it could be disastrous. Even crew members had to be aware when working cargo that the winches could set things such as large hydraulic cylinders in one spot on deck temporarily before moving them to their final locations. If another heavy item was then lifted, the vessel would roll, and the cylinder, not yet secured properly, could move around and catch someone. Watching for these things became instinctive when the men had been at the job together for a time, but new men—and certainly passengers— could easily be caught in these situations.

When we went alongside floats to make a quick stop, we often tied up with just one spring line amidships and steamed slowly ahead on it to hold the vessel in for the short time necessary to discharge a passenger or a small amount of cargo. Then we had to make sure that the passenger had not stepped into the centre of the coil of line that was about to run out. The lines for this purpose were always three-strand nylon, an inch and a quarter in diameter with a maximum one-in-three stretch capability, so they were not likely to break, but whatever they are hooked onto ashore can come adrift when the line comes taut. Then the line becomes a slingshot. The five-pound hook at its end whips through the air and can do real damage to people or things. The sailors know this and know to keep out of the line of fire, but passengers often don't have the instinct to be in the right place.

There was also room for trouble when people would appear on the wharf looking for information, trying to find someone to talk to or just hoping to see what was going on, wandering through all the activity as freight trucks pulled in and turned around and towmotors buzzed around everywhere. The problem was even greater during refits when visitors came around; at times like that there could be big holes in the deck planking or other parts missing and gear and tools lying everywhere, and all the while there would be a lot of clattering machinery and tools.

For many years the lighting on the work deck of the *Uchuck III* was provided by one two-hundred-watt light bulb backed by a white-painted reflector on the mast above the winchman's head and two one-hundred-watt bulbs in cages under the fo'c'sle head. This lighting was barely adequate for our on-deck work, but when we were alongside a float at a logging camp, the shadow cast by the ship's rail created a black space below it. If the vessel was hanging off even a little from the float, it was quite possible—and it did happen—for someone to walk to the edge of the float and step right into the water. That problem was solved after we got more AC power generation on board and were able to get new brilliant lighting.

Woman Overboard

It was New Year's Day 1974, a clear, cold night at the dark of the moon. The *Uchuck III* had sailed at 17:00 from Gold River on a scheduled run carrying cargo and passengers bound for Nootka Sound ports. There were visitors in the wheelhouse, still buoyed up and cheerful from the holiday but quite happy to be going home and back to work. As we approached Tahsis, the lights of the town and the mill twinkled ahead in the sharp winter air. With the exception of the coloured navigation lights, all the vessel's outside lights were off in order to preserve the night vision of the people on watch, so the main deck below us, which can't be seen from the wheelhouse, was a very dark area.

A little after 21:00 when we were about a third of a mile out from Tahsis, I rang up "Standby" on the engine room telegraph and reached behind to turn on the main deck lights. The clanging of the engine room telegraph bells, which could be heard throughout the ship, was the signal for the crew to appear on deck to prepare to go alongside. As the steel fo'c'sle door banged open against its stop and the first man came out on deck, I heard the unexpected sound of pounding boots and a great shout of "Hey, stop!" Then the cry went up, "Man overboard." Always in the back of my mind had been the fear that one day I might hear that cry and now here it was.

We had practised procedures should we be faced with this "man overboard" situation, procedures that took into account the size of the crew and the equipment we had at our disposal. First, though, everything froze for a split second, the heart stopped and then got going at a hell of a lick as the shock of the cry hit home. I felt hot and cold at the same time, then the brain engaged and I went to work, dealing with the situation with its particular details of darkness and cold. Had the woman jumped two minutes earlier, no one would have known, but as it was we could do something.

First, one of the hands threw overboard one of our three life rings that had a light attached. At about the same time, I swung the four-foot wheel hard over to starboard. When the vessel reached sixty degrees off the course line, I spun the wheel the five turns to the other stop. The vessel heeled sharply to starboard and swung fast around to port. As she came around, I began to ease the wheel until we were steadied up on the reciprocal of the original course, having completed a Williamson turn, a manoeuvre that caused the vessel to be headed back down her own wake and aimed for the lighted life ring. We had been travelling at twelve knots, and the woman had jumped from about amidships, so she would have passed the stern in three and a half to four seconds. By the time we got turned around, she was almost a quarter of a mile away.

As we passed the life ring, I had already slowed the vessel and had turned on the searchlight, which was mounted on top of the wheelhouse. I ordered some passengers who had been standing outside on deck to watch Tahsis get closer to act as lookouts now, and soon in the beam of the light we could see the woman in the water. She was lying on her back amid patches of floating ice, breathing out puffs of vapour into the cold air, the whole scene brightly lit by the focussed beam. She made no sound or any movement but she was obviously breathing. I stopped the vessel nearby while in the meantime the two hands on deck had readied the twelve-foot rescue boat for lowering over the side. The mate operated the cargo winches while one hand rode the boat into the water. His job was to go to where she was and keep her afloat. I worked the vessel closer to the boat so that the hand on deck could throw a heaving line over the rescue boat and draw it in alongside. Now that the vessel was stopped, the engineer and I were free to go on deck to get involved.

The man in the boat, his hands and arms going numb in the frigid water, was supporting the woman. With the rescue boat now alongside, the other hand dropped down into the boat to help. But as soon as they started to move her, she began to sink, feet first. She had only been float-ing because of the air trapped in her winter clothing, which by now had soaked up much water and was nearly saturated.

Meanwhile, a small crowd of passengers had gathered at the gate in the rail to watch. Among them was a man who suddenly realized that the woman in the water was his wife. He had no idea that this had happened.

Together, the two hands were able to roll her into the boat, which we lifted aboard with everyone in it and landed on the cargo hatch. Fortunately, there was an industrial first-aid person among the passengers, and he was able to help the woman once she had been moved into the warmth of the cabin. I returned to the wheelhouse to move the ship over to the wharf, and as her circulation started up again, I could hear her moans coming through the deck under my feet. Within an hour, we were docked in Tahsis where she was able to walk over the gangway with a little assistance.

But there is a sad postscript to this story: a year later she finally did manage to take her own life.

CHAPTER THIRTEEN

The Highways and Byways

Communication

Until the beginning of the twentieth century, when a ship left her home port, nothing could be known of her until she returned unless another ship, passing her at sea, took word back. Some ships just disappeared forever without a trace. The West Coast of Vancouver Island is littered with two hundred years worth of unidentified pieces of ships that never arrived at their destination ports.

When wireless communication equipment was first brought on board around 1900, things began to change. The wireless operators, employees of the Marconi Company, were given working space to operate the new communication technology, and for the first time shore-bound ship owners could know where their ships were and begin to control their movements. Masters were divided on this new development, some viewing it with suspicion as they considered the loss of control over their ships. Even today masters resent interference from ashore to a certain degree.

By 1946 when Esson and George acquired the *Uchuck I*, not much had changed where communication was concerned. Many small vessels still had no radio equipment although it had been in wide use in the war just ended. The first radio transmitter in the No. 1 was an aircraft unit that had been converted for use in the marine radio spectrum. It was moderately successful and was used to call in the estimated time of arrival when the ship was within range of the wharf, that being about ten miles out. But at this time marine radio transmitters could not legally be installed in shore establishments, so Esson and George had to be satisfied with installing a good Phillips receiver that could be tuned to the marine frequencies in the company's dock office. Later they replaced it with a marine radio telephone installed out of view under the desk because the government radio licence people drove around with direction-finding equipment, searching for illegal transmitters.

Near the beginning of the *Uchuck II*'s service in 1948 she was fitted with a Spilsbury Hepburn twenty-five-watt AM transceiver. This was a big step forward, allowing the master to talk easily to other vessels and to people ashore with information on cargo, ETAs and other business. The equipment had a good range of operation so that occasionally in the 1960s we could even communicate from Nootka Sound with vessels in Vancouver harbour.

The next innovation in the industry was to connect these radios up to the land telephone system. The Department of Communications set aside a few dedicated frequencies for use by the telephone company through which a ship could connect with a marine operator in Vancouver who would then connect the vessel to the land system and ring the number requested. Now tugboat company dispatchers could hold conference calls with their fleet skippers, and shoreside people could have the telephone company connect them with a ship, provided that the vessel was standing by to hear it on the frequency selected. The operators would try the call several times at intervals before giving up. After Zeballos became our home port in the 1960s, the *Uchucks* would have their twice weekly harbour days there. Often on those evenings, people would come down to the wharf, usually at suppertime, to ask to use our radio to get phone messages out. At that time we had the village's only radio/telephone connection to the outside world.

The *Uchuck III*, when out on charter to Murray Marine Services Ltd. of Alert Bay in 1960, was outfitted with a VHF radio, which had very short range by the nature of the wave propagation. But this went a long way toward reducing the clutter on the air, which by this time had made the old AM radios almost useless. Then the government changed the regulations, putting an end to the licensing of AM sets and enforcing the use of single sideband radio, which, while still AM, made less clutter on the

Main Street, Zeballos, a rough West Coast town in 1938 when in the midst of a gold rush, and still a small, rough place thirty years later. IMAGE C-06075 COURTESY OF ROYAL BC MUSEUM, BC ARCHIVES.

airwaves but still maintained or increased the distance capability. We installed such a set in the *Uchuck III* to satisfy the safety regulations that said we had to be able to reach a government shore station in the event of an emergency, but as no one else in the area had a single sideband radio, it was useless to us in our day-to-day business.

While this was happening, the local small boats and logging camps in Nootka Sound were using citizen's band (CB) radio, another high frequency type that was used first and extensively by truckers in the US because the sets were unregulated and cheap. Although it was also a very short-range system, it worked well, so we adopted this for our working business communication. By coincidence this was a good time for CB radio as there was not much atmospheric interference, but we soon learned that the signal could bounce off layers in the atmosphere so that a transmission that should only travel a few miles was being received as far away as the opposite corner of North America. The resulting babble soon became incomprehensible on all forty-one available channels. We had experienced some of this problem on the AM sets in the evenings, receiving the Los Angeles police broadcasts and the Tijuana taxi cabs loud and clear, but this had not stopped our regular daytime usage of the system, and in fact, we had usually been able to blast through it anyway.

In the early 1970s we were able to satisfy the Department of Transport regulations regarding ship safety using the VHF radio system instead of the single sideband, provided that we had two separate units. These rules were especially stringent for vessels that were licensed to carry passengers. The change came about because by this time the government had installed VHF equipment in the coast radio stations and established a system of peripheral sites controlled by the central station, which in our area was at Tofino. Through the peripheral sites they could now broadcast into, and hear from, most parts of the West Coast of Vancouver Island. They also established a duplex system using two VHF channels to provide a telephone service that allowed a link to the land telephone network, much in the same way as the original BC Tel system had worked. Now we were able to talk to other vessels, the coast stations and the camps and villages that we serviced while at the same time being connected to the telephone network again. It became a workable system as long as one knew where the radio dead spots were and planned around them.

VHF radio became the standard way for people in vessels and ashore all around the sound—and indeed all the sounds—to communicate, and except for the problem of not carrying over long distances, it worked well. Meanwhile, the Tahsis Company's Gold River Logging Division had its own land-based VHF system that used radios with frequencies not included in the marine spectrum and a repeater situated on a hill so that the office in Gold River could talk to all of the company's contractors in both Nootka and Kyuquot sounds. After some lobbying we were able to get that crystal and the separate radio to install in the *Uchuck III*, which meant that we could also be in contact with those contractors from most locations. Now we could make sure that all camps had what they needed in the way of boom chains, swifter wires and bundling wire because we could hear their gear orders when they called the Gold River office. The gear for all of them was delivered to the wharf there once a week, but sometimes there was not enough to go around. By knowing who had extra supplies accumulated, we could sometimes rob Peter to pay Paul. We kept track of these movements and were careful to bring replacements from the next orders being shipped. The switch was not done in secret and the Gold River office knew what was happening, but in this way we could help out in times when things were not running smoothly.

Having the Tahsis Company VHF radio also helped in ways other than those related to business; for example, when some emergency arose, we could be reached quickly once everyone knew that we too were in the system. But atmospherics still created transmission anomalies with the Tahsis radio; one night while we were berthed in Kyuquot I was treated to a half-hour news broadcast in English from Beijing, China, until it faded out and fell silent.

In villages up and down the west coast, the marine VHF soon came to be used as a phone system with radios in each house. Technically this was not legal but, as these were short-range units, they didn't interfere with other traffic, so the rules were not enforced. We could call people at home to tell them what we had on board for them, and they could call us to say they had freight for us. We couldn't help overhearing other people's conversations, especially since we could scan several channels for different reasons, but we learned to tune it out of our conscious minds until the right call sign came up amid the chatter.

After BC Tel began installing microwave towers on Vancouver Island in the 1970s, signals could be sent from major phone exchanges and then from tower to tower into valleys and around mountains that would have blocked high-frequency signals. The signal, when received, was fed into the local phone system of the village, camp or work site to provide a phone system just like those in major population centres. That was how the villages of Gold River and Tahsis came to have telephone systems although the central exchange for both of them was at Campbell River. At first only the village was covered by the Gold River network, then the line was extended to the pulp mill, and later an underground line was run to the airline office just up the road from the wharf. We still had to walk up to the airline office after we had docked to ask the airline representative if there were any messages for us.

Later when a telephone line was extended to the wharf, a public phone was installed there along with a phone jack for us to plug into so that we could have our own phone number. We were now able to run our own affairs from the ship, organizing cargoes and all manner of business rather than just waiting to see what arrived at the ship's side. After we built a small dock office in Gold River with a man stationed there, we were able to call him by VHF from fifteen miles away and exchange messages to and from the outside world. This was a great help because at that time Tofino did not have a VHF peripheral site that would reach into the harbour at Gold River, so we had not been able to use the new Coast Guard duplex telephone service.

At about the same time, BC Tel replaced their system based on AM radio and operators in Vancouver with a new system using VHF transmission. This was made possible by the installation of transmission towers at prominent places along the coast so that they had a fairly complete coverage of all the waterways. Each tower had a different frequency, and ships and land stations were provided with maps showing where the towers were located and what their frequencies were. A vessel radio operator pushed and released the transmit button on the radio phone's handset and waited to see if the signal was strong enough to trip the switch in the selected tower. If it did trip, an operator came on and asked for the vessel's BC Tel "N" number, which was in effect a telephone number. The operator would then connect the caller to the land system and to the number requested. This system worked quite well except for the usual VHF problems. BC Tel had also established a second mobile system, again using towers, called Autotel, an automatic system similar to cellular but intended for outlying areas not covered by the cellphone system. We could use this for connecting to the outside or with some of our customers locally as well as our own dock office but now from much farther away, although coverage was still not complete. By this time the *Uchuck III* was able to use all three systems, plus the Coast Guard duplex system and the BC Tel "N" number type, but not the cellular system, there being no coverage in Nootka or Kyuquot sounds. And because of the convoluted geography, the reception was still a little spotty for each of the others in different places.

After a time BC Tel stopped taking new subscribers to its original VHF "N" number mobile system because the new cellular and Autotel phone systems provided coverage to most of the areas covered by the VHF system. We on the West Coast were at a disadvantage with this development as cellphones still didn't work on our part of the coast and Autotel coverage was limited.

The new century saw the disappearance of the Coast Guard duplex system of public correspondence for the same reasons that BC Tel had ceased theirs. Satellite phones are the latest system in place for ships and they provide the best service so far, but there are still problems and the system is the most expensive yet to operate. Not every ship has them, but it seems that they will become necessary because the other systems will be phased out of service some time soon.

It seems very strange and wonderful to me that we went from having no marine communication when Esson and George started the business to being almost continually connected to the outside world in the space of just forty years.

Traffic Control

Most vessels moving near the shores of the west coast of Vancouver Island are bound for ports on the island, but other vessels appear there, too, because this is where the Great Circle routes from the Orient converge and make landfall. These other vessels travel east to the Strait of Juan de Fuca and go on to destinations in both the US and Canada, but from points along the coast, you see a few of them as they come up from or disappear over the horizon. Before a traffic system was set up to monitor ship movements, ships would arrive unannounced with only the agents for the shipping lines knowing where they were or when they were due. As a result, in 1962 the Greek ship *Glafkos* got lost and fetched up on Jenny Reef just outside Ucluelet harbour, but no one knew where she was until a local fishing vessel was asked to go out and look for her. The bulk carrier *Treis Ierachai*, a new ship, landed on Ferrer Point on the west corner of Nootka Island in 1969, and the car carrier *Vanlene* grounded in 1972, well inland of Cape Beale in Barkley Sound. Had a traffic system been in place then, none of those events would likely have happened.

By November 1978 the government had instituted a system of traffic monitoring all over the coast from several traffic centres, now called Marine Communication and Traffic Services (MCTS) centres. The one for the West Coast is at Amphitrite Point at the western edge of Barkley Sound. It answers on VHF channel 74 to "Tofino Traffic," and it covers an area from the middle of the Strait of Juan de Fuca to a section of ocean north and west of Vancouver Island. By using VHF radio and radar, Tofino's job is to watch and listen for new arrivals into the system, especially deep-sea traffic, as far as Estevan Point. Vessels are warned of other traffic moving in their vicinity.

All vessels above a certain size are required to report at fixed "call-in points" with course and speed information as well as port of destination, purpose and anything else that is pertinent to safe passage. This is much like air traffic control but doesn't carry the authority to definitely order traffic movement. Small vessels and vessels travelling close to shore do not have to participate, but if they don't, then they must stay clear of those that do. Participating vessels have charts showing a grid of sea lanes for their coast area and for those inside waters where traffic converges, creating congestion. They are also given a set of rules to be followed to keep the system operating properly. As we travelled along the coast between Esperanza Inlet and Kyuquot Sound, we participated in the program and were told what other traffic was in our area.

We often passed deep-sea cargo ships in Barkley and Nootka sounds as they came for cargoes of lumber, plywood, shingles, pulp and paper, and minerals. In our early years in Port Alberni, these ships were wartime-built, small by today's standard, so there could be up to ten ships at a time in the harbour loading or anchored and waiting to load. In Nootka Sound, when we arrived there a few years later, the ships were bigger so there were fewer coming and going for the same amount of product, lumber from Tahsis and pulp and later paper from Gold River. In the end the ships were so large that one could load everything in the yard at the Tahsis mill wharf. We heard these ships being assisted in and out of the loading berths as the pilots talked to the assisting tugs on VHF, and we knew that if one was leaving, we might encounter her somewhere in the inlets. We travelled close to the beach so when we cleared a point we might suddenly find one of them steaming by at fifteen knots. That's when they seemed to take up all of the available space. In the late 1960s, ore carriers that were twice the tonnage of the lumber carriers and seven hundred feet long were going to Zeballos for iron ore, but that only lasted for five years.

In 1972 at Head Bay we came across a huge tanker, the *Mandoil II*, which had been in collision with a Japanese cargo ship off Cape Flattery and had a fire as a result. She had been towed to Head Bay as that was deemed a safe and remote enough place to transfer her cargo of ten million gallons of mostly gasoline. We went once to take supplies to the crew working on the job. We lay alongside the tanker, working our DC electric winches, which were arcing and sparking, until someone explained the situation to us.

Tugs and Barges

We met tugs and tows nearly every day while we were en route. Tugs have been around since propulsion engines were put into vessels, and they tow and push all descriptions of ships, barges, booms, rafts and anything else that floats. We saw equipment, chip, fuel, log and aggregate barges constantly coming and going, and we saw them holed up half a dozen at a time in Mooyah Bay, waiting for favourable weather to let them carry on down the coast. We watched log barges being loaded in camps and dumping at the mills. We saw fuel barges, looking like half-tide rocks, surging in the swells as they were towed up the outside. There were local small barges used to move equipment from camp to camp and bigger ones coming in from outside the Sound. By the collision regulations, we were required to stay out of their way, which makes sense as the tows are subject to the effects of wind and tide and can be moved in directions that the towing vessel has to counter in order to bring them back in line.

The Port Alberni harbour, when the company first arrived there, was full of small low-powered tugs, working as many as fifteen at a time, yarding flat booms from the storage grounds to the mills, pushing ships in and out of the loading berths, towing rafts with boom gear on them, and any other job where things had to be moved. On big jobs several would gang up and work together. Everywhere in the inlets and sounds we saw larger tugs towing booms of bundled logs from logging camps, to and from sorting and storage grounds, and to the mills. There were multitudes of very small boom boats and the so-called sidewinders, working in booming grounds, shunting and sorting logs.

By the mid-1960s a new breed of tug appeared called "hot rods," so named because "package power" had come into use. These engines were much smaller in size but still had the same or more power, so could be fitted into smaller, more nimble vessels with smaller crews. But I remember hearing a disgruntled skipper complaining on the air that the only things that worked on them were the men. These more powerful vessels, instead of holing up and shutting down so often to wait for a break in the weather, kept circling, ready and waiting for that short break to happen that would let them continue their journey. Now Mooyah Bay didn't get such a collection of weather-bound tugs except in the most extreme conditions.

Moving logs from the north coast down to the mainland and island mills was a daunting task, especially in winter because of the open water passages and severe weather. Some early attempts involved using old sailing ship hulls that were modified to be able to have logs loaded inside. This was time consuming at both ends of the run. Then a system of large rafts called "Davis rafts" was developed that involved using wire to weave a mat of logs onto which thousands more were laid, and the whole structure was lashed tightly with more wire. In Port Alberni we saw the last of this type of transport in the 1950s.

Log barges appeared next. The earliest, converted from old tankers, were made to be loaded by shore facilities and unloaded at the other end of the run by other shore facilities. Then they were made self-dumping by using a system of floodable tanks in the hull that could be filled on one side of the barge, causing the logs, which were loaded athwartships, to slide off in one great splash. Later these barges were fitted with cranes so that

A sidewinder stowing bundles in the bag boom close beside us in Gold River.

they could be self-loading. It was reasonable to move logs this way for even short distances because it was quick. We saw one barge make three trips in a week from Nootka Sound to Port Alberni, moving close to two million board feet of wood at a time.

On any meeting with these large barges, we had to keep in mind that, even when loaded, they could move almost as fast as our speed of twelve knots.

The chemical barges that we encountered were dual purpose vessels, developed to carry the chemicals used in pulp and paper making to the mills and afterwards to take the product away. The pulp mills at Port Alberni and Gold River each had two of these constantly being towed to California and back.

Fuel and other oil products have been moved from Lower Mainland refineries for a hundred years by coastal tankers to over two hundred places. These ships were up to two hundred feet long and had a tradition of being kept in excellent condition, but they were expensive to run as they required full crews. Shell Oil, Standard Oil and Imperial Oil all had their own tankers plus there were a couple of independent carriers as well, all serving the coast up to the late 1960s. One night I passed three in a row in Tahsis Narrows going about their business of delivering product to tank farms belonging to logging camps and to the fuel stations located at all the villages.

Fuel barges took the place of coastal tankers as they were a less expensive way to move product. As they were flat-decked, they were equipment carriers as well so that machinery coming from the Lower Mainland could be taken directly to outlying places. We saw these barges everywhere on our runs until logging began to tail off, and after that, fuel delivery became a problem. As the frequency of barge deliveries slowed down and eventually dried up, the *Uchuck III* began to carry much more fuel in barrels. She also carried fuel in her own tanks that could be pumped off in smaller quantities for small operations.

Fish Boats

The salmon troll fishery had a bigger effect on us because when we first arrived in that area the season lasted for more than half the year. The larger West Coast troller of that time, a wooden boat thirty-eight to forty-two feet long, would load tons of shaved ice and head out for an eight- to twelve-day trip farther out to sea. The fishermen would fish all day and then clean their catch and load it into the ice before turning in to sleep for the night. Often the boats would just drift in the night in groups, each with a light to advertise its position. They fished up to forty miles offshore, often in the fog, only coming in if the weather deteriorated into gale conditions when fishing became impossible. Some might heave to and wait it out if it was not too bad, but usually they ran in for shelter. One such place was Kyuquot because it was sheltered but near the fishing grounds and so was a relatively short run in for the boats.

Around the late 1960s the boats became bigger and machinery was developed that could freeze fish at sea or create a brine system that kept the fish in good shape. The vessels became bigger and more complex so they could fish until full and then go to a major centre and sell for a better price than selling to a middleman local buyer. These vessels became very expensive to build, and a costly licensing system had been put in place that made this a seriously expensive way to make a living.

We only encountered the trollers when we were on the outside part of our runs. They travelled at a speed of two or three knots and went in straight lines, their turns slow and gradual so as not to tangle up the many lines they were towing. Usually we saw them when they were heading to and from the grounds, but we had to be a little careful with them because with a small crew they might not be watching closely as they worked on the afterdeck, trusting the boat to its "iron mike" or automatic pilot. Sometimes when a single-hander was running in, he would fall asleep after a long and arduous trip and run up into the trees, being carefully steered there by his iron mike.

Gillnetters were the other common vessels that we encountered. These were smaller than the trollers and simpler with usually one man on each. Their one thousand- to fifteen-hundred-foot-long nets were run out from the drum, and a marker was put on the end in the daytime or coal oil lantern at night. (These net lights would usually go out before morning so we had to be especially careful moving around them.) The cork line, the top edge of a net, was held up with small wooden net floats painted black and therefore impossible to see at night and difficult to see in the daytime. The net hung down thirty to forty-five feet, held there by the lead line.

Running into fishing nets was always trouble. Here, in 1953, a hard-hat diver is going down to clear nets from a propeller.

Sometimes the boat would be disconnected from the net, leaving just a marker at each end so that they could run up and down the length of the net to help direct fish into it. This actually advertised the position of the net to us, which was a great help.

The boats in Barkley Sound fished the sockeye runs as they were headed for the spawning grounds in the rivers, so they were only out fishing for short intense periods. I ran over a net off Uchucklesit Inlet in the *Uchuck I*, and when I realized what was about to happen, I tried to turn away. Wrong action. The correct procedure when you saw that it could not be avoided, was to run at ninety degrees to the cork line, only cutting the power as you crossed it. In so doing, the odds were that you would only cut the cork line, leaving a simpler repair job to do. What I did caused the web of the net to be wound up in the propeller, stopping the engine in the process. That meant limping back to Port Alberni and having a hard-hat diver go down to cut it out. Fortunately, the nets in those days were made of cotton line and not the modern nylon. When a nylon net is caught in a propeller, it will melt into a solid blob and cause a really big problem.

Gillnetters later switched to fast aluminum boats so they could get from one opening to the next quickly. In Nootka Sound, when we moved there, the fall chum salmon season was a big fishery, attracting a hundred or so net boats. They set their nets at the prearranged signal in limited

A drum seiner making a set in Kendrick Arm for chum salmon.

areas, usually opening at 18:00 on the first day. For those of us just try-ing to get from here to there in the Sound, they posed a special challenge because there would be forty or fifty boats fishing in one small area, each boat with a white light on it and another white light on the end of its net. Often boats and nets overlapped, so our system was to head for each boat in turn until we could determine which net light belonged to that boat, get around it and go on to the next.

When the fishery closed after a day or a few days, the boats ran in to unload their catches, but since they were small and could not make the run to Vancouver, they would unload to trucks on the wharf at Gold River. If there was to be a further opening some days later, the boats would just be left there while their crews went home for a timeoff. As there was not much moorage space available, they were left tied to the wharf, floats, log booms and each other. We had to make sure that they left us enough room to wriggle in and out as we went about our normal work, day after day.

We encountered seiners fishing chum and pink salmon, which travel in schools near the surface when they are returning to the rivers in the fall, making them available to the seiners. A seine net is much bigger than a gill net and the boats average eighty feet or more. When the school is located, the boat makes a fast circle around it, reeling the net off the drum as she goes. Once around and the ends are connected, the line on the bottom edge of the net is "pursed up" creating a big bag and hopefully containing the fish that was detected with the boat's electronic gear. We always had to be aware that these boats were setting their nets as they would be travelling quite fast in a large circle.

A small fleet of longliners work off the west coast on the continental shelf in waters over sandy bottoms. They use a weighted ground line that has a great many short leaders with baited hooks on them to catch halibut and cod. These boats drop a long string of gear and put a buoy with a flag on a pole at each end to mark the position while they move on to drop more gear elsewhere. They let it sit for hours or a day before coming back to retrieve it, finding the locations with Loran C or GPS. But while their flags are quite visible in calm seas, they will disappear from view as the big swells roll by, so we had to be aware and watching when that fishery was in progress.

For years there were a couple of prawn fishermen making a decent living in Nootka Sound. They used baited traps set in strings of thirty at depths of around three hundred feet by boats looking like gillnetters or trollers, each having a side-mounted winch to pull the strings. Each string had a scotchman, a large red and blue inflated ball, at each end of his string. As they set their strings in different places each time and left them for most of a day and they concentrated their efforts near the heads of the inlets, right where we operated, we had to be continually watching for them.

Then the price began to rise when the Japanese market discovered the local prawns, and soon there were two or three more fishermen. And it seemed that every time they brought their catches in, the price was a little higher, which encouraged yet more to come. At one point in the 1980s there were thirteen seasonal prawn fishermen fishing with at least ten strings of thirty traps each for a total of nearly four thousand traps. The resource was taking a hit. Later that fishery died away until there was once again only a couple of full-timers working in the Sound in ever-shortening seasons. We tried not to pass too closely when they were actively pulling or setting traps, so as to not roll them around too much, and we had to determine which direction they would be moving and set our course accordingly.

Other Traffic in the Sounds

We also saw the mission boats of all the major churches. In our time, the major player was the Shantyman's Christian Association, a non-denominational Christian missionary group. We encountered their fifty-foot *Messenger III*, which began service in 1946, travelling between Victoria and Cape Cook, bringing medical supplies and spiritual comfort anywhere they found small groups of people living. That vessel was in service until around 1968. An offshoot of the Shantyman's Association, the Nootka Mission Association, also had a boat, the smaller, faster *Bruce McLean*, which served the Nootka Sound to Kyuquot Sound areas from their base hospital at Esperanza.

Up to the 1950s the BC Telephone Company had a fleet of small vessels in Barkley Sound that was used by the linemen servicing the phone line that ran along the shore from tree to tree to Bamfield and other places on the inlets. This fleet was not needed after microwave towers were installed.

The BC Forest Service also had a fleet of thirty-five- to fifty-foot wooden vessels to carry their timber cruisers, forest engineers and scalers to the many sites of current logging operations and projected logging. But roads, aircraft and fast boats changed how the work was done, and those boats disappeared. Ex-BC Telephone and Forestry boats went onto the market to become pleasure boats, well equipped to do that job just by being what they already were, so we still saw some of them from time to time.

Just after the war, Canada still had many naval vessels in service, and they roamed around the coast, visiting and "showing the flag." They were still in training but that died away quite soon and they were laid up to be scrapped. New destroyer escorts were built in the 1960s that would be able to operate in the radioactive fallout from a possible nuclear attack. These vessels had a very different look; they looked round and smooth, the better to wash them down of radioactive contaminates. No one was visible when they moved as they were controlled from deep within. Once, I had just sailed from Gold River toward Friendly Cove and was following behind one of these ships when she went out of sight behind Bligh Island. When we went around the point at the far end of the island, she reappeared at speed and did a circle around us before speeding away. I was told later that, if we had not been carrying passengers, she would have had her main armament trained on us throughout the exercise.

One day we encountered one of these vessels stopped in the middle of the Sound with a smaller private vessel close by. On approaching, we saw armed men holding weapons on people in the smaller vessel. This was the arrest of a drug carrier of which a number have come into the Sound, thinking that they can off-load their product quietly out of sight in such a relatively unpopulated place.

There is still much traffic on the West Coast but it is more seasonal now. Toward the end of Walter's and my time, there were days in winter when we went into Kyuquot Sound and saw no other moving traffic except for a few small craft travelling in very local areas.

CHAPTER FOURTEEN

The Final Years

The Office

It wasn't until 1985, twenty-five years after leaving Port Alberni, that we finally had a little dock office and a shed man on the wharf in Gold River. Back in 1966 when I became master of the *Uchuck III*, the company office had been in Port Alberni, run by our very competent bookkeeper, Audrey Peterson. She had retired in February 1967, at which time Florence Kapchinsky, who was trained by Mrs. Pete, took over. Florence remained in the job for seventeen years, which meant that the office stayed in Port Alberni. It was in this period that once a month Esson and I would have a day at the office together. I usually arrived there first and got my business with Florence done, and when Esson came in, we had a three-way session. Then it was time for Esson and me to have lunch at the Beaufort Hotel, this nearly always consisting of a roast beef sandwich and a bottle or two of McEwan's Strong Ale.

Esson's stroke in May 1976 ended his sailing days, but when he recovered, he was still in charge of the company, and we decided to move the office to Courtenay to make it easier for him to get to there. It was also a good opportunity to change company accountants. Over the years the running of the company had become more complicated as, for instance, we were dealing with subsidy contracts that involved government-required reporting, so the services of the accountants were needed more often. My friend Ted Cowan, the senior partner in our new accountancy firm, specialized in helping small business people to run their businesses more effectively. As he also took an interest in the workings of our ships, he made many trips with us, giving him a very good feel for what the business entailed outside of the figures alone.

We rented office space in downtown Courtenay, and Florence agreed to come to Courtenay four days a week, living in her motorhome there and travelling back to Port Alberni for the rest of the week as she was a long-time resident of that city with family and social connections and her own home there. This situation existed until November 1977 when Esson died. Now there was less reason for the office to remain in Courtenay and we moved it back to Port Alberni and into Florence's basement where it stayed until she retired in 1984. When Florence retired, there was no understudy waiting in the wings to take over her job, so the chain linking us to that city was broken.

Walter and I, now being the owners of the company, decided to base everything in Gold River. We canvassed the town and from a few possibilities found Eileen Erb, who had experience in bookkeeping with the village of Gold River and only had to learn the particulars of our business. Once again we moved the office into the bookkeeper's basement, but within a year we rented space in the Village Centre and, for the first time since 1960, had an office with a sign on the door. It became an administrative as well as a bookkeeping centre now that it was located where the company operated.

The final progression for our office came when we moved our bookkeeper to a space at the far end of the government freight shed on the dock. Her new office was built rather like a bomb shelter in order to carry the weight of our equipment and lumber on top, the lumber being part of the 10,000 board feet of edge-grain that was air-drying on racks for later use in our ship repairing. Space was tight in the freight shed as all the cargoes coming and going were also stored there, but our new office there was modern, with all the business machines and computers and communication equipment that we needed. Now there was someone to send and receive cargo while the vessel was out and to talk to anyone who needed information. We already had a little dock office for our shed man, and we provided him with a VHF radio to talk to us while we were out on the run. Walter and I could get up-to-date reports on whatever we needed at any time. The whole company operation was now in Gold River for the first time since we came to Nootka Sound.

Advertising

Advertising became an important factor in these later years. Up to this time there had been very little money for this, although we had always contracted with a commercial printer to prepare a simple one-page brochure, at first not even in colour. Starting in 1986 we engaged Havers Design of Courtenay to develop a better brochure and then to handle our advertising in general. For the new four-panel brochure, I supplied photographs of the vessel and scenes around the Sound. To get the photos of the vessel, I was put over the side in the aluminum rescue boat, and I had Keith sail around me in two complete circles so I could get a variety of shots with different backgrounds and different lighting. Havers directed our efforts to likely markets so as not to waste our resources.

Each year we changed some of the photos to keep the brochure interesting and in time also included paintings of the ship. When in 1984 Florence, our long-serving bookkeeper, had retired and remarried, we had commissioned a painting of the *Uchuck III* by Maximick Originals

One of the paintings that Bill Maximick did for us of the *Uchuck III*.

as a retirement and wedding present for her. This turned out so well that my wife and Walter's wife both wondered aloud why Florence should have such a painting and not us, so there were two more created. When we decided that employees who had served with the company for fifteen years had earned a painting, four more were created and in the end there were a total of thirteen. Reproductions of some of them were incorporated into our new information brochures to make a striking and original production.

Travel writers had often come on trips on the *Uchuck*, but one in particular had a bigger effect than most of the others. Doris Kennedy from Colorado, a well-known syndicated travel journalist, along with her photographer husband, Gary, sailed with us about this time. They were in the area for several days of writing and photographing, and soon their first article appeared in a Seattle paper, creating a flood of phone calls from people wanting to make reservations to travel with us. For months afterwards, as other papers across North America ran the story, more people called. We always knew where the story had last appeared by the area codes of the calls that we received. Even a year later those same articles were generating calls, and then Doris updated the article and away it went again. We could never have bought this kind of coverage.

Passengers

Passengers had always been welcome in the wheelhouse while we travelled, so we continued to meet interesting people from everywhere who had done everything. You could never tell by just looking at the stooped old man standing on deck contemplating the scenery what he had done before he looked like that: he may have invented the equipment that you were using at that minute. Some people had done research and knew what they were coming to see while others had no clue, discovering things of which they had never dreamed before they came on board. Very often when we landed at a camp, we were close to the log dump and booming ground, so our passengers were able to see how that end of the logging operation worked. Coastal logging equipment is bigger than that used anywhere else because the trees grow so big.

In 1988 a paper machine was added to the pulp mill at Gold River, creating a need for more workers and generally increasing the activity in

Comfy and warm inside the passenger accommodation, but still with a good view of the outside. ANDREW SCOTT PHOTO.

the area. During construction of the addition we ran a couple of evening trips out toward the coast for the workers. They brought enough booze to have a drink but not enough where anyone would get hurt. On the way back to Gold River, some of them began playing in the rigging, climbing fifty feet up the mast, then hand over hand out along the derrick topping lifts and finally sliding down via the cargo runners, hooting and hollering in the dark. I knew they were all high steel workers so I didn't worry about them falling off, but it was a little disconcerting to have all this going on while we were travelling.

The Forest Industry in the 1990s

Tree planting had begun about 1955 in a desultory way as it was then the responsibility of the individual forest companies. At that time loggers had rated the people hired to do this work as one notch below a whistle punk, the lowest in the logger hierarchy. And perhaps it was no wonder, since these first groups of planters had been poorly equipped and disorganized, looking like bands of gypsies complete with pregnant women, kids and dogs, and all of them lived in tents. But the work became more important after environmentalists, government and others got involved, and loggers began to understand its value when the new forest tenure licences were predicated on a sustained yield model, making replanting essential to the overall plan.

The Tahsis Company used one contractor for tree planting and thinning over its entire tree farm licence, and for years this contractor had its headquarters on a float, which was towed from camp to camp according to the company's reforestation plan. The work opened up in 1971 when other contractors were allowed to bid on the jobs, so we began to field calls about our rates for moving equipment in and out. But we saw our first real increase in work from this sector after contracts were let to companies whose only job was replanting. Thinning jobs were separate contracts. Gradually the companies coalesced into larger units and became properly organized under a few smart men. The crews of six to twenty-five workers began travelling with all their equipment, which had been trimmed down to the essentials. The planting site for which they were destined determined whether they had to take their camp with them or use the logging camps for housing. For a time distrust between the planters and loggers remained, but their relationship improved as the planters became accepted as professionals.

The planting contracts, which ranged from two weeks to two months, began in January on the coast where it was warmer and snow-free sooner and then spread into the interior as the snow melted. The cargo for these groups consisted of the planters' vehicles, food, personal stuff and many thousands of boxes of seedlings sent out by the logging company's forestry division, which in turn got them from the tree nurseries. While they worked, we kept the supplies coming and finally took the whole lot out again in May when they were finished. After some years of this, the planting was catching up to the accumulated backlog of denuded lands and was just behind the actual logging, so the contracts began to be smaller and fewer.

Cutting Back

The forests on the west coast of Vancouver Island had been worked over extensively, so toward the end of the 1980s the forest companies were given smaller quotas of timber to work. By that time each of the major forest companies had developed a helicopter logging arm because log prices had risen to the point where it was economic to log small cutblocks by helicopter. Our part in this was to haul fuel and boom gear and occasionally parts for the machines, but since they were flying anyway, for the most part they could look after themselves.

All of this meant fewer people employed in the logging industry and longer shut-down periods, therefore less traffic for us. This change was gradual, but the time came in 1991 when we were not carrying enough cargo and passengers to support a full schedule and two crews. We decided to reduce to one crew only, leaving the vessel tied up from Friday evening to Tuesday morning. The company was virtually shut down for that time with no one on board. This was the first time this had happened since we started in 1960 and it was not a good feeling. Good men were laid off. Continuity was broken. The crew coming back on Monday night came back to a cold, dead ship, something I never liked or got used to.

Now I left my house on Monday evening at 19:30. Often it would be dark, raining, blowing and cold. I would start the truck, drive out of the yard, shivering until the heater kicked out enough heat to make a difference. On the highway there might be rain, fog and dazzling headlights to deal with as I headed for Campbell River to pick up Angie, my cook, at the Super Valu in Discovery Plaza. She was there to buy the groceries for our next five-day trip and would have just about finished shopping when I arrived. I would load the dozen or so cartons into the box of the truck and then we would head for Gold River a hundred kilometres away in the night. A little Dixieland jazz helped the situation along, making the kilometres roll under the wheels a little faster, and in due course, we arrived in the village. I would stop at the company office to pick up the mail and paperwork for the next trip and then we would drive the last fourteen kilometres down to the wharf.

The ship would be lying in her berth out at the ends of her mooring lines, held there by the brisk off-shore wind that blows steadily out of the valley. Everything would be dark except for the single dock light casting its wan yellow glow over all. Once I stepped out of the truck, the wind would carve through my jacket, biting as if I were naked. I would unlock the warehouse and start the towmotor, which was parked just inside the door, and move it out to a point opposite the stern of the vessel. With the stern line looped over a hook on the machine, I would back it up, pulling until the ship came alongside the wharf. Then I would jump off and take a turn on the cleat with the line to hold the vessel in tight.

Next I had to get the end of the gangway from the boat deck to the wharf. The tidal range in that area is about thirteen feet and averages ten feet, and when the tide was high, the main deck of the *Uchuck* was about level with the surface of the wharf, so I could just open the lift gate in the vessel's main deck rail and step aboard. When the tide was low, I had to scramble aboard however I could. Sometimes if I walked forward, I could grab hold of some of the cargo gear and swing aboard. Then I would toss the two lines from the end of the gangway up over the foot-high bullrail on the edge of the wharf. I would then climb back up after them and, hoping my back would stand the strain one more time, give a big heave and up would come the end of the gangway.

Ships, especially wooden ships, are living things. They are meant to have machinery running, making heat and light. There should be the sounds of large fans forcing air into all the spaces on board, keeping the wood healthy. When we were gone from Friday to Monday night, there was none of that. The whole vessel was cold and dark and it smelled. So we got our gear on board and, while Angie put her groceries away, I went through the vessel unlocking doors while looking to see that all was as it was supposed to be. The rest of the crew would trickle in over the next couple of hours, and in the morning we would start up and set out on the day's run. By the end of that day, the vessel would be alive again.

Just after we made the move to the reduced schedule, Hayes Logging opened up a new area and decided to use our service exclusively, while at the same time other camps had a revival that made us frantically busy for nearly a year. But we knew that this would be temporary so we stayed with the reduced crew and service level. As expected, activity did even out again in the following year and returned to the 1991 level. From then on business waxed and waned but we were busy enough that we did not slide back into the situation of not being able to keep up with the repairs and maintenance, a state that had nearly sunk the company a few years earlier.

Selling the Company

After three years of this reduced routine, I was fed up with it, but business was such that this was still the route we had to take. Then one day at the end of March 1994 the phone rang and on the other end of the line a voice announced that he was a lawyer representing a client who wanted to buy the *Uchuck III*. By June 30 the company was sold.

In the meantime we carried on as usual. In these last years, there had not been the same rush to get going to Victoria for the annual refit since our current reduced sailings and the scheduled time for our haul-out often meant that we had a day in hand before heading out. By leaving on that day, we had found that we could break the run into two parts and spend a night somewhere along the route, rather than going as fast as possible to Victoria to just make our haul-out time as we had in years past.

My partner, Walt Winkler, had always wanted to go to Hot Springs Cove, so in 1994 that is where we planned to make our overnight stop. We sailed from Gold River in the afternoon of the day before we really had to leave and headed for the hot springs. On the way out of Nootka Sound, we met Bob Leduc in his prawn boat and got from him a bucket of prime prawns, still jumping around in their bucket and telling us that they were very fresh. We tucked them away for the trip around Estevan Point and into the entrance to Sidney Inlet where Hot Spring Cove lies.

It was late afternoon on a sunny day in early May when we arrived, picked up a buoy and settled in. For a while we sat about in the sunshine, enjoying a beer or two. Supper came, based on a tureen of cooked prawns along with bread and salad. Our group worked through the prawns and then sat back to rest. The empty tureen was removed. Shortly afterwards it came back again full to the brim. This was too much for David McGinnis, one of the regulars on these trips, who left the table to go below to find his camera saying, "I'll never see this again in my lifetime." We worked on the second tureen but didn't manage to get to the bottom of it. The remainder would have to wait for breakfast, but prawns in an omelet are just as good.

Evening was coming on, so before sunset we launched the rescue boat to take the whole crowd to the park float at the shore. From there we walked the mile over the boardwalk to the hot spring for a dip to top off the day. On the following morning we sailed for a leisurely run down the West Coast to Victoria, arriving well before sunset to begin the refit and inspection. It was a very pleasant interlude before the real work began.

❀ ❀ ❀

The sale of the *Uchuck III* was carried out so smoothly that some of our customers were not aware for months that a change had been made. The accountants and lawyers for each group agreed that they had never before been in negotiations that had gone that smoothly. The last two weeks were strange because, although we had sold the company at the end of June, we had been asked to stay on for another two weeks while the new owners finished up other work. During those two weeks I found myself becoming very conservative, taking the vessel where the passage was widest and deepest, risking nothing; this was no longer our vessel and already I felt a bit of a stranger. But the work on the wharf was the same, people collecting their goods and boats coming alongside to have pallets lowered into them to be taken to other parts of the bay. There were the usual camaraderie and friendly insults being shouted around. Everything was normal.

The last two-day trip for Walt Winkler and me ended on a beautiful July 15, 1994. In most respects that day was no different than all the others on which we had travelled together, nor did it feel any different; the mix of cargo was the same and so was the routine. Few people in the ports we visited knew that the faces were about to change, so there were no teary farewells, no solemn handshakes.

There was one exception. At the end of the previous day when I steered into Walter's Cove and headed for the wharf, I saw balloons hanging from the sliding freight shed doors and a banner strung above to show that, yes, they knew something was changing. When the vessel was alongside and secure, I tidied up in the wheelhouse and then gathered up the freight manifest and packing slips from my desk in preparation for going ashore. Suddenly I found that I had to hold back for a bit while I composed myself as it struck home that this was it. It was over. I had been looking forward to this day, but now that it had arrived, I didn't feel quite how I thought I would. I found that I was getting a little emotional and it wouldn't do to show too much of that as it is not in line with my Scottish and English heritage.

That day in Walter's Cove we finished up the work and had supper as usual, but later people began to trickle down to the wharf, bringing things—a large cooler of cooked crabs, smoked salmon, pies and all kinds of other good things, including beer and a bottle of good scotch. As the sun set, there were twenty-five or so people gathered on the main hatch and work deck having a party on this beautiful warm evening in summer. The chatter went on till the wee hours when gradually people drifted off until we were alone again.

The next morning we sailed at 08:00 into a thick fog. One more time we felt our way out of the bay, easing between the various rock piles on our way up into Kyuquot Sound for that day's deliveries, carrying with us fond memories of the previous night. The rest of the day went by uneventfully and, as we approached Gold River, there was a final salute. From behind, so I couldn't see it approaching, came the Beaver float plane owned by Frank Beban Logging, CF-SCM, right on the deck and very fast until, right alongside us, Louie pulled up in a climbing turn at full throttle with lots of pitch, so that the engine was snarling like I had never heard a Beaver snarl before, and then with a "That's for you!" on the VHF, he disappeared.

We finished up the trip and shook hands all around. It was done

On the day after our last official run, we organized a picnic for the old crew, the new crew and all the families. We went to Friendly Cove for the day, just as on a tourist trip, only this time we brought along a cooler of beer and our big old barbecue plus a borrowed one for our traditional harbour day feed of steaks. The new owners, Fred and Sean Mather and Alberto Girotto, were not strangers to us. Sean had sailed with us off and on for some time as a relief mate, and we certainly knew the others before. For this trip, Fred was skipper, and Walter and I stood by to answer any questions, but there were very few, so we were just passengers.

It turned into a good day for all. The crew members who were staying on with the company began to fit in with the new owners. This type of situation can be difficult as some things will certainly be done differently as new ideas come on board but nothing changed much for some weeks. The new owners wanted to get used to how we had done things before making changes, and they knew that a slow change is better for the customers as well.

While we were in Friendly Cove, Walter and I made a small presentation, another Bill Maximick painting of the *Uchuck*, this time to Glen Pollock, to recognize his fifteen years with us in this vessel. This was the fourth time that someone had qualified for this award.

When the new owners took over, they hosted a party to mark the occasion. Note the barbeque, made in twenty minutes one evening at Gold River from pieces of scrap and then used for the next twenty years. One new engineer on first arriving thought that it might be a forge. From left: Ron Fast, Glen Pollock, Walter Winkler, Ross Manton and Alberto Girotto.

For years I had been taking a body of time off in summer to go sailing, so I went home that day as if I was going on holiday, and although I knew I would not be going back, everything felt all right. It didn't begin to feel strange until two months later. It wasn't that I missed worrying about the business or the crew troubles or cargoes or passengers, but I did miss the feeling of being at the centre of things and being one of the two to whom crew and passengers and customers in the ports turned to for answers. Suddenly there was a large hole in the middle of my life.

I waited for the phone to ring with someone asking what he should do about something or other. It didn't happen. Walter was called on more often than I was and worked a lot of shifts over the next couple of years as his work as chief engineer had involved such an intimate knowledge of all the systems on board, knowledge that was not so easily handed over. Vessels like the *Uchuck* are one-offs that grew into what they became by degrees and stages, becoming a unique combination of elements. Local knowledge is required to keep them in shape.

Epilogue

In 1995 I was asked to go to Victoria to help with the new owners' first refit period because I was familiar with the people and procedures of the shipyard. I was quite happy to do this and planned to be there for a few days, but after the vessel was hauled up on the ways, there was a phone call for me. It was the Coast Guard wanting to know if I was aware of the problems encountered by the sixty-six-foot *High Seas Drifter,* which was owned by my daughter, Tracy, and son-in-law, Randy. They had been about to leave an anchorage near Namu to get ready for their next charter when Randy had fallen off the wheelhouse and onto the anchor windlass, which with all its protruding gears and levers had hurt him badly. Tracy was left with engines running, ready to move, but was stuck there. She contacted Coast Guard, asking them to call in an aircraft to take Randy to the hospital at Bella Bella, and a Beaver was dispatched with a paramedic on board. Tracy and the two on the plane managed to get Randy into the skiff and over to the aircraft. Then Tracy had to get the vessel to Bella Bella, twenty-five miles away. She found, again through the Coast Guard Radio, a seiner that was waiting for weather nearby and one of the crew was willing to help her get going. She really only needed a hand to get the anchor up and then would be able to run the vessel herself, but the company was appreciated.

By the following morning I was in Port Hardy where I caught the scheduled flight for Bella Bella, but as we flew over the harbour there, I couldn't see the *High Seas Drifter*. It turned out that Randy, after about twenty hours of sleep in hospital, had checked himself out, determined not be stuck there, and now the vessel was floating around out in the channel while they waited for me to show up. They were due to go out on charter soon, but Randy was in no condition to do that, so they asked if I would do it while he went to Royston to allow my wife look after him for a few days. And so I went out for the two weeks of the charter. For the next ten years I went off on charters in the mid-coast area with Tracy whenever Randy was busy and couldn't be there. This was a lifesaver for me because I had not taken up another line of work and at times found that the days went slowly.

Five years after leaving, Nootka Sound Service asked me to do a spot of relief work, which turned out to be two full weeks. I set off for the ship hoping I would remember how to do all the necessary things and hoping my judgment for making the landings and machine driving and so on was still intact. At sailing time that first day I went into the wheelhouse and prepared to get us moving, and as soon as I put my hands on the engine room telegraph, it all fell back into place. It could have been yesterday that I had made that last trip. There were several more relieving spots in succeeding years, which I enjoyed immensely. All I had to do was drive the boat and tell sea stories to the crew, most of whom I had sailed with in the years before.

My third saviour in those early retirement years was *Abalone,* my sailboat. Nancy and I got out onto the water and made several trips to the real West Coast, visiting old friends and becoming reconnected with real life there.

Now, eighteen years after selling the *Uchuck III*, I probably won't be asked to relieve again, although I could, as my certificate is up-to-date as is my medical. But I am beginning to think that at seventy-four, I might not want to do it anyway. And for now, I am reliving the whole fifty years as I write it down.

Acknowledgements

I laboured away in my garret for seven or so winters writing the words to go into this book, sharing pieces with my wife, Nancy, to whom I owe my first thanks. Carol Sheehan of CS Communication Strategies in Comox, BC, read the manuscript and has been a great mentor. Eventually I read some of the stories at the Comox Valley Elder College's Writers Workshop course, which I attended over several semesters, and to my fellow members of the Comox Valley Writer's Society. I was in the third year of this process when I approached Harbour Publishing, who took a personal interest in helping me to bring the project to a publishable state. Harbour's managing editor, Anna Comfort O'Keeffe, oversaw the process and educated me as to how book publishing works. Many thanks go to Betty Keller, who edited my manuscript and made some sense of its organization. A first-timer certainly doesn't create a book by himself and I was truly amazed and grateful at the number of dedicated and talented people who came forward to help me get my rough manuscript to the finished book you now hold in your hands. Thank you all.

Index

Photographs indicated in **bold**